JAZZ DIASPORA

Jazz Diaspora: Music and Globalisation is about the international diaspora of jazz, well underway within a year of the first jazz recordings in 1917. This book studies the processes of the global jazz diaspora and its implications for jazz historiography in general, arguing for its relevance to the fields of sonic studies and cognitive theory. Until the late twentieth century, the historiography and analysis of jazz were centred on the US to the almost complete exclusion of any other region. The driving premise of this book is that jazz was not 'invented' and then exported: it was invented in the process of being disseminated.

Jazz Diaspora is a sustained argument for an alternative historiography, based on a shift from a US-centric to a diasporic perspective on the music. The rationale is double-edged. It appears that most of the world's jazz is experienced (performed and consumed) in diasporic sites – that is, outside its agreed geographical point of origin – and to ignore diasporic jazz is thus to ignore most jazz activity. It is also widely felt that the balance has shifted, as jazz in its homeland has become increasingly conservative.

There has been an assumption that only the 'authentic' version of the music – as represented in its country of origin – was of aesthetic and historical interest in the jazz narrative; that the forms that emerged in other countries were simply rather pallid and enervated echoes of the 'real thing'. This has been accompanied by challenges to the criterion of place- and race-based authenticity as a way of assessing the value of popular music forms in general. As the prototype for the globalisation of popular music, diasporic jazz provides a richly instructive template for the study of the history of modernity as played out musically.

Bruce Johnson is Adjunct Professor in the School of Communication, University of Technology Sydney, Visiting Professor and Docent in the Department of Cultural History at the University of Turku, Finland, and also Visiting Professor in the Department of Music at the University of Glasgow.

Transnational Studies in Jazz

Series Editors: Tony Whyton, Birmingham City University, UK, and Nicholas Gebhardt, Birmingham City University, UK

Transnational Studies in Jazz presents cross-disciplinary and global perspectives on the development and history of jazz and explores its many social, political, and cultural meanings.

Jazz Sells
Music, Marketing, and Meaning
Mark Laver

Austral Jazz
The Localization of a Global Music Form in Sydney
Andrew Robson

Jazz Diaspora
Music and Globalisation
Bruce Johnson

Voices Found
Free Jazz and Singing
Chris Tonelli

Remixing European Jazz Culture
Kristin McGee

For more information, please visit: www.routledge.com/music/series/TSJ

JAZZ DIASPORA

Music and Globalisation

Bruce Johnson

Routledge
Taylor & Francis Group

NEW YORK AND LONDON

First published 2020
by Routledge
52 Vanderbilt Avenue, New York, NY 10017

and by Routledge
2 Park Square, Milton Park, Abingdon, Oxon, OX14 4RN

Routledge is an imprint of the Taylor & Francis Group, an informa business

© 2020 Taylor & Francis

Library of Congress Cataloging-in-Publication Data
A catalog record has been requested for this book

ISBN: 978-1-138-57754-1 (hbk)
ISBN: 978-1-138-57755-8 (pbk)
ISBN: 978-1-351-26668-0 (ebk)

Typeset in Bembo
by Newgen Publishing UK

MIX
Paper from
responsible sources
FSC
www.fsc.org
FSC® C013985

Printed in the United Kingdom
by Henry Ling Limited

To Mandy
1958–2019

CONTENTS

TRANSNATIONAL STUDIES IN JAZZ

Since the 1990s the study of jazz has changed dramatically, as the field continues to open up to a variety of disciplinary perspectives and critical models. Today, as the music's meaning undergoes profound changes, there is a pressing need to situate jazz within an international research context and to develop theories and methods of investigation which open up new ways of understanding its cultural significance and its place within different historical and social settings.

The Transnational Studies in Jazz Series presents the best research from this important and exciting area of scholarship, and features interdisciplinary and international perspectives on the relationships between jazz, society, politics, and culture. The series provides authors with a platform for rethinking the methodologies and concepts used to analyze jazz, and will seek to work across disciplinary boundaries, finding different ways of examining the practices, values and meanings of the music. The series explores the complex cultural and musical exchanges that have shaped the global development and reception of jazz. Contributors will focus on studies of the music which find different ways of telling the story of jazz with or without reference to the United States, and will investigate jazz as a medium for negotiating global identities.

Tony Whyton
Nicholas Gebhardt
Series Editors

INTRODUCTION

Diaspora and New Jazz Studies

This book is about how jazz circulated beyond its accepted site of origin. In global terms, that means jazz outside the United States, but in intra-national terms it can be jazz outside New Orleans. My emphasis will be on the former, though this will require also some reference to the latter. At some point I shall explore the inadequacies of the concept of nation as a discriminator in the attempt to understand the global jazz diaspora, but those inadequacies are far less apparent in the primary distinction between jazz within and outside the US, simply because that distinction is so deeply etched in the discourse of the music. Jazz studies presented as 'histories' are overwhelmingly dominated by the US, with some passing references to such outlanders as Django Reinhardt or Antônio Carlos Jobim, exceptions who prove the rule.

More recently there is growing recognition of the broader category of jazz beyond the borders of the US, but generally as something of a footnote to the 'real' story, adding some names as an appendix to the US canon without fundamentally questioning its ideological underpinnings (see further Schenker 2019). Of Kirchner's 850 or so pages (2000), apart from African and European roots, there are also chapters on jazz in Europe, Africa, Japan, Canada and Australia, as well as Brazilian and Latin music, a total of less than 80 pages (it is notable in this structure that Africa's participation thus concluded in a pre-jazz past). In Shipton's nearly 1,000 pages (2001), fewer than 70 are explicitly devoted to jazz outside the US as a category. Out of around 500 pages Gioia (2011) spends seven on 'The Globalization of Jazz' within a final chapter on 'Jazz in the New Millennium', implying that globalisation is a recent footnote. DeVeaux and Giddins (2009) devote none of their 600 or so pages specifically to the international diaspora. The assumption is that only in the US do we find what Zwerin calls 'the real thing' (Zwerin 2000: 537), undergoing its authentic and largely autonomous development, ready for export. This US-centricity hovers over the phrase 'America's classical music', which not only underlines jazz's seminal centre, but also its status as America's unique equivalent of the Western art music tradition. Underpinning the various understandings of 'classical' in this context is neo-Kantian dehistoricisation, music of 'permanent interest and value' (DeVeaux and Giddins 2009: 538). Such music is the end product of a hermetically sealed aesthetic teleology.

All this is something of a trailer for later discussion. But the point of raising these issues briefly here is to situate this study in contemporary jazz scholarship. A sea-change in jazz studies over recent decades has begun to dislodge it from the discourse of autonomous music, of a European high art form *manqué*. Thus located, jazz aspires to a status in which the music must be inherently second-rate, because the category 'art music' was tailored to a very different historical and cultural moment. Ironically, as jazz relinquishes its tenuous hold on the aesthetic high-ground, it gains increasing cultural weight. In a process maturing in the 1950s, advocates of jazz sought to quarantine the music from the vulgarity of rock baying at the gates, by seeking sanctuary in the temple of art music. In doing so they also consigned it to a below-the-stairs existence, a slightly gauche imposter (see further Johnson 2002B). In the recent migration from a self-contained aesthetics to a broader cultural landscape, scholars are disclosing the profound importance of jazz in the formation of international modernity, as manifested in its means of production, dissemination and consumption, in the global negotiation with the local: the first new music of modern glocalisation.

In this way, jazz is richly instructive as a template for studies of subsequent twentieth-century popular musics, and also of cultural globalisation more generally. In his Introduction to a collection of bench-mark essays in recent jazz scholarship, Tony Whyton put the case that in many ways 'jazz served to shape the ways in which popular music is discussed and understood today as historical writings on jazz have offered a legacy which is now embroiled in the critical tensions of broader popular music scholarship' (Whyton 2011: xi; see similarly Dorin 2016: 6–7). The relationships between popular music, modernity, place, space, politics, identity and the high/low cultural binary that have become perennial fields for researchers can find prototypes in the century-long history of jazz. Likewise, the plasticity of generic distinctions in a field so deeply traversed by cut'n'mix modern mediations. Indeed, like other contemporary jazz historians including (Tucker (2011: 146–147) and Whiteoak (2009: 33), I consciously refrain from attempting to legislate any particular definition of jazz in this enquiry, because I am more interested in recognising the bewildering range of musics that have been performed and conceptualised under that label as jazz circulated internationally. As discussed further below, I think it tells us more about the history of the music to try to understand why the word 'jazz' was applied to musics that we would no longer recognise as such, than to simply declare them to be wrong, from our own lofty but historically situated position. A history of jazz that pivots on a dogmatic and *ex post facto* definition of jazz screens out the history that preceded the music's international codification. I am looking for, rather than seeking to erase, 'difference' in the understanding of the music, both in terms of character and supposed quality. That is, my interest includes music called jazz that doesn't sound like what we think of as jazz, music that by the 'canonical' standards is mediocre, corny, quaint and misconceived, but which has been presented under the name jazz. My objective is not to disdainfully dismiss it as failing to conform to the criteria of the canon, but to think about why it was called jazz, how it served its functions for the musicians and audiences who enjoyed it as such. I believe that in doing so, we not only learn more about the history of the music, but also about the various diasporic cultures with which it negotiated.

The reservations I am articulating regarding the 'canonical' disclose where this study stands in current debates regarding jazz history. Until the late twentieth century, the dominant and barely challenged jazz narrative was based on the foundation of a canon wholly constructed within the US and then exported internationally. By contrast, I set out the basic premise of this study in an article published in 2002: 'jazz was not "invented" and then exported. It was invented in the process of being disseminated' (Johnson 2002A: 39). It is a proposition given increasing buoyancy over the intervening 16 years by the developments under what has become the rubric of the 'New Jazz Studies' (NJS). This provides a hospitable climate for the argument that diasporic jazz has its own integrity, as well as holding valuable lessons regarding the processes of cultural globalisation and diffusion, and syncretisms between musics of the supposed centre and peripheries. This has been accompanied by challenges to the criterion of place- and race-based authenticity as a way of assessing the value of popular music forms in general. As the prototype for the globalisation of popular music, diasporic jazz provides lessons regarding the history of modernity as played out musically. Indeed, this monograph itself sprang from seeds in the NJS garden. Asked to provide a chapter on the diaspora for the *Routledge Companion to Jazz Studies*, edited by Gebhardt, Rustin-Paschal and Whyton, I found that preparation of that 5,000-word essay generated enough raw material to warrant a full-length book. That essay is thus in part the structural platform for this much more fully developed study, which also adapts some material from a lengthy essay on 'Jazz Outside America' completed for a volume of the *Encyclopedia of Popular Music of the World* which is still in press, and I thank the editors, represented in this case by David Horn, for permission to draw on that article.

Clearly, the focus of these publications is a significant departure from the older US-canon-centric historiography, in which the 'primary texts' are recordings, especially of the solos, of US masters of each successive development, exemplified most authoritatively in *The Smithsonian Collection of Classic Jazz* assembled by Martin Williams in 1973 and still providing the primary texts internationally for jazz education programmes (Gabbard 1995 A: 13). The overt features of this historiographical model include a teleological trajectory, moving from the primitive toward a perfection of form.

> After an obligatory nod to African origins and ragtime antecedents, the music is shown to move through a succession of styles or periods, each with a conveniently distinctive label and time period: New Orleans jazz up through the 1920s, swing in the 1930s, bebop in the 1940s, cool jazz and hard bop in the 1950s, free jazz and fusion in the 1960s.
>
> *De Veaux 1998: 483*

Each of these stages is completed in the work of a master figure whose achievement is summarised in a body of recorded masterpieces (see further, for example Rasula 1995: 136, 138). Work since the late twentieth century has identified canonisation and its corollaries as the central project in the formation of the traditional narrative of jazz. Useful overviews, and therefore documentation of the general points made below, may be found explicitly and implicitly in the work of jazz scholars over recent decades, including, *inter alios*, in chronological order De Veaux 1998 (originally 1991); Johnson 2011 (originally 1993); Gabbard 1995B; Ake 2002; Gennari 2006; Hersch 2008; Whyton 2011 and 2012; Cherchiari et al. 2012; Bohlman 2016.

The specific contents of the canon are determined by the drive to locate jazz as a high art, as defined by European traditions. Drawing on those traditions, the canon presents a very particular profile of the artistic process through which the jazz trajectory is navigated: the heroic individual *agon*, in this case through the fetishisation of the soloist and his (the gendering is pointed here) struggle with musical form, in the endless quest for artistic purity and authenticity, free of both generic and commercial contaminations. And the record of this quest is to be found in the texts which make up the canon itself, which thus become the subject of close formal analysis, which has now been raised to the highest level of detail by calling on computational musicology, as in Weimar's 'Jazzomat' project (Pfleiderer et al.: 2017). All of these features are clearly appropriated from Eurocentric high art discourse: 'As a canonical art, jazz is portrayed as a universal and transcendent music, mirroring the ideals of Western classical music and, therefore, continues to reinforce the constructs of high and low culture' (Whyton 2011: xiv). Of course, that Old World construct must be adapted in its specific detail to the New World situation. This entails foregrounding distinctively US features: the male artist is most often black American, whose African roots provide an 'Other' to European culture and whose history in the US provides a particularly potent image of heroic struggle against mainstream society.

> The added twist is that this new American classical music openly acknowledges its debt not to Europe, but to Africa. There is a sense of triumphant reversal as the music of a formerly enslaved people is designated a "rare and valuable national American treasure" by the Congress, and beamed overseas as a weapon of the Cold War.
>
> *De Veaux 1998: 484.*

The model is mediated at every level of jazz commentary, from journalism through polemic to academic scholarship, a range exemplified in the work of such writers as Barry Ulanov and Albert Murray, as well as Martin Williams and Gunther Schuller who 'sought to map across the value system of the great literary tradition and the formalist methods of classical musicology to demonstrate how serious and enlightening jazz was, and to write about works that constituted the essential building blocks of jazz history' (Whyton 2011: xxiii). This canon-centric narrative has been publicly institutionalised through such forums as college education programmes, the high profile collaborations between Wynton Marsalis and the Rockefeller Centre in New York, film and TV documentaries (see, for example, the Joe Williams's introduction to Part 1 of the *Jump for Jazz* series www.youtube.com/watch?v=zaUwd_lTNoA, accessed 28 July 2018), and most famously Ken Burns's 2001 television series *Jazz*.

In spite of its continuing public authority, this canonical model is pervaded by aporias. By this I mean both disruptions of its internal logic and also unresolved disparities between the discourse and actual jazz practices. The former include the tension inherent in an aesthetic based on improvisational performance but which centralises static texts; a discourse that assesses a performer's *oeuvre* on the basis of an infinitesimal proportion of his performance output (that is, in both cases, recordings); and criteria of quality that sacralise solo brilliance in a music for which collective improvisation is regarded as a primary discriminator. But the canonical *mythos* also fails to correspond with the realities of jazz practice. Like any putatively master narrative, and especially one so susceptible to romanticising, it inevitably submerges what Wall and Long described as the 'potentially interesting paradoxes, inconsistencies, and incongruities of the past' (Wall and Long 2011: 523). The need to maintain the satisfying symmetry of the narrative is not hospitable to musicians who disrupt the neat teleology of a succession of 'giants'. As Whiteoak reminds us, a '"who's who" is by default a "who's not"' (Whiteoak 2009: 19). Even in a city as important to the music as New Orleans, Sudhalter provides numerous examples of highly active white musicians who have been ignored (Sudhalter 1999: 82–3), as have entire stylistic communities, as experienced by English reed player Bruce Turner, both individually and as a member of various bands. He recalled the way the revivalist pundits 'closed in' on his playing, through a critical discourse which finally determines who shall get work and who not, and how they seek to freeze the music (Turner 1984: 106–107). Discussing the Freddie Randall groups, he laments the fact that the 'important role played by this band in the revival was never clearly understood' (Turner 1984: 110). Similarly, when Acker Bilk recruited him and moved into a more Louis Prima/Slim Gaillard/Louis Jordan-based jump style, playing largely to non-jazz purist 'squares', the 'critics kept away' (Turner 1984: 175). But examples of 'who's not' are generally reflections of issues other than musical, including gender, ethnicity, race, place and even commercial success as entertainers, as in the cases of Louis Prima (Sudhalter 1999: 80–81; Raeburn 2011: 392 n. 6) and Louis Jordan, whose successes coincided with 'the emergence of bop ... the seeming lightheartedness of Jordan's music flags him as a problematic figure for critics attempting to paint jazz since the 1940s as a serious art form' (Ake 2002: 43). Or, as in the case of Ethel Waters, at one point by her own account the 'best-paid woman in show business' (Waters n.d.: 170), a combination of several of these issues.

The canon has developed a protective carapace, and it is only with great difficulty that it can be prised open to admit new insights. It can be added to on its own terms – new 'masters', for example – but as a closed structure, it is difficult to build on conceptually. It has thus produced an ossified jazz narrative that tends to turn back on itself, retelling the same tales:

> the problem with writing about a world of twentieth-century jazz is that *the* history of jazz (one located almost exclusively inside the geopolitical boundaries of the United States) has already been written, and repeatedly replayed, reproduced, and displayed. It has created for itself a state of equilibrium.
>
> *Ake 2002: 289*

To re-invigorate jazz discourse it has become necessary therefore to stand outside those boundaries. A rapidly growing body of literature has explicitly and implicitly addressed the aporias in the canonical narrative from a range of perspectives (for some overviews of this literature see, for example, Whyton 2011: xv–xvii; Whyton 2012: 36–37; Bohlman and Plastino 2016A: 7–8). This has involved a shift along the spectrum from 'text' to 'context' toward the latter, which in turn has enlarged the disciplinary base (see, for example, Dorin 2016: 8); it is notable that Tucker identifies the inclusion of a jazz panel in a conference of the Modern Languages Association in 1988 as a significant moment in giving momentum to NJS (Tucker 2011: 138). Jazz studies have increasingly supplemented text-centred music aesthetics with broader perspectives from fields ranging from cultural theory to anthropology and detailed ethnography. In so doing they have made space for voices of jazz actants previously marginalised by the boundaries, exclusions and schematic binaries of the canon. The counter-narratives emerging from NJS question to a greater or lesser extent each component of this discourse, including US-centricity, 'blackness', an aesthetic teleology and the fixation on the recorded solo and its attendant figure–ground model. There are few assumptions cognate with this canon-centric narrative, both explicit and implicit, which do not come under challenge from NJS, in relation, for example, to gender, race, and the cultural and geographical origins of the music.

This is not to place NJS and its cognate discourses beyond critique (see, for example, Nicholson 2014: 117–127). And the deeper current of the canonical model remains tenacious. Reviewing the progress of NJS, Tucker raises the questions: 'To what extent *has* New Jazz Studies diverged from the jazz tradition narrative? To what extent does New Jazz Studies continue to reify the Jazz

Tradition as an object of study [?]' (Tucker 2011: 139, emphasis in the original). The question is timely. The established canon against which NJS locates itself is the outgrowth of a deeply rooted aesthetic going back the Enlightenment that seeks coherent narratives of the sublime and hierarchies sustained by neat *schemata*. As soon as jazz aspires to the legitimacy of high art, it becomes enmeshed in that historically specific paradigm, which is in fact inapposite to the specificity of jazz (see Johnson 2011). Ultimately this goes to questions more fundamental than changing the story. As I discuss in more detail below, there is an epistemological question here, of how we know, represent and construct the history of cultural practices. For the moment, however, the point is that even with a conscious agenda of challenging the content of the canon, it is still difficult to unmoor ourselves from the ideologies that underpin it, including the assumption (or wish) that history is orderly and linear, governed by legible relationships between cause and effect, and able to be represented in terms of neat binaries.

The deeply embedded and widely reticulated roots of the canonical model continue to condition even the challenges articulated by NJS:

> Jazz history textbooks, despite stated claims about problems with and alternatives to the canon, have almost universally shied away from a sustained critique of the idea of a canon itself; nor have they made a serious attempt to offer alternative methods and perspectives on how to approach jazz history from a broad non-canonical standpoint.
>
> *Prouty 2010: 23. NOTE: my citations from this article are*
> *from the online text which is not paginated, and my page numbers*
> *are based on those appearing in the scroll column, which begin at 1).*

And in his benchmark essay on the jazz tradition, DeVeaux observed that 'The crisis of the current jazz scene is less a function of the state of the music ... than of an anxiety arising from the inadequacy of existing historical frameworks to explain it' (DeVeaux 1998: 488). Yet Prouty, among others, notes the fact that DeVeaux's and Giddins's 2009 high-quality textbook *Jazz* itself exemplifies the tenacity of the canonical, great man/great work, teleological model:

> The text of *Jazz* seems, for the most part, to be organized along the same lines as previous studies, breaking down jazz's history roughly by decade-based stylistic categories, and emphasizing the contributions of major figures like Armstrong, Ellington (who are described as jazz's 'pre-eminent' soloist and composer, respectively) and Coltrane, who headline individual chapters. While the thoroughness of the narrative is impressive, DeVeaux and Giddins take us through a relatively familiar path, the 'official history' that has defined jazz scholarship for so long.
>
> *Prouty 2010: 21*

He concludes: 'by and large the book offers a narrative that is strikingly similar to the "official version" that DeVeaux decried in 1991' (Prouty 2010: 22; see also Perchard 2015: 8; Bohlman and Plastino 2016A: 9 and 43 n. 2; Pfleiderer et al.: 2017: 29). It has been pointed out that the undertow of the canonical model has led to an unsteadiness in the critical engagement with more recent developments, particularly fusions that are in tension with the criterion of generic purity. It is only when these developments can be sucked back into the traditional force field, rather than interrogating the template itself, that the story regains its composure (see, for example, Bohlman and Plastino 2016A: 9–10). This raises the question: is it possible to pursue a trajectory of jazz history and analysis without becoming a satellite whose orbit is shaped by a canon that is clearly itself an inadequate and misleading model? What would a history of jazz that steps outside the US-centric canon look like and what are its larger implications, not just for jazz studies, but for studies of music in the era of mediatised globalisation?

The point of this study is to get outside the closed room of the established jazz narrative, enclosed by such boundaries as blackness, masculinity, canonical aesthetics and textuality. There are many ways in ways in which this is being done within NJS: along gender lines, along racialised lines, by going beyond recordings-as-autonomous-texts to production contexts. All of these, if explored far enough, will open up vast and overlapping continents that disclose the limited horizons of the model from which they have departed. One of the positions from which these challenges can be mounted is from outside the US axis. Tipping (2016: 103) lists significant recent publications in jazz scholarship, but in which there is negligible if any reference to jazz outside the US, and he cites Travis Jackson's declaration that studies of jazz outside the US 'act as supplements that mildly challenge the standard narratives without necessarily expanding the geography. ... The master narrative, however, remains intact – at least in the United States – and isn't subject to modification or elaboration' (Tipping 2016: 104). I argue however that in neglecting and even completely ignoring the story of jazz beyond the borders of the US, the established canonical account seriously limits our understanding of the cultural work that jazz could perform, and falsifies what it did perform, as a global force. To view the history of jazz from, so-to-speak, the 'outside' is potentially to fundamentally rearrange the whole historical landscape.

The relative neglect of the diaspora and its paths outside the US represents a fundamental contradiction that is all the more striking in the context of cultural globalisation. It is ironic that a music so widely hailed for its international scope, is largely explained through an insular narrative. The canonical account of the history of the music itself relies on the recognition that jazz was in a process of continuous formation in the diaspora *within* the US. The distinctive regional (Chicago, New York, Kansas City, West Coast) and individual voices are deeply valorised – until we hit the US border. What are regarded as enriching early developments in the internal US diaspora are ignored or anathematised when they manifested themselves at the global level, even though it is at that level that the importance of jazz in modernity is articulated. Apart from the logical problems in that asymmetry, in brute quantitative terms, neglect of the global diasporic process is deeply misleading. In 2003, Jerome Harris reported an estimate that jazz in Europe 'generates $250–300 million per year' and in assessing the global presence of the music predicted that 'elsewhere' would account for more jazz activity than its place of origin (Harris 2003: 106, 124). Michael Pronko argues that the 'largest home' for jazz outside the US is not in Europe, but Japan (Pronko 2019: 271). On the basis of demographics alone, it seems reasonable to assume that more hours of jazz are played outside the US than inside it, enough to provide US jazz musicians with most of their living (Rasula 2002: 68).

The potential benefits of studying the global jazz diaspora, however, go beyond that simple calculus. Few of the issues that traverse jazz can be adequately contextualised within modernity while the story of the music remains confined within the US. The complicity of 'blackness' with the history of the music, for example, is a larger story than can be told without engagement with its global routes. Paul Gilroy noted that confining our perspective within the terms of nation 'impoverishes modern black cultural history because the transnational structures which brought the black Atlantic world into being have themselves developed and now articulate its myriad forms into a system of global communications constituted by flows' (Gilroy 1999: 80). Apart from the complexities of the broader black diaspora, at the same time, jazz itself has broken out of the confines of US-centric canonicity. As is now increasingly recognised, there are thriving jazz formations that owe relatively little to US models (see Cherchiari et al. 2012; Arndt 2012; and see further discussion below). Indeed, a number of writers now argue that the centre of gravity of the music may no longer to be found in the US, that today 'it is in countries outside the United States where the most profound changes in the music are occurring' (Nicholson 2005: xii; see similarly Harris 2003: 128, n. 31). Nicholson cites sources from both within and beyond the US declaring that the country's thriving jazz education industry has institutionalised a form of conservatism that makes institutions basically 'trade schools' dominated by the objectives of technical mastery, leading in turn to the fixation on fluency and speed in the deployment of a standard vocabulary and grammar (Nicholson 2005: 76, 101, 117, 118, 120; Nicholson 2014: 30–32). Attention is thus turning to the question of how to break away from these US-bound models of practice, historiography and pedagogy: 'How … do we understand the enormously complex globalization of jazz?' (Bohlman 2016: 155). Born and Hesmondhalgh (2000A) provide an overview of theoretical approaches to the study of transcultural musical migrations, and participant-observer ethnographic anthropologists like Steven Feld provide models in action, including specifically for jazz. Feld's study of jazz in Ghana in particular is marked by an inspirationally robust, close-quarters engagement with the local specificity of the subject (Feld 2012).

While NJS has raised the profile of diasporic studies, they can be traced back many decades. In their overview, Tackley and Whyton (2013: 6) list David Boulton's

Jazz in Britain of 1959, nearly 60 years ago. An early monograph on the jazz diaspora was Goddard 1979. Pioneering though this was, its scope was not global,
and like the later Moody 1993 and Larry Ross 2003, its primary objective was to
compile a chronicle of US jazz musicians travelling outside the US. The pioneering
academic multi-authored collection of essays on diasporic jazz in various regions is
Atkins 2003. Most recently Philip V. Bohlman and Geoffrey Plastino (2016) edited
a collection of essays on various diasporic jazz regions. A sudden surge of collections
covering the whole of Europe is to be found in Martinelli 2018, Wasserberger, et al.
2017, and the forthcoming multi-volume *Oxford History of Jazz in Europe* edited
by Walter van der Leur. There are collections of essays on jazz in specific regions,
such as Johnson 2016, which includes essays on both Australia and New Zealand,
and Toynbee, Tackley and Doffman 2014 on black British jazz. *Jazz Research Journal*
has recently produced special issues on diasporic jazz (Johnson 2016, above, first
appeared in a double of issue of the journal), and the May/November 2016, double
issue 1/2 was on 'The global circulations of jazz'. Nicholson's 2005 monograph
specifically surveyed aspects of the international diaspora and in some respects
overlaps with this study, though we extrapolate in different directions.

There are essay-length surveys on the general phenomenon of diasporic jazz,
as for example Johnson 2002A and Harris 2003. Currently in print or recently
published are my essay of around 50 pages, 'Jazz Outside the US' (Johnson
Forthcoming A) and an essay for the 2019 *Routledge Companion to New Jazz Studies*.
Some coverage of diasporic jazz has begun to appear in general histories of the
music, as for example in Shipton 2001, and Terry Martin 2000 writes on Canada
and Australia. For the most part, however, such coverage remains negligible even
in the most recent general histories, as summarised above. There have been book-
length academic studies of particular regional and national jazz histories, a sample
of which includes a recent flurry of studies of the UK, for example McKay, 2005;
Gelly, 2014; Parsonage (now Tackley) 2005; Moore, 2007 and Heining 2012; and
also jazz in France (Nettelbeck 2004 and more recent studies include Mawer 2014
and Braggs 2016) and Sweden (van Kan 2017). Other region-specific collections
include Atkins 2001 on Japan. The pioneering scholarly study of jazz in Australia
was that of Andrew Bisset 1979/1987, followed by Johnson 1987, 2000, 2016 and
Whiteoak 1999. There are also chapters on regional jazz in collections of national
musics, for example on jazz in Spain (Alonso 2013; Iglesias 2013, 2017; Pedro
2017). The various volumes of the continuing work-in-progress, *Encyclopedia of
Popular Music of the World*, also include entries on regional jazz. Broader studies, in
regional terms, include Heffley 2005; Cerchiari et al. 2012. These are just a few
examples of proliferating studies of jazz in particular diasporic sites. There have
been studies of jazz in totalitarian regimes. The pioneering monographs were Kater
1992 on the Third Reich and Starr 1983 on the USSR. More recent collections
of essays include Pickhan and Ritter 2010 on the Soviet Bloc; Pietraszewski 2014
on Poland; Kajanová, Pickan and Ritter 2016 on jazz under state socialism; and
Johnson 2017C on jazz under various totalitarianisms.

There is thus a burgeoning literature on diasporic jazz, but most often it consists of historical accounts of region-specific jazz outside the US, rather than focused explorations of the actual diasporic process more generally. It is my hope that this book will extend the conceptual and disciplinary range of jazz studies in general, bringing them into mutually illuminating convergence with other fields including acoustic ecology and cognitive theory. When I began publishing on any form of diasporic jazz in the early 1980s (see for example Johnson 1982), it was still possible to read everything in the field. As the foregoing selective list suggests, that is no longer so. There are therefore inevitably partialities in my emphases, particularly related to region. Most of my miniature case studies are from the UK, Australasia, South Africa the Nordic region and the former Soviet Bloc, for the simple reason that I feel I can speak on these with more detailed and often direct knowledge. But this is not intended to be a country-by-country overview, for which in so many cases now there are detailed and intimately informed studies. My interest is rather in the diasporic process and the larger historiographical, cultural and epistemological issues it raises. Most fundamentally, as a counter-narrative to the dominant historiography, a sustained analysis of the jazz diaspora releases jazz studies from a range of conceptual limitations which are largely inappropriate to the specificity of jazz as a practice. In so doing it enormously enlarges the potential of jazz studies as a vehicle for the productive engagement with a range of other fields, from methods of cultural analysis to cognitive theory. At the same time, this is emphatically not presented as a new 'master narrative' – the whole spirit of this study is to challenge and identify the limits of an existing canonical narrative, 'THE history of jazz'. One of my conclusions will be that while there are broad patterns in the global jazz diaspora, there is no single master narrative, and the future of an effective jazz historiography must include detailed local micro-histories.

Apart from certain regional emphases, there is also a weighting here toward the interwar diaspora. There are several reasons for this. First, this period has been least studied in the literature, and more generally somewhat disdained as producing tepid and unconvincing iterations of the US 'original'. I don't share that view. The relationship between US and non-US jazz has gone through several stages. First exposure, indirect and direct, to the US source material was followed by more or less convincing attempts to approximate that model, impeded by problems of access, ingrown training and musical memory. As those obstacles were overcome, as the music became internationally codified, a point was reached by about the late 1950s when diasporic jazz for the most part was becoming indistinguishable from US jazz, globally placeless. This near-total assimilation was then followed by 'fusion' – by attempts to go beyond the template – leading in time to a situation where non-US musicians were producing striking locally distinctive innovations. This stage is being increasingly respected and documented, often in association with the World Music scene. But I would like to put in a plea for the same level of respect and recognition of that first stage, the supposedly clumsy work outside the US in the interwar period, a plea for the value of what is almost always overlooked as misconceived jazz, partly because I think it has its own 'authenticity' and also because it is such an instructive site of the diaspora in progress, jazz 'in the making'. In many ways this is the most instructive period in the encounter between jazz and its diasporic destinations, with the strongest lessons for hybridisation and glocalisation. It is here that we see jazz coming into being, the mechanics of its negotiations with the world.

A further aspect of the structure of this study is that, compared with the general pattern in studies in cultural history, there might appear to be a certain untidiness, asymmetries between chapters and sections, recapitulations. I certainly came to this work wishing to produce a neat arrangement of material, but as in all such projects, the subject itself should be allowed to dictate structure as well as content. I did not want to force the material into a neatly pre-meditated structural model; the whole argument is based on the proposition that seeking to fit the study of jazz into a standard model is misconceived. So I must own any apparent structural untidiness, and declare that, paradoxically, it required considerable intellectual discipline to allow that untidiness to prevail. In other publications I have discussed the difficulties of deciding on the most appropriate 'voice' for representing the distinctive character of jazz (see Johnson 2011, 1994, 2000: xv–xvi), and suggested that it needs many. The point is reflected in the mix that constitutes this study. It combines more or less chronological narrative, cultural analysis, first person accounts, and the interpolation of micro-case studies that disclose the local specificities out of which jazz cultures emerge, the way regional cultural dynamics relating to for example, ethnicity, gender and politics traverse and shape jazz in ways that gratifyingly coherent canonical narratives elide.

I want to conclude this Introduction with a case study that exemplifies arguments I have been making, and foreshadows the scope and intent of this study: that is, to try to demonstrate what might be added to our understanding of jazz history by shifting our vantage point outside the canonical US-centric narrative, to the global diaspora. My case study here is from Australia and the UK, and it bears on a number of schematic binaries that sustain the authenticity of the canon, including black/white, art/entertainment and US/the rest. The idea of 'True' jazz has in some cases turned the diaspora into a story marked by deficit or absence. It is common to note that the 'masterwork' recordings by Oliver, Armstrong and Morton were not readily available as models for jazz musicians and communities outside the US until around the early 1930s. Thus, the work of benighted musicians throughout most of the 1920s begins with the assumption that it must be deficient, and it is already consigned to that category before any considered analysis (if any) even begins. Their exposure to US jazz was to rather pallid white bands, and their own efforts were therefore at least third hand from the fountainhead. This explains why these early diasporic jazz communities are perceived as slightly risible, so lacking in conviction according to our standards. And this, be it emphasised, is because they were deprived of exposure to the authentic black jazz, that is, not validated in terms of the canon.

For many Australian jazz writers, the 'father' of Australian jazz was either Graeme Bell (1914–2012) or Ade Monsbourgh (1917–2006). Both of these musicians are unquestionably among the most important jazz figures ever to emerge in Australia (see further Johnson 2000: 147–163). But the particular honorific 'father' arises from the parallel circumstance that they were of the generation first schooled in the 'classic' US recordings of the 1920s. While advertisements for Hot Five, Bix Beiderbecke and Joe Venuti recordings were appearing as early as 1932, committed jazz musician Benny Featherstone was still complaining in 1934 about the shortage of 'hot records'. These only became available to the burgeoning revivalist coterie in quantity through the private collection of Bill Miller, which he brought back in 1938 from England where he read law at Oxford, and through systematic reissue programmes like EMI's Hot Jazz Classics series from 1941 (See Johnson 2000: 17; for a broader overview of the early Australian record industry see Laird 1999). The members of the 'Mouldy Fygge' community (who constituted the most influential, articulate and vocal historians of the music), who rank Bell and Monsbourgh so highly have also been wont to declare that there was *no* Australian jazz prior to that period. Apart from dinner, bar room and gig conversations, this debate was primarily conducted in jazz club publications and small journals such as *Jazz Notes*, inaugurated by Bill Miller in 1941; the debate is alluded to in Linehan 1983. Interestingly, Bell himself modestly declined paternity and declared that the 'father' of Australian jazz was trombonist, trumpeter and bandleader Frank Coughlan (1904–1979) (Johnson 1987:135). He referred to him as 'the great Frank Coughlan', always looked forward to sharing the bill with his orchestra and was honoured when Coughlan sat in with the band (Bell 1988: 65, 273). Coughlan also recorded six sides with the Bell band in 1942.

Emerging from the rural brass band movement, Coughlan arrived in Sydney in either 1922 or early 1923 (Johnson 1987; Ford 1995: 80. The main sources drawn on here for information about Coughlan's career are Bisset (1987), Johnson (1987), and especially Ford (1995). On matters of detail, they do not always agree. In this account I have drawn only upon material on which they are unanimous, or at least not in open disagreement). Coughlan's exposure to jazz was first through recordings of white jazz musicians, particularly the Original Memphis Five, whose trombonist Miff Mole deeply impressed the young trombonist and became his primary jazz inspiration. Coughlan soon gained a strong profile in the local dance band scene, particularly as someone able to deliver 'hot' choruses.

In April 1923 the first visiting US band billed as jazz arrived in Australia, in the form of Frank Ellis and the Royal Californians, to open Sydney's new Palais Royal where they played a season from 5 May to 28 February 1924 (the main sources used for the movements of the Californians in Australia are Sutcliffe 1982 and Ford 1995). With his trumpeter brother Tommy, Frank made their acquaintance, enjoyed lengthy discussions of jazz, and were often invited to sit in with the Americans and join post-gig jamming. Frank was invited to join the band for a St Kilda Palais de Danse engagement in Melbourne, from 1 March to 8 May

1924, to be followed by a further six-month engagement back at Sydney's Palais Royal ending on Christmas Eve 1925. With some changes in personnel, including Ellis's return to the US by the end of 1925, the Californians continued to work in Sydney until the expiry of their contract on New Year's Eve 1926. Recordings Coughlan made with the band in that year demonstrate that not only did he fit in, but in many respects, his solo work is more supple and harmonically informed than some of the Americans, for example as compared to the US trumpet soloist on 'Milenberg Joys' from August 1926.

Over the next few years Coughlan worked in Australian dance bands at the top of the profession, then sailed for England in November 1928, carrying letters of introduction to bandleaders from Californians trumpet player Eddie Frizelle. Arriving on 10 December, Coughlan immediately found work in clubs including the Kit Kat, and the Piccadilly with Al Starita. Jack Hylton's manager heard Coughlan on a broadcast from the Kit Kat and invited him to audition for Hylton's orchestra, at that time in Hamburg in the midst of a European tour. The audition was successful, and Coughlan joined them for the remainder of the tour. Back in England, he auditioned for Fred Elizalde, at that time at the Savoy, and was engaged for a lengthy season, starting that night, reading the sax part of Adrian Rollini who was temporarily on a recruitment visit to the US. He went on to work with Al Collins's Dance Band at Claridge's in Bond Street, playing for dancers from nine to midnight, then jamming for an hour with some members of the band, sessions which gained a following of fans. 'Picking up their chairs, they would gather round the band to listen whilst it jammed away on the latest hits of the day' (Ford 1995: 113). It is worth noting in passing this early example of jazz performed for listening rather than for dancing. Coughlan returned to Sydney, arriving in January 1930, and went on to become, along with Melbourne-based Jim Davidson, the most successful Australian dance orchestra leader over several decades, retiring from full-time music in December 1970.

In the 1920s this was a glowing CV. But of course, this was with white English hot dance orchestras (and that an Australian with his non-black jazz education should be so successful becomes also an implicit reflection on the standards of UK hot dance). In all this, there is no reason that post-war jazz commentators would expect, and therefore little encouragement for them to hear, anything but lukewarm third hand jazz – after all, all of this is without exposure to the black US 'classic' recordings, the *sine qua non* for fully-fledged jazz credentials. Yet, throughout these stages of his career, careful listening reveals a jazz-literate agility that would be impressive even in a black US jazz trombonist of the 1920s. This high level of competence is barely explicable within the framework of the canonical narrative.

But let us look more closely at these white musicians he heard on record and worked with in Australia and the UK. Coughlan's primary inspiration, heard on recordings, was Miff Mole, one of the early trombone jazz virtuosi. It is hard to think of any black trombonist of the 1920s whose harmonic agility came close to

Mole's, incidentally prompting a hypothesis that the 'tailgate style' of New Orleans jazz trombone, drawing on the brass band tradition (see Sudhalter 1999: 103), was an obstacle to the harmonic suppleness of the white northerner Miff Mole. Coughlan's first experience of performing with US musicians was many months with Frank Ellis and His Royal Californians, and he roomed with one of their trumpet players, Paul Whiteman alumnus Eddie Frizelle, who 'took him under his wing' during the St Kilda Palais engagement (Ford 1995: 95). Canadian-born Australian entrepreneur J. C. Bendrodt had already been importing US musicians when he travelled to the US searching for a band for the 1923 winter season. He heard Ellis in San Francisco and signed him for six months (Sutcliffe 1982: 22). Frank Ellis has no presence in jazz historiography, but the band members, including Ellis, were in fact from Art Hickman's dance orchestra. Hickman had led the band at the Rose Room in the St Francis Hotel since February 1915, starting with six, and expanding to ten pieces by 1919. They had recorded extensively before Hickman turned the band over to Ellis in late 1921, and this was the band Bendrodt heard in 1923. And except for the Australian bass player Bob Waddington, who was recruited in Sydney, it was the band he imported, promising 'jazz numbers of the orchestra that has moved a million feet' (Sutcliffe 1982: 22).

Under erstwhile leader Hickman, this band enjoys some notice in US-centric jazz histories, but being white and from the West Coast, the allusions are usually *en passant* (see, for example Collier 1981: 217). Sudhalter, however, has documented the revolutionary innovations Hickman's band introduced, including horn counterlines, the orchestrated 'break', and especially the incorporation of a section of what has become the iconic jazz instrument, the saxophone (Sudhalter 1999: 88). Hickman's arranger was Ferde Grofé, whose work would later leave its stamp on Paul Whiteman's orchestras. Hickman's band

> shaped the modern dance orchestra and laid the foundation for the entire field of big band writing, foreshadowing even the swing bands of the 1930s. As arranger Robert Haring Sr. told James H. Maher, "Everybody – and I mean players, arrangers, and leaders of bands – was talking about Hickman. What he was doing was utterly unprecedented."
>
> *Sudhalter 1999: 160*

And, incidentally, one of the significant participants in these innovations was saxophonist Bert Ralton who joined the band in 1919. Ralton would go on to London's Savoy, leading the Havana Band which, along with the hotel's restaurant staff, was then brought to Australia to open the Ambassadors nightclub in 1923 (Johnson 1987: 69), remaining as an influential presence for several years.

Coughlan went on to work in England and Europe, including with the orchestra of Fred Elizalde, 'a figure unique in dance band history' (Sudhalter 1999: 174). Born in the Philippines, largely raised in the US, Cambridge educated, studies with Ravel, and professionally based in England, Elizalde's profile has little to recommend him to the attention of canon-centric historians. Yet far from being a run-of-the-mill dance band leader, Elizalde had very advanced ideas about the future of jazz, visualising 'a music that made free use of various time signatures, abandoned the traditional verse–chorus structure of pop songs, and even dismissed the idea of melody as "an entirely secondary consideration"' (Sudhalter 1999: 175). Unlike other British hot dance bands of the period, Elizalde's featured a number of innovations including extended improvisations (Parsonage 2005: 209). In addition, he recruited a number of US musicians who were highly influential. Most prominent was New York born, of Italian extraction, Adrian Rollini, recruited along with Chelsea Quealey and Bobby Davis in 1928 (Sudhalter 1999: 189). They had been central to one of the most popular bands of the 1920s, the California Ramblers, a stopover for most white New York musicians of the time. It was perhaps their popularity with white collegians that has led to its neglect by purist jazz historians (Sudhalter 1999: 160). In 1929, they were joined by reed player Fud Livingston, whose work as an arranger in the Bix–Trumbauer coterie made 'a deep impression … on all arrangers of the late '20s, black and white' (Sudhalter 1999: 342). These musicians played a major role as models for British colleagues. London violinist George Hurley recalled the enormous admiration in which Rollini was held by the Elizalde band at the Savoy, 'it was like going to school again' (Sudhalter 1999: 175); for Harry Gold, whose 'Pieces of Eight' would become so prominent in post-war Britain, Rollini 'was the greatest influence on … shaping my style' (Parsonage 2005: 215).

Rollini is one of the most extraordinary figures in jazz history. He adopted bass saxophone as an alternative to the string and brass bass, bringing a new suppleness and drive to the music's bass lines (Sudhalter 1999: 162). He exploited novelty instruments like the Couesniphone (aka the Goofus) and the 'Hot Fountain Pen' (Sudhalter 1999: 166–167), further reasons that it was probably felt his status as a serious musician was compromised. Yet on his arrival in the UK, he had just come from a central role in some of the latest, and now 'classic' jazz recordings of the 1920s, in the company of Bix Beiderbecke, Frankie Trumbauer, Eddie Lang and Joe Venuti. Given his profile, as Sudhalter notes, as long as we remain enclosed by canon-based chains of influence, Rollini –like Eddie Lang – 'makes no sense' (Sudhalter 1999: 166, similarly 169), and, we may add, nor does Coughlan. But there they all were.

The influence of the US-centric canon tended to consign a white, non-US dance band musician like Coughlan to the trivial margins of the music, while in fact he was exposed to and working with some of the most 'advanced' jazz exponents of the 1920s. But the blackness fetish has occluded this, and while his contemporaries clearly recognised his abilities as a hot player, subsequent historians, falling under the umbra of 'blackness', have seen little reason to recognise and reassess his stature. There is much talk of how little direct contact diasporic musicians had with important US sources; but the word 'important' derives its weight from canonical criteria, by which Coughlan's career profile has little to recommend it to serious consideration. This situation is not just a reflection of the 'anti-white' tendency in the canon, but also its reluctance to accept the utilitarian functions and corporeality associated with dance bands, especially 'society bands' and their class associations, and its focus on the New Orleans/Chicago/New York axis for acceptable jazz routes. The fact that Coughlan was appointed bandleader for the high profile Trocadero dance palais back in Sydney in 1936, also consolidated his link with dance music just at a time when the emerging and highly vocal revivalist coteries were so stridently opposed to commercial Swing, a position that was as much to do with broader historical background, including the rise of Fascism in Europe as with music.

Coughlan was only one of a number of antipodean musicians from the interwar period who were successful at the highest professional level in the northern hemisphere. Australian trombonist Clarrie Collins reportedly coached the Basie and Ellington brass sections (see further Johnson 2000: 145–147). Like Coughlan, they demonstrated that in order to participate convincingly in the 'jazz-world' even during its earliest phases, it was not necessary to have travelled the route of New Orleans/Chicago/New York black musicians that is constitutive of the canon. Sudhalter's monumental study has clearly established that race and place within the US are neither exclusive nor essential elements in the tradition, identifying alternative routes. The global diaspora makes that case with even more force. It is harder to be more remote from the jazz circuit than Australasia in the 1920s, yet from that region comes a dramatic lesson in the multiple paths of globalisation. Studies of the extra-US diaspora are revealing both the infinite and increasing multi-directionality, the 'polysporic' character, of that phenomenon – including the *two* way traffic between 'source' and 'diaspora' – and its potential as a site on which a distinctive jazz discourse can be constructed, one which in turn can provide a template for the subsequent developments in the twentieth century. What follows reinforces the proposition that 'One of the strengths of jazz is its sheer diversity and ability to keep reinventing itself through time, location and cultural context' (Mawer 2014: 168).

PART 1
First Eight

Global Jazz Diaspora

1

GLOBAL JAZZ DIASPORA

A Chronicle

Introduction

A chronicle is an account of historical events in the order of their occurrence. I begin with what is primarily a chronicle of the international jazz diaspora, to provide a foundation on which to build subsequent arguments about the cultural and political dynamics of that process. Given the recent spate of books on jazz in Europe listed above, I have tended to provide examples from regions that have been receiving less attention. Much of my supplementary material arises from one of the arguments prosecuted in this study and articulated explicitly below. That is, that one of the most serious deficiencies in the standard jazz historiography is that in the interests of a 'grand narrative' it elides the crucial importance of micro-histories and local dynamics in the formation and dispersal of the music. I therefore pause in my narrative from time to time for exemplification.

The diverse landscape of jazz outside the US exhibits both general patterns and regional variations at key moments in the internationalisation of the music. For the sake of coherence it is necessary to invoke various taxonomies, such as the concept of nation or blackness. But the investigation itself will disclose problems with such models, and these will be explored in more detail in later sections, as will other implications of a diasporic frame of reference. This opening chronicle will be structured around apparently unitary episodes which have framed the music, such as the Great Depression, two World Wars and the Cold War, reflecting the fact that the internationalisation of jazz has been aligned with the trajectory of various Euro-US imperialist enterprises, and these can therefore be seen as reference points in the exploration of its history. Jazz has also been in continuous exchange with antecedent and collateral streams of American music such as minstrelsy, gospel and ragtime, and although these are beyond the scope of this discussion occasional cross-referencing is useful.

International Migration – The First Phase

Both discursively and as a social practice, jazz was internationalised with a rapidity unprecedented for any music. 'The jazz audience, from the very beginning, has been global' (Rasula 2002: 68; Johnson 2017C: 10). This proposition, which only a couple of decades ago would have required considerable citation from primary sources, can now be succinctly reviewed with a festoon of secondary citations, the dates of which testify to the extent to which the field has been recently populated.

The year 1917 is pivotal. It was the year of Passchendaele which, for many, marked the point beyond which World War One could no longer be justified by reference to the idealisms of the nineteenth century. The French army mutinied, the generals began to realise that the heart had gone out of the armies and the Pope called for an end to hostilities (McDonald 1993: 166; Johnson 2000: 20). Germany's declaration of unrestricted submarine warfare and its first air-raids on London herald the unchivalric era of total war. It was the year proclaiming a revolutionary new order, literally in the case of Russia, but also in the publication of T. S. Eliot's 'Prufrock' collection, the coining of the word 'surrealism' and the foundation of Mondrian's journal *De Stijl*, in Europe, and the advent of female suffrage in the 'New World'. The entry of the US into the war in 1917 helped to end it, and also led to the closure of the red-light area in Storyville in New Orleans, laying the foundations for one of the central mythologies in the dissemination of the music. In 1917 the Original Dixieland Jazz Band (ODJB), from New Orleans via Chicago, famously opened at Reisenweber's Restaurant in New York, converting a puzzled crowd by declaring that jazz was for dancing. It was the year that the band made what are regarded as the first jazz recordings. It is thus an appropriate year from which to date the international jazz diaspora.

Intimations of the new music were circulating internationally before the cessation of hostilities in November 1918. An account of the Arras offensive of April 1917, only months after the first jazz recordings were made by the ODJB, includes mention of a Royal Flying Corps squadron mess with its own jazz band to boost morale (Hart 2005: 288). By 1920 jazz had become a pervasive presence in Europe, including in Spain, France, Germany, Italy and the Nordic regions (Iglesias 2013: 101; Plastino 2016: 315; Johnson Forthcoming B). In the UK it now supplanted the fashion for ragtime, and in London song-writer Ivor Weir, a member of the service entertainment unit the New Zealand Pierrots, was enjoying great success with his 'Mad Jazz Razz' (Parsonage 2005: 27; Bourke 2010: 7). The antipodean connection proclaims the geographical extent of the new craze. In August 1919 the New Zealand *Dominion* announced that a group of Wellington musicians had formed a jazz band, whose rehearsals produced 'the weirdest effects imaginable', which could scarcely be termed music, but nonetheless, could 'make people dance to its quaint rhythms and amazing pauses' (Bourke 2010: 7). In Finland references to jazz, and the ODJB in particular, were appearing in the press as early as May 1919 (Johnson Forthcoming B). The first 'echoes of jazz' in Brazil had been in 1917 when *The American Rag Time Revue*, presented in Rio de Janeiro, featured the shape of things to come in the form of 'imposing drums that took centre stage', the 'show-stopper' according to a press review, 'the most fascinating part of the show' (Fléchet 2016:16). The following year the word 'jazz' first appeared, with the announcement that 'the famous American dancer Miss Della Martell would perform a traditional dance 'and American Jazz Music' at Rio's Moderno theatre (Fléchet 2016: 17). By 1926 the music was being advertised in Azerbaijan as performed by 'the first Caucasus Eastern Folk Symphonic Orchestra' (Naroditskaya 2016: 100). In 1922, in an article published in *New York Times Book Review and Magazine*, journalist Burnet Hershey reported that in his recent journey around the world he found the 'zump-zump-zump and toodle-oodle-doo' of jazz everywhere (Walser 1999: 26). The speed of its international circulation tells us as much about modernity itself as about the music which became its anthem.

Physical Migrations

The dispersal of jazz through physical migrations was crucial in internationalising models of a music so rooted in live performance. In spite of the perceived connection between jazz, blackness, Africa and primitivism, in many cases, especially Anglophone countries and regions like the UK and Australasia, the first live exposures to US acts presented as jazz musicians was to white performers. The ODJB in London in 1919 is generally cited as the benchmark, but I want to consider the case of Sophie Tucker, because it carries our attention forward to a number of issues to be explored later regarding the diaspora narrative, all of which cast light on later elisions relating to vaudeville, Jewishness, dance and gender, and how the historian is to deploy the term jazz. Tucker's New York formal performance debut was in 1906, in blackface coon singing with a thick southern accent (Tucker 1948: 44). In 1910 or 1911 she had shared a bill with Art Hickman, referred to above, in San Francisco on the Pantages Circuit, and she recalled also visiting Purcell's, 'the hot coloured joint' (Tucker 1948: 102).

In her memoir Tucker recalls the beginning, in what must have been about 1916, of what she referred to as her 'jazz' period, billed as 'The Queen of Jazz' with her band, 'Five Kings of Syncopation', recruited from local New York musicians (Tucker 1948: 137), including drummer Dan Alvin who 'could do a mean shimmy and still beat his drum … [and] … could throw the sticks up in the air and catch them without losing a beat' (Tucker 1948: 143). Following an Orpheum circuit tour which included Chicago, where they enjoyed outstanding reviews (Tucker 1948: 140), her agent booked her for an eight-month season at Reisenweber's, opening on 23 December 1916, playing both as a show and for dancing (Tucker 1948: 152). By this account, Tucker's 'Queen of Jazz' season, with white New York musicians led by a Jewish woman, opened before the ODJB's season at the same café began in January 1917, often mythologised as New York's first exposure to jazz. Regarding the international diaspora, Tucker left for England in March 1922, taking with her two pianists, Ted Shapiro and Jack Carroll (Tucker 1948: 181, 197): 'I wouldn't risk being stranded and having to break in a British piano player who might not be up on American jazz rhythms. I would show the folks over there what American jazz was like' (Tucker 1948: 171). To open one of her programmes, she decided on what was felt to be 'a jazz song', 'Dapper Dan' (interestingly, this music hall item was also in the repertoire of the Australian Graeme Bell band in the UK several decades later); the 'audience liked the jazz' (Tucker 1948: 182). Her Jewishness was a prominent feature of her presentation, especially the song 'My Yiddisher Mama'; she identified as a 'Jewish' performer and she attracted a large proportion of Jews in her audiences (Tucker 1948: 195). She recalls that the English audiences 'seemed crazy about everything American and eager to take up American jazz, American dance steps, American slang, and American mannerisms' (Tucker 1948: 189, see also 193). She also toured Europe, and returned to London in August 1925, following Ted Lewis at the Kit Kat Club, then in 1928 and 1930 (Tucker 1948: 203, 230, 237). She identified herself as a jazz performer, and audiences, promoters and reviewers evidently agreed. But we will look in vain for reference to Sophie Tucker in histories of jazz and its diaspora. There was at one time a humorous website that explained how to play the blues, and it included the injunction that if your name is Damien and you live in an ashram, then it doesn't matter how many men you killed in St. Louis, you can't be a blues singer. Nor, it seems, if you are a female Jewish vaudevillian from New York, can you be a pioneer jazz performer, no matter how many people thought you were. I spend time on this case at the outset to prepare the ground for arguments running through the following chapters about the inadequacy of the canonical 'who's who'.

The physical and cultural mobilisations of World War One played a significant role in the music's migration. James Reese Europe's sixty-piece black band of the 369th US Infantry ('The Hellfighters') was both embodiment and instrument of the multi-directional migrations feeding into all jazz. The nineteen among its musicians recruited in Puerto Rico by its leader included many who would settle in New York, the vanguard of a greater influx from the 1930s (Shepherd et al. 2005: III: 88). In 1917 Europe's orchestra arrived in France where it presented jazz and ragtime repertoire to civilians, allied soldiers and even German POWs. They were followed by similar US military bands, one of which included Sam Wooding, who returned with his own jazz group in 1925 to tour Europe including Sweden (van Kan 2016: 39). Louis Mitchell's Jazz Kings (1917), the ODJB (1919), Will Marion Cook's Southern Syncopated Orchestra with Sidney Bechet (1919) and Paul Whiteman (1923, 1925), were all seen by British and European audiences. Wooding also visited Tunis and South America, and Josephine Baker visited Finland with a sixteen-piece orchestra in 1933 (Kernfeld 1988: I: 502; Nettelbeck

2004: 16–28, 37–41; Goddard 1979: 9–78; Shepherd et al. 2005: VII: 263; Nettelbeck 2004: 37–41; Johnson Forthcoming B). Baker had electrified Paris with the *Revue Nègre* company in 1925 (Nettelbeck 2004: 37–41), and the same company had also premiered its show *Black People* in Berlin in 1926, and under the name *Black Follies* in Lisbon in 1928, with music composed by Spencer Williams and Joe Solmer and performed by the Neger Jazz Orchestra (Roxo and Castelo-Branco 2016: 205–207; Cravinho 2016: 90–91). Other early European exposures to visiting US jazz-oriented performers included in 1923 in London the revues *The Rainbow* of which James P. Johnson was a member, and *Dover Street to Dixie* which included Johnny Dunn (Parsonage 2005: 179). Parsonage provides a detailed account of similar visits and their impact (see also Parsonage 2012). She argues that the ODJB and the Southern Syncopated Orchestra in particular were 'vital to the evolution of jazz in Britain' (Parsonage 2005: 160).

By the 1920s there were well-established Southeast Asian dance band circuits used by musicians from the Philippines, Russia, Britain and Japan, as well as the US. Sidney Bechet and Buck Clayton were heard in the Soviet Union and Shanghai, which boasted its own highly paid black American jazz community servicing its prolific entertainment industry. Teddy Weatherford settled in India and performed in Japan, China and Southeast Asia (Atkins 2003: xv; Jones 2003: 231; Pinckney 2003: 62, 231). White US Jazz bands began touring Australasia in the early 1920s and were extremely important as models for a less frantic and chaotic performance style than earlier vaudeville-based local acts that had been based on second-hand exposure in print formats (Johnson 1987: 3–13, 64–73). Under the influence of the first US jazz group, Frank Ellis and his Californians, Frank Coughlan recalled that sax players began to use vibrato, bass players more often played pizzicato, and the rhythm section began to include 'drumming for rhythm instead of noise' (Boden 2016: 112). In New Zealand early personal contact with US performers came in 1923 with the arrival of ex-US navy musician Dick Richards who joined the Ambassador Musical Trio, billed as a jazz specialist, creating a sensation with his 'stomp arrangements' and 'eccentric' banjo style (Bourke 2010: 21). Of particular importance was Sammy Lee and his Americanadians, who arrived in 1938 and stayed for 18 months of residencies in Wellington and Auckland, whence they also broadcast (Bourke 2010: 91). Lee later settled in Australia where he became a very successful nightclub entrepreneur.

An invaluable first-hand account of early contacts between US jazz musicians and Europe is provided in reed player Garvin Bushell's memoir *Jazz from the Beginning* (Bushell 1988; the page references below are to this edition). Few if any jazz musicians could have a broader panorama of the history of the music, ranging from participation on what are regarded as the first jazz/blues recordings with Mamie Smith in 1920, through work with Ethel Waters, the bands of Fletcher Henderson and Cab Calloway, and the 'rediscovered' Bunk Johnson in the 1940s, to Eric Dolphy, John Coltrane and Gil Evans in the 1960s. His career spanned early black vaudeville and circuses to orchestral settings on double reed instruments. He also accompanied an international tour that lasted just over two years from May 1925 to July 1927 in Sam Wooding's band with the *Chocolate Kiddies* revue. It opened in Berlin and took in Sweden, Denmark, Czechoslovakia, Spain, France, Switzerland and Russia, then back to Germany where the band split from the revue to become a touring orchestra that went on to England, France and then Argentina. As a further reminder of the international dispersal of his colleagues, in the course of his travels he met other expatriate US musicians. In Budapest he heard Palmer Jones and his black American band playing at the Moulin Rouge (61). In Vienna he first heard the now largely forgotten Arthur Briggs: 'What a beautiful trumpet player! He was in an orchestra with some Austrians, some French, and a couple of Senegalese. His trumpets made ours sound like beginners' (62; on Briggs's importance in Europe see also Johnson 2017C: 10). And he met the 'great clarinet player from Florida', J. Paul Wyer, aka The Pensacola Kid in Argentina where Wyer had bought a huge ranch (70). Bushell also recorded some of the impressions he formed and that the band left. In Prague Bushell was also engaged to play in a Czech dance band which played US dance music: 'they were interested in knowing how American jazz musicians played. They were a few years behind our things in New York. Rudolph Friml's "Indian Love Call" was very popular then, also "Whispering," "Avalon," and "St. Louis Blues."' (61). And it is an instructive disclosure of the stereotypification of early black jazz that the band (*sans* revue) did not go over well in London; Bushell speculates that it was because they were a 'classy organization'; that the British 'would have accepted a black orchestra doing comedy and slapstick' (68).

But what exactly were these 'jazz' audiences responding to? It is worth taking some time to discuss this, as it throws so much light on these early diasporic dynamics. The revue troupe consisted of an eleven-piece orchestra and more than thirty chorus girls, dancers and comedians. The revue, which was in two sections, 'with sketches, dance numbers, and comedy bits' (55), including: a plantation sketch; a 'jungle number' which gave the opportunity for 'jungle music: tom-toms and hoochie-coochie'; the interior of a Harlem cabaret, in which Adelaide Hall sang and an Apache dance was presented (55–56). The show 'was built around the team of Greenlee and Drayton, "a big-time" US vaudeville act who had been in Europe pre-war. They would dance and talk in Hungarian, Russian, French, Yiddish, English and German' (56). Willie Robbins and Chick Horsey did a black-face act that included very popular trumpet novelty imitations of their singing; Three Eddies did a comedy song and dancing routine in blackface; Jessie Crawford did a 'strut dance and drill with a chorus line' (56). Lest it be thought that all this was 'for export only', many of these acts had been presented at New York's Club Alabam (56), where Bushell had worked with Sam Wooding in 1924. The band played in the pit for the first half, then on stage for the second, without written music; the programme order would be changed according to audience response (56). They would use a wide range of instrumental combinations, including even an oboe trio (57). This 'revue' format was the norm. When Ellington toured

France in 1933 the concerts were in two parts, the first music, the second dancers and comedy. It was not until his 1939 tour that the format was what we would now recognise as a jazz concert (Hasse 2012: 192). The format of a tour by a black US jazz act as we are now accustomed to is very unlike the interwar period, when the vaudeville and variety roots of jazz were still much in evidence, as documented further below.

The importance of such direct contacts is reflected in the cases where it was not available. Finland was generally bypassed in early American tours of Scandinavia. Finnish jazz recordings as late as 1939, when compared with those of Swedish bandleader Thor Ehrling of the same year, indicate a much closer correspondence between Ehrling's work and US source materials (Johnson 2002A: 35). In Australia the deportation of Sonny Clay's Plantation Orchestra from the visiting revue *The Colored Idea* (see further below) was the last official live exposure for the general public to black US jazz musicians until 1954, and over the same period there was a dearth of any visiting US musicians (Johnson 2004: 10). England received a steady stream of major US jazz performers until 1935 when the Ministry of Labour placed a ban on US groups without appropriate reciprocity (see further on the Australian and UK bans below). The effects of these proscriptions were ambiguous, starving locals of up-to-the-minute exposure except for contacts during the periods of activity of US service musicians during World War Two, but also fostering locally serviced jazz scenes. Some sense of the significance of these circumstances can be gained by reference to the mirror image of France, which suffered no prohibitions on imported US musicians except during the period of German occupation (Johnson 1987: 23–32; Godbolt 1984: 236–274; Nettelbeck 2004: 37–80). The tours of visiting US bands, and of a local, albeit small visiting and expatriate community of US jazz musicians including a high proportion of African-Americans, affected interwar Parisian culture in a range of ways. Apart from simply being visible as a stimulating (if often ambiguous) presence, they 'coloured' the local jazz scene, and particularly its emerging discourses (see below). As metropolitan cohabitants they nuanced the music's exoticism and became a significant element in the city's radical intellectual life (see for example Nettelbeck 2004: 31–52). The significance of protracted and close exposure would be dramatically confirmed from the late 1950s in the case of the Montmartre Jazzhuset in Copenhagen, where front-rank US jazz musicians were available as models for musicians and audiences on a nightly basis over several decades (Büchmann-Møller and Welsgaards-Iversen 2008: passim).

Regional jazz development was also affected by the migration of audiences. Prohibition in the US made Tijuana to the south and Montreal to the north attractive destinations for US citizens seeking less constrained forms of leisure, and these visitors helped to stimulate local jazz activity. Jelly Roll Morton found work in a Mexican border town, and the relatively liberal milieu of Montreal sustained a strong jazz scene until the 1950s. With the opening of the Panama Canal in 1914, an army of labourers, followed of course by the new traffic, turned Panama itself into a cosmopolitan centre where jazz was a strong presence (Shepherd et al. 2005: III: 146; V: 64–65; III: 180). As this last case reminds us, in a pre-aviation era of rapidly developing international trade and tourism, shipping lanes were the essential conduit. Peter Linebaugh declared that 'the ship remains perhaps the most important conduit of Pan-African communication before the appearance of the long-playing record' (cited by Gilroy 1999: 13). Thus transnational ports in many ways constituted a more coherent jazz network than many 'national' scenes. Port cities like Barcelona, Goa, Hamburg, Kobe, Marseilles, Montevideo, and Sydney were important jazz incubators. Finland's jazz scene began in the port towns Helsinki and Kotka (Haavisto 1996: 10, 11). In 1936 American composer/arranger Claude Lapham, observing Shanghai's night life, declared that 'the Orient is MORE interested in jazz than all of Europe with the exception of England' (cited Atkins 2011: 469).

The importance of access to shipping lanes of course increases with trans-oceanic remoteness. The case of New Zealand is illustrative. Before the advent of radio, the country's main contact with the rest of the world was via shipping. The steamer routes, which took in Vancouver, San Francisco, Honolulu, Suva, Sydney and Auckland, gave shipboard musicians exposure to the latest styles; drummer Bill Egerton recalled that in this way he learned modern drumming from US nightclubs (Bourke 2010: 51). The most famous of the steamers was the 'Niagara', by which recordings arrived, particularly through members of the ship's orchestra led by Birmingham born pianist Edgar Bendall, who joined in 1917 (Bourke 2010: 24). At 15 years of age, Maori George Campbell joined the 'Niagara' as a deckhand, where he listened closely to the Americanadians rehearsing on their way between the US and Australia, an experience so powerful that he then quit the 'Niagara' to become a full-time musician (Bourke 2010: 106) and with his brothers Phil and George went on to make a 'lasting impression on New Zealand jazz and popular music' (Bourke 2010: 104). New Zealand-born Abe Romain as a teenager served as a musician on the 'Tahiti' travelling to San Francisco, where he was able to hear 'live jazz and buy the latest records'. He later migrated to Australia, thence to the UK where he worked with Jack Hylton and Harry Roy, with the former of whom he accompanied Armstrong for the London debut in July 1932. He returned to Sydney in 1940, becoming one of Australia's most important bandleaders (Bourke 2010: 25).

Media

Ships of course also carried commodities, including those for mass mediation. Printed reports of the word 'jazz' and its antecedents predate the first recordings of the music in 1917, perhaps as far back as the 1870s (see, for example, Holbrook 1974; Nettelbeck 2004: 2–6). Printed commentary reported jazz activity and provided the earliest definitions; it was the 'vibrant print culture of the period' (Jones 2003: 234) that provided the basis for an understanding of early jazz in

China (Kernfeld, 1988: I: 593–594; Walser 1999: 3–70). *Melody Maker*, founded in England in 1926, was taken internationally by subscription, and local journals like Finland's *Rytmi* magazine (established 1934) and the Australian journal *Jazz Notes* (established 1941) played central roles in shaping local perceptions of jazz (Kater 1992: 10; Haavisto 1996: 17; Johnson 1998: 26–37).

More useful for actual performance was sheet music which, by the early 1920s through an expanding global music publishing industry, shipped jazz repertoire as far afield as New Zealand, Russia and South Africa. Estonia's first professional jazz band began in 1918 using sheet music brought in by crews of ships to the port city of Tallin (Starr 1983: 26; Ballantine 2011: 484; Shepherd et al. 2005: VII: 4). Although we now think of this as offering little more than templates for a music that is centrally improvisational, sheet music conveyed something of the new rhythmic qualities of jazz, already foreshadowed in banjo music (Parsonage 2005: 14). In addition, song lyrics and the cover illustrations were essential in constructing public understanding of jazz prior to radio and recordings (Parsonage 2005: 13). Indeed, it seems arguable that these largely inspired the grotesque antics described in reviews of the earliest diasporic performances.

Such images of performance rhetoric were also internationally circulated by early silent film. As an inexpensive mass-circulated recreation, film was important in democratising access to the modern imaginary, its lifestyles and popular culture. Until the arrival of talkies, the only way the onscreen performers could identify themselves as jazz musicians was by extravagant gestures, which confirmed the good-time zaniness so ubiquitous in sheet music lyrics and graphics. In Sydney, as early as 1919, a 'Jazz Week' at Sydney's Globe Theatre advertised 'Jazzy fun … Jazz dances, jazz music, jazz movies' (the poster is reproduced below, p144). One of these movies was a local production, now lost, *Does the Jazz Lead to Destruction?* Apart from the intimations of heedless hedonism implied in the advertising, it also constructed jazz as a potential path to 'destruction'. In the poster announcing the event, a male narrator talks darkly of the temptations of jazz; a week later he is cheerfully confessing that he has succumbed. Throughout the 1920s movie plotlines involving the dangerous temptations of modern urban sophistication included sequences in formal and informal jazz venues as imagined by local directors. While many of these movies have not survived, we still have archived posters, synopses, shooting scripts and some extant footage, for example the Australian film *Greenhide* (1926), which includes an extended sequence of a jazz band and 'jazz' dancing (discussed, with stills in Johnson 2000: 69–76). The sequence establishes the heroine Margery as a risk taker, preparing us for a defiance of paternal authority which underpins the plotline. The unrestrained physical deportment of both the band and of Margery signals a lack of restraint and decorum.

The presentation of the 'New Woman' in so much early silent film underlines its role as a conduit of modernity (see further below). The silent movie was mediated acoustically through local cinema musicians who often incorporated contemporary

US jazz material in their collages. Parsonage reports that from the opening of the first English cinema in 1907, 'there is evidence of use of new American music to accompany films' imported by a ship's musician (Parsonage 2005: 10). The director's synopsis for *Greenhide* suggests that the cinema musician(s) play 'That Certain Party' over the dance sequence, a song which had just been recorded in Sydney by the visiting US band, the Palais Royal Californians (Johnson 2000: 72). These convergences between vision and sound played a major role in the way jazz was imagined in diasporic destinations. Movie accompaniment was also one of the most important public workshops for developing improvisational practices, which as we shall see, implicated the issue of gender (Whiteoak 1999: 61–66). US films became major sites for the global circulation and construction of the jazz imaginary.

Radio provided a further mass medium for the internationalisation of jazz; 'By the late 1920s it is likely that more people were hearing music on the radio than in any other way' (Wald 2009: 93). In 1928 the first Greek radio station was established, including jazz in its programming (Anagnostou 2016: 67). In Brazil In 1926 Radio Sociedade de Rio presented a daily 15-minute slot by the Oriental Jazz Band (Fléchet 2016: 18). In the UK, 'Jazz was present on the BBC from the very first broadcast on 1 January 1923, and in February 1923 Marius B. Winter and his orchestra featured a program of British jazz' (Wall 2019: 67), and it is estimated that by the end of 1926 about 20 per cent of British households possessed radio (Parsonage 2005: 45). As a domestic technology it became for many their first contact with the music, as in the case of later bandleader Chris Barber during the war (Barber 2013: 1). Radio was of particular effectiveness in a number of ways. Although a household technology, from the beginning it broke down isolation on a transnational scale. In New Zealand listeners could pick up transmissions from the West Coast of the US – Los Angeles, Oakland – and Honolulu, which gave access to the latest US songs (Bourke 2010: 67). While gratifying to many, among others this led to complaints about Americanisation, that 'ghastly croon-jazz-blare-baby-doll American rubbish', in the words of one writer to the Christchurch Press, signing himself 'British', and the 'uncivilised din of Negro bands' (Bourke 2010: 68). Radio also helped to sustain the link between jazz and dance; on the BBC programmes of uninterrupted dance music 'were advertised in advance so that evening dances or afternoon *thé dansant* parties could be planned' (Parsonage 2005: 46–47). New Zealand radio presented jazz for dancing in the home including an experiment with a 'special jazz programme' in 1927 consisting of a three-hour broadcast with Allen's Dance Orchestra, which in rural areas was also danced to in public halls (Bourke: 2010: 38). This service –virtually free, after the initial purchase of the receiver – became particularly important during the economic austerities of the Great Depression.

Originally most jazz content was provided by broadcasts from public venues like restaurants and cabarets. Until 1926, BBC dance music was broadcast mainly from the Savoy Hotel, beginning with the Savoy Havana Band from 13 April 1923 (Parsonage 2005: 164). From its opening in 1926, the Finnish Broadcasting Corporation presented jazz from restaurants on Saturday nights (Haavisto 1996: 63). In New Zealand, by 1924 dance band music was broadcast from cabarets, and also from cinema orchestra overtures to silent films, and from December 1925 trans-Tasman links enabled broadcast exchanges with Australia (Bourke 2010: 30). Radio also produced permanent studio orchestras. In Barranquilla, Columbia, radio theatres with in-house studio orchestras were major disseminators of jazz in this early period (Shepherd et al. 2005: III: 300). In Portugal broadcasting administrator António Lopes Ribeiro at first maintained that local musicians were not of sufficient calibre compared to US musicians to form such a band, but the first Portuguese radio jazz orchestra broadcast live on Saturday 2 November 1935 (Cravinho 2016: 94, 95). The first radio dance band in New Zealand, the Plume Melody Makers, was sponsored by Plume Motor Oil Company, broadcasting a weekly three-hour show (Bourke 2010: 73). Jazz programmes were also sponsored by Swing clubs, as in Luis Villas-Boas's programme Hot Club in Portugal from 25 November 1945 (Cravinho 2016: 100). The case of Portugal reminds us that radio was not necessarily an open conduit, but depended on broadcasting policy and philosophy. On National Radio Broadcasting, inaugurated in 1933, jazz was at first 'virtually nonexistent' (Cravinho 2016: 93).

The BBC played a major role not simply in presenting jazz, but in how it was understood by its audience. In the words of Tim Wall, radio was 'more than a channel though which jazz flows; it is an active mediator, selecting what could be heard of jazz and contributing to defining what jazz actually is' (Wall 2019 65). The policy of the BBC cultivated a more acceptable image of jazz that separated it from the connotations the music had acquired from dubious nightclub culture; in 1932, for example, it replaced Jack Payne with Henry Hall to create a Paul Whiteman-style orchestra, a '*sweet* soft sound' (Parsonage 2005: 164, 252). The conservatism of the New Zealand Broadcasting Service (NZBS) affected music programming, culminating in a censorship process in the 1940s targeting songs likely to cause offence (Bourke 2010: 263; on radio as a filter, see further below). Many of these issues converge in the case of Germany, which is of particular interest because of the strategic role that would be played by radio in the Third Reich. Beginning in 1923, the first jazz broadcast was from Munich in 1924, the format gaining momentum after Paul Whiteman's Berlin performances in 1926. Stronger receivers gave access to foreign stations including the BBC, Radio Luxembourg after its establishment in 1930, and Poste Parisien. This gave influential exposure to black US jazz, sowing the seeds of a dilemma that would haunt Goebbels's radio propaganda policies (Kater 1992: 12–13, 89; see further below). The effects of radio and the rhythms of Harlem in displacing 'grandfather's pianola', were explicit in an advertising jingle for the Swedish 'Radiola' in 1939, concluding: 'I go from Vienna to Berlin and from Paris to Tunis and back to you' (Fornäs 2003: 213).

All these conduits for the jazz diaspora converged in various permutations. Jazz arrived in Japan before the first US jazz recordings of 1917 through a combination of migration, sheet music and film. The members of the five-piece Hatano Orchestra worked for a Japanese shipping company from 1912 to 1918. In San Francisco they bought the latest sheet music, on which they then based their performances back home as an intermission band in cinemas (Atkins 2001: 53–54; Shepherd et al. 2005: V: 136). In New Zealand, influential jazz proselytiser Arthur Pearce began bringing in jazz recordings through personal connections in local shipping from the late 1920s. Following an on-air debate about crooning in early 1937, Pearce was asked by Bruce to host a weekly dance programme, 'Rhythm on Record' which ran for 40 years; he became 'New Zealand's most influential broadcaster' (Bourke 2010: 69). He also travelled to Sydney where he mingled and recorded with members of the country's leading Swing orchestra led by Frank Coughlan (Lewis 1996: 35, 50, 52–67).

Pearce's case introduces the single most significant medium for the internationalisation of jazz, proclaimed in an advertisement in an Australian trade journal of 1921: the Melola record player was vaunted as being 'as effective as a full jazz band' (Johnson 2000: 9). In the 1920s, outside the US, that would most often of course be a white jazz band (Lotz 2012: 143). The recording industry globalised with impressive speed (Johnson 2002A: 36–37) and in spite of the slump in the early 1930s the sound recording had already had a decisive effect across the globe. When Ahmet Ertegun, later the co-founder of Atlantic Records, arrived in the US from Turkey in 1935, he was already deeply familiar with American jazz from recordings (Shaw 1977: 342). Contemporary Ghanian musician Nii Otoo's musical education has been 'permeated' by modern sound recording technology, from which he absorbed the influence of US jazz musicians like Elvin Jones (Feld 2012: 138, 141), a useful reminder that Africa is more than a static jazz 'Ur'.

New Zealand provides a useful case study. By the mid-1920s most households owned a record player (Bourke 2010: 29). In 1925, the value of imported gramophones and records overtook pianos and player-pianos (Brown 2017: 43), and with the abolition in 1928 of government duty on recordings their popularity soared. Recording of local popular music began in 1927 by technicians from Parlophone's Australian branch (Bourke 2010: 41, 33). Although the country did not have its own commercial recording industry until 1948 (Bourke 2010: 151), the 'first jazz recording' made in New Zealand was in fact a short promotional film, or 'early music video' (Ward 2015) made for the New Zealand Tourism Board, featuring Epi Shalfoon and his Melody Boys from Rotorua in December 1930 (Bourke 2010: 61). Shalfoon himself was of Syrian or Lebanese background, married to a Maori wife. For that clip, now lost although stills survive, they dressed (bearly/barely) and black-faced as indigenous warriors, but about a week later they made another in their usual attire as a band promotion, paid for at a discount by the Board (this clip can be seen at www.youtube.com/watch?v=bm-wTQaKNdw, accessed 21 July 2019; my thanks to researcher Aleisha Ward, personal communication 30 April 2018, for much of the information given here). Announcing the band to the camera as 'Rotorua's famous ja[zz band] (there is a brief sound dropout), Shalfoon then leads the band in a jazzed version of a sexually themed Maori song locally popular at the time, called 'E Puritai Tama E'. At the end the leader addresses the camera: 'Watch the newspapers. This band will be playing REAL dance music in your town soon'. There is an air of self-conscious 'music *du jour*' about the clip, not least in the change of costume. Shalfoon's band had played at a welcome party in Rotorua for pioneer aviator Charles Kingsford Smith, who joined them on one of the signature jazz instruments of the time, the banjo (Bourke 2010: 62). Ward has written further about this, including an account of legal action regarding payment and strident press coverage (see www.audioculture.co.nz/scenes/new-zealand-s-first-jazz-recording, accessed 25 September 2018). I have dwelt on this for several reasons: it is of interest as a rare example of early film and sound recording of jazz in a country far distant from the US, yet participating vigorously in the most up-to-date forms of culture, technology and media coverage. And sound recording, in this case as film soundtrack, is central.

But recordings did not simply circulate jazz, they largely created its cultural politics. Elijah Wald has discussed the ways that sound recordings reconfigured relationships between songs, singers and other music media (Wald 2009: 84–96). Further to such arguments: until the late nineteenth century, the mass dissemination of culture was dominated by print. The advent of sound recordings bypassed notation and released music from the limits of its symbolic order and specialised knowledge restricted on grounds such as class, gender, ethnicity and physical location, giving direct access to music as sound. They also transformed an evanescent oral music in a commodity, shifting it into a different political economy. Garvin Bushell recalled his first experience of jazz on his family's new Victrola, directed into the street as a sign of social 'rating'. Similarly, among urban black South Africans, ownership of the latest record was valued not only as a music delivery system but as a marker of status. For the white Anglophone bourgeoisie the 'rating' of the record player – and the music associated with it - was likely to be *déclassé*. A 1907 an English gramophone advertisement noted that, designed to look like elegant furniture, it was for an 'educated class' who preferred that their neighbours not be aware that they owned a 'talking machine'. *Gramophone* editor Compton Mackenzie condemned the 'abominable' new electrical recordings because of their association with 'an American accent' and 'Yankee clarinets'. The recording and other technologised music media became ways of distinguishing high from low culture (Johnson 1987: 212–3; Starr 1983: 119; Bushell 1988: 1; Ballantine 2011: 484; Johnson 2000: 83).

For the first time, sound recording also enabled the close and detailed study of unscored musics that otherwise vanished with the performance moment. There are many accounts of early jazz recordings being worn white by repeated playing for the purpose of imitation, and this was especially useful in diasporic sites, as in the case of Japan in the 1920s (Atkins 2011: 470). From the first jazz recording made in Japan, a song called 'Walla Walla', by the Nitto Jazz Band in 1925, 'almost all of the jazz in Japan was more or less imitative of the jazz heard on records' (Koyama 2000: 566). From the UK to Brazil bands were able to produce what we now call covers of songs shortly after their appearance in the US (Parsonage 2005: 61; Fléchet 2016: 18). As in that case, the globalisation of recording also meant the internationalisation of American music, since the industry was controlled to a significant extent by the US (Gronow 1996: 40). US popular music influences were largely introduced to Argentina in the 1930s by recordings, which led to the incorporation of a jazz component in most public dances (Shepherd et al. 2005: III: 187). Early record manufacturing facilities in Shanghai were crucial conduits of modern music into China and Southeast Asia, and the establishment of German Brunswick by Deutsche Grammophon under license from American Brunswick in 1926, opened the country to the most recent work of Duke Ellington and Louis Armstrong (Jones 2003: 229; Kater 1992: 10–11). In a noteworthy contrast with the niche marketing of US 'race' record catalogues, English enthusiasts enjoyed specialist jazz or hot series from Columbia ('Hot Jazz Records') in 1927 and Parlophone ('Rhythm Style') in 1928 (Shepherd et al. 2005: VII: 332). Australians could buy predominantly white US jazz performances from the early 1920s and, with the local introduction of Parlophone's 'Rhythm Style' in 1930, a growing sample of black jazz musicians (Johnson 1987: 72–73, 133; see similarly Gronow 1996: 21–24). The link between jazz internationalisation and the record industry was equally striking when it was severed. The isolation that followed the Revolution seems to be one reason for the difficulties Russian musicians had in assimilating the non-notatable aspects of the music (Starr 1983, 48). As discussed below, access to jazz at an international level via modern media including recordings was highly erratic, at least up to the 1950s. This would be crucial in its diasporic history and would be decisive in the dissemination and understanding of bop.

The international jazz diaspora is thus a case study of the negotiation between local cultural practices and global cultural processes, between culture and mass mediations. As both idea and practice, jazz came into being through negotiation with the vehicles of its dissemination, and with conditions it encountered in any given location. The complexities of diasporic reinvention are not simply the outcome of which particular versions of jazz were exported. The conditions these exports encountered reconfigured the music and its meanings even further.

Cultural and Political Reception

Each diasporic site required negotiation on its own unique terms; in the 1920s post-revolutionary Russia, Weimar Germany, post-war France, South African urbanisation and race relations all brought very different sets of attitudes to bear regarding both the US and blackness. (Johnson 2017C: 11). The history of

European occupation in Australia since 1788 engendered anxiety about alien contamination. The Musicians Union had been influential in the deportation of Sonny Clay's Plantation Orchestra in 1928 (Johnson 2010 and see further below), and the following year declared its formal support for the White Australia policy (Whiteoak 2009: 31). Although New Zealand had its own machinery to prevent 'coloured' immigration, the history of its relations between settlers and Maoris allowed the formation of generally admired indigenous jazz bands, in complete contrast to Australia (Whiteoak 2009: 31). In Finland the reception of jazz was determined by such diverse factors as the Finno-Ugric language, the history of Finnish emigration to the US, the country's recent independence as a sovereign state (1917) and the ensuing brief but savage civil war (see further Johnson 2002A: 39–40; Johnson Forthcoming B). In many respects Finland's newly emerged status invites comparisons with Greece. The two countries also shared a peripheral status within Europe, no imperial history or strong connection with two important diasporic sites, England and France, little or no touring by US performers and no black community (see further Anagnostou 2016: 55), hospitable conditions for the formation of a distinctive local jazz culture that incorporated local musical traditions.

The reception accorded US performers themselves, particularly for black musicians after the treatment they had experienced in their home country, often augured well for the reception of the music and foreshadowed the hospitality accorded black jazz musicians in many parts of Europe from the 1950s. Rex Stewart recalled that 'for the first time in my life I had the feeling of being accepted as an artist, a gentleman and a member of the human race' (Bushell 1988: 192), and Bushell encountered the same respect in Russia, which appeared to be 'colour blind' on matters of race as compared to France,. In Germany the band encountered examples of xenophobic racism which involved violence (Bushell 1988: 66, 57–58, 65). The issue of race is central to some of the most incandescent debates in jazz discourse, and the relevance of a diasporic perspective will be explored further below.

Everywhere on its diasporic journeys it was agreed that jazz became the music of urban modernity. The alignment between jazz and modernity was a determining force in situating the music (see further for example Appel 2002; Johnson 2000: 7–26; Johnson 2017C: 14–18; Nicholson 2014: 155–252). In Columbia, Barranquilla was a major centre of the country's modernisation, incorporating a number of features that often contributed to that profile: it was a port with close ties to the US and became a major centre, along with Cali, for Columbian jazz from the early 1920s (Shepherd et al. 2005: III: 299). Similarly in Japan, jazz spread from the port cities as the bearer of 'cosmopolitan modernities' (Atkins 2011: 467). The music found common cause with complementary modernist impulses and arts, from Finland to Brazil to Portugal (particularly through the writing of surrealist António Ferro), and later became a marker of modernisation in Iran (Johnson Forthcoming B; Cravinho 2016: 87, 88, 91–92; Roxo and Castelo-Branco 2016: 205–207; Nooshin 2016: 126). Its friends included the progressive and the avant-garde. Apart from oft-mentioned names like Hindemith, Milhaud, Ernest Krenek, Kurt Weill and Stravinsky, they included Eberhard Breussner, Hans Heinz Stuckenschmidt and Alfred Baresel, a piano teacher at Leipzig Conservatory who published an instruction manual on jazz improvisation (Kater 1992: 16–17). Australian modernist painters and writers embraced jazz while largely ignoring modern developments in art music (Johnson 2000: 31–52).

In these cases jazz was treated as a music having cultural gravitas. Elsewhere, however, in its earliest diasporic manifestations it was trivialised as too deficient in dignity. In England the highly conservative BBC sought to invest its hot dance orchestras with greater dignity, rejecting the label of jazz in favour of 'Syncopation … a real music, not just a collection of noises'. These were the words of the conductor of the Savoy Orpheans (they 'played like Gods – like Orpheus') (Parsonage 2005: 167) and it was this band and also the Savoy Havana Band that the BBC contracted for broadcast. In this way the BBC promulgated an understanding of hot dance music that was a more chastened version of American syncopated music, with a British inflection (Parsonage 2005: 172). This was not to say that the music entirely abandoned its good-time spirits, and it was reported in the *Radio Times* 19 March 1926 that 'While syncopated music comes from America, the Savoy Orpheans are particularly anxious to add a British touch to it, by adding some characteristic humour and comedy' (Parsonage 2005: 172). Implied here is a constraining of affective range as compared with much of the jazz being recorded in the US during the 1920s. Outside the paternalistic custody of the BBC, early diasporic jazz was generally narrowed emotionally to low comedy, and musically to extroverted novelty routines, a music exclusively of insouciance, high spirits. In Australia, 'lots of clowning and mirthmaking' (Johnson 1987: 10), and in Japan the coinage 'jazuru' meant 'to make merry, to mess around, to talk rubbish, to be noisy, to live without cares dancing nonsensically, like jazz' (Atkins 2003: 102).

For many, jazz was thus a threat to traditions, not just of music, but of responsible citizenship (see further Johnson 2017C: 15–17). The jazz band formed by Bauhaus students caused alarm among local parents: 'we were the punks of Dessau' (Whitford 1994). While living with an aunt in Scotland in 1932, Bruce Turner would listen to popular music on the radio: 'If it was harsh and syncopated, it was jazz, and Auntie May felt obliged to frown upon it. Jazz was something anti-social and vaguely irreligious – not the sort of thing for decent law-abiding folk' (Turner 1984: 9). On the other side of the world, in Wellington New Zealand (but, as it happens, populated by a high proportion of expatriate Scots), the scholar Edward Tregear complained of being kept awake by jazz coming from the nearby nightclub, The Cabaret. In a press report of his complaints, jazz became implicated in the noise of modernity: reporter Pat Lawlor described 'the beginning of the era of barbarous jazz bands, the grinding orchestrations of motor gears and motor horns on nightly joy rides – a new age of ungodly noises'. Tregear sold up and moved (Bourke 2010: 10). In France Paul Claudel castigated its machine-like character, 'rhythmic pulsation and nervous uniformity of the pistons of a steam-engine interrupting the cyclical roaring of the dynamo that one feels across all American life and of which jazz is the supreme expression' (Jackson 2011: 448). These anxieties disclose the other side of the coin. Conservative cultural power blocs agreed that jazz was the music of modernity, but read it as threat rather than promise.

The threat which jazz presented to law and order was registered in New Zealand as early as June 1918 in a report that police had gone to arrest seven men who had failed to appear at the medical examination for military conscription. One of them, a Maori king, was protected by 'a bevy of Maori girls, a number of whom were equipped with brass band instruments, from which they produced music of a somewhat uncertain tune'. The headline was 'Maori Maids' Jazz Band' (Bourke 2010: 7). The report, however, was in a Sydney newspaper, and, like one of the earliest references to jazz in Finland (Johnson Forthcoming B), perhaps included an element of tongue-in-cheek. Not so, however, the initial reluctance of the BBC's John Reith to engage American Bert Ralton to lead the Savoy Havana band on the grounds that jazz musicians were 'eccentrics and madmen' (Parsonage 2005: 165). The belief that jazz musicians could not be trusted with serious music projects was tenacious. At what was billed as 'Auckland's first jazz concert' in August 1950, presented in the Town Hall, the city fathers forbade the use of the Hall's Steinway. In 1961 at a jazz performance given by Bryce Rohde at the University of New England in Armidale, New South Wales, the mayor first tried to ban the concert, then gave in but for the stipulation that Rohde (a pianist) could not use the piano (Johnson 1987: 54). The university vice-chancellor over-rode him. Highly respected Melbourne-based composer, musician and educator, Tony Gould, in his 2018 memoir recalled that when playing a concert with another pianist at a Melbourne university conservatorium, 'we were not to improvise on the Steinways' and in fact they 'were not permitted to play the concert'. He declares that in some institutions this proscription still stands (Gould 2018: 94, 101).

The most deeply seated objections to jazz however were more culturally and politically grounded, especially among authoritarian power blocs such as the church. The Portuguese Catholic church (as well as the state-controlled radio) was opposed to jazz and modern dance (Roxo and Castelo-Branco 2016: 200–201; Cravinho 2016: 96). Their objections were multi-faceted, and included the contamination of national identity and moral values, vulgarity, and the fact that the music was associated with blackness (Cravinho 2016: 84, 87, 97). The threat to national identity via its musical traditions would lead ultimately to the establishment of the Music Studies Bureau within State Radio, in 1942, to foster 'a Portuguese music idiom grounded in "folklore" (considered the foundation of nationalist music) to shield audiences from the negative and potential transgression – social, racial, and sexual – represented by foreign popular musics such as jazz and tango' (Roxo and Castelo-Branco 2016: 213). In New Zealand, responses to the threat to musical standards included calls for a conservatorium where British music was taught (Bourke 2010: 21). The reference to 'British' here proclaims a general nervousness about cultural heritage. But where there were very distinctive and specific local music formations the anxieties were more focused, for example in relation to gypsy/Romany music in Hungary, Brazilian rhythms, and in Lombardia, Northern Italy, where the arrival of jazz in the interwar period actually extinguished local viola and cello playing (Havas 2018; Fléchet 2016: 24; Bohlman and Plastino 2016A: 23). Regarding local trumpet-playing traditions, a Serbian on-line commentator recalled earlier times:

> Back in those days, by listening to music, you felt how it was lifting you from the ground, how your heart was jumping with joy; but nowadays everyone is trying to become a trumpet virtuoso, everyone would like to emulate those stupid Americans. Why? We have our wonderful music and our wonderful people and customs, so why not let them return and help us preserve our tradition.
>
> *Cited in Gligorijević 2019: Chapter 4, p. 39*

At the same time, however, in some regions local music traditions were such as to form a comfortable symbiosis with jazz; the most celebrated example is Manouche jazz, exemplified most famously in the work of Django Reinhardt, but this was by no means the only example. Elsewhere in Italy such as Naples local traditions found a comfortable juxtaposition with jazz. Similarly Azerbaijani jazz was from the beginning 'closely linked to native musical traditions' (Naroditskaya 2016: 99). Further examples of fruitful syncretisms are explored below.

As in the case of Portugal, above, much of the opposition to jazz was related to transgressive activities associated with the music, including indulgence in drugs, alcohol and promiscuity. The English *Dancing Times* in 1919 declared 'The Jazz … was a word which to some suggested the acme of poetical motion, while to others it conveyed conceptions of the lowest depths of immorality and degradation' (Parsonage 2005: 14). In 1922 it was reported of the Dixieland Cabaret in Auckland New Zealand that, during a charity ball alcohol was consumed without a license 'in cuddle cubicles' filled with 'young jazz weeds, dashing sheiks, effeminate nincompoops and frivolous flappers'. Modern dancing was itself highly suspect: at that time in Auckland new dance styles came under review by the Board of Health's Committee on Venereal Disease (Bourke 2010: 20, 21). As late as 2000, at what was billed as a 'jazz concert' in Tehran (in which most of the programme consisted of covers of Western pop artists like Paul Simon, Lennon and McCartney), Laudan Nooshin observed officials watching from the side 'to make sure that order is maintained and no one tries to dance' (Nooshin 2016: 125).

For both friends and enemies, blackness was an authenticating marker of jazz, and in ambiguous ways: it was both American modernity and a signifier of primitivism. Together, they represented a threat to European civilisation (see further Johnson 2017C: 15–16). In England eminent writers including John Buchan, Aldous Huxley, Eric Linklater, J. B. Priestley and Aelfrida Tillyard regarded ragtime

and jazz 'as symptoms of mass-produced, corrupt, sex-ridden culture that was con-
taminating an ageing European culture, fatally weakened by the First World War';
in 1919 Canon Arthur Hislop Drummond spoke against the arrival of jazz bands
in his parish Maidenhead, characterising the 'art of Jazz dancing' as 'the dance of
low niggers in America, with every conceivable crude instrument. Not to make
music, but to make a noise', a 'symptom of a grave disease which was infesting the
country' (Lawson-Peebles 2013: 23). Germany's Admiral Raeder was offended
at the decadence of the Weimar Republic as a 'distortion of social life'; 'jazz and
modern dance for example, were not symptoms of a nation resolved to shake off
the chains of a national humiliation but of moral decay, manifestations of a society
that had lost its bearings' (Dimbleby 2016: 19). In a government notice circulated
to radio stations in Spain in 1943 it was declared that there was 'nothing further
from our virile racial characteristics than that dead, sickly-sweet, decadent and
monotonous melodies, which, like a cry of impotence, soften and feminize the
soul' (Iglesias 2013: 102). Apart from the reference here to feminisation, to be
taken up later, all these diatribes invoked the imagery of decay and disease that
has perennially intersected with various forms of music, and which invites further
investigation in the specific case of widespread interwar discourses of eugenics
among intellectuals (see further Kennaway 2012; Carey 1992, for example 13–14).
The association between jazz and blackness was one of the objections to jazz in
Brazil, a matter of particular sensitivity given that slavery had been abolished there
only three decades before the arrival of the music and there were still tensions
regarding those descended from Africans. It was not until the thirties that Afro-
Brazilian music began to be accepted as integral with national identity (Fléchet
2016). In general, blackness did not become a predominantly positive authentication of the music until the publication of work by writers such as Panassié
from the late 1930s, a provocative area for further enquiry in light of the political
dynamics at work in Europe through that decade.

Jazz was also regarded as an economic threat. Everywhere, professional music
sectors were being destabilised by an array of cultural and technological changes
that gathered critical mass in the wake of the war, including the onset of a festive
iconoclasm and the growing popularity of cinema, radio and recordings. While
many of these created expanded work opportunities, the effects were ambiguous.
In a foreshadowing of what later became the 'jazz dilemma' (see below), notwithstanding the opposition from various power blocs, jazz was wildly popular
with significant sections of the public. As such, the established music sectors felt
that the new dance craze threatened their own employment, and to add insult to
injury, jazz performers were earning far more for what was often seen as highly
questionable musical competence, for example in England (Williamson and
Cloonan 2016: 69). In Finland by the end of the 1920s it was complained that jazz
performers were making twice as much as members of the Helsinki Symphony
Orchestra (Johnson 2002A: 41). By the 1930s, in the Donbass region of Russia/
The Ukraine, jazz had significantly displaced classical music in many areas of life,

a problem aggravated by the fact that 'jazz musicians earned up to ten times as much as classically trained musicians' (Lücke 2010: 88–89 n. 26). In many cases they were aided and abetted by dubious intruders from the US who as visiting performers were also seen to be stealing employment from the locals. In Paris in 1924, following complaints from local musicians, the police confiscated the working permits of some two dozen US jazz performers and gave them a deadline for leaving the country (Jackson 2011: 157). In New Zealand the 'intruders' were also encouraged by the enormous trans-Tasman disparity between the costs of joining the musicians' unions: 21 pounds and six months waiting in Australia, five shillings and no waiting period in New Zealand (Bourke 2010: 49).

The economic grievances of locals were also able to wrap themselves in cultural objections arising from nationalism and race. Mentioned briefly above, in 1928 a black US revue called *The Colored Idea* arrived in Australia for seasons in Sydney and Melbourne. The revue incorporated a jazz band, Sonny Clay's Plantation Orchestra, press reports of which emphasised that this, the first coloured American jazz band to visit Australia, was a revelation for local musicians. Its members however were discovered by police cavorting in an alcohol-fuelled party with local women in an apartment in Melbourne. The fact that the apartment had been under prolonged surveillance and that the press were in tow adds to the evidence that the raid arose from lobbying by the Musicians Union, communicated via the government to Australia's intelligence agency, the Commonwealth Investigation Branch, who had then initiated the action. This in turn discloses the complicity of the whole event in the larger cultural history of the country, particularly in regard to issues of popular leisure, sexual politics and race. The ensuing scandal ('White Girls With Negro Lovers', screamed the headlines), led to the cancellation of the band's engagements and to its deportation. The ban on 'negro' jazz bands officially remained in place until Louis Armstrong toured in 1954, although Rex Stewart had been smuggled in in 1949 by Graeme Bell who simply failed to disclose the fact that Stewart was black when he applied to the Union for Stewart's admission (see full details of these episodes online at Johnson 2010). The country was thus deprived of systematic live exposure to the 'revelations' of black jazz performers for two and a half decades of crucial developments in the music. Indirectly this also had impact across the Tasman. New Zealand had a far less overtly racist history, with freely integrated bands all enjoying the same level of popularity. But because it was not economically viable for a US band to make the visit to the region without including Australia, New Zealand was equally starved of exposure.

In England a similar dynamic produced a similar ban. In January 1926 the journal of the Musicians' Union reprinted an article from the *Empire Record* that declared: 'a revolting phase of this alien competition is that in some cases – all too frequent – the British musician has to give way to a negro … Or again, he may have to submit to being trained by a black' (cited Williamson and Cloonan 2016: 83). Anxieties about imported US competition more generally grew with the Depression, aggravated by a lack of reciprocal exchange. While there was never a 'blanket ban', from 1935 heavy restrictions were imposed on foreign musicians. There were loopholes that enabled individual musicians to perform in certain circumstances and under non-jazz billing – for example Duke Ellington in 1948. But in effect the restrictions prohibited general British exposure to US jazz bands, not significantly easing until the 1950s (Williamson and Cloonan 2016: 99, 138–139). The effect of these measures was made especially evident by the stimulating impact of the few who were able to circumvent the conditions, as in the case of Benny Carter in 1936–1937 (Parsonage 2012), and also by comparison with the Parisian jazz scene where no such restrictions obtained.

The emancipatively modernist coding of diasporic jazz attracted the attention of partisan political oppositional interests from the personal to the collective (see further Johnson 2017C: 17). This relationship was intersected by other forces, however, particularly those of (post)colonialism. A colonialist history could work to the benefit of the music by providing reciprocal pathways for musical migrations, and scores of antipodean jazz musicians worked at the highest professional levels in England, enabled by the fact that as members of the British empire/commonwealth, they were not subject to bans on 'foreign' musicians that excluded US performers. But the colonial connection could also work against jazz. Jazz introduced issues of race that were particularly sensitive in countries with histories of African colonialism. In the 1930s in Portugal for example, the colonial policies of Salazarism fortified official opposition to jazz and its African associations (Cravinho 2016: 79–80, and see further below). In China the socialists opposed jazz because its main point of entry and active centre, the treaty-port Shanghai, carried colonialist baggage (see further Johnson 2017C: 17; on the later reception of jazz in China see also Portugali 2017). Yet blanket generalisations, again, need to be nuanced to local conditions. It all depended on who had been colonising whom, and paradoxically, the jazz culture in Shanghai could not have come into existence without a regime of colonial oppression inflicted on China by the Japanese (Atkins 2011: 465–466).

In regions under some form of colonial administration, like India, Papua New Guinea and Zimbabwe, jazz tended to remain an Anglo-outsider recreation for colonial administrative communities and visitors, enjoyed primarily as a link with 'home' that distanced themselves from the native culture (the irony of British administrators in Africa being reminded of 'home' by listening to jazz, invites further reflection). The local clientele therefore mainly comprised groups that had prospered through the colonial connection. Jazz (djaz) bands formed in Haiti's Port-au-Prince in the 1920s played mainly for the local elite as well as for the occupying US garrison. Access to colonial indigenous audiences was therefore constrained by custom and economics, and by laws that enforced segregation (including by restrictions on alcohol consumption), or by rank as recognised by the colonial authorities (Shepherd at al. 2005: III: 56–7; Jones 2003: 226–228; Pinckney 2003: 60–63; Crowdy and Goddard 1999: 49–51, 56–58, 60–61; Williams 2003, 97).

The political formation which has been most schematically read as antipathetic to jazz is totalitarianism, and for very strong reasons. Jazz and totalitarianism are both, to use Philip Morgan's term, 'alternative modernities' (Johnson 2017C: 8), twins both fostered by modern media, but each signalling the two opposing directions in which modernity pulls, one towards mass culture, the other towards individualism. Just one year after Burnet Hurshey's report of the globalisation of jazz, the term 'totalitarianism' was coined in 1923 by Giovanni Amendola. While totalitarianism is oriented to regimentation, standardisation and homogenisation, jazz valorises spontaneity, freedom of expression and individuality. As such it set up an 'imaginary' that contested state repression by creating a place for individualism (see for example Iglesias 2017, Pedro 2017; Roxo 2017; Cravinho 2017). That totalitarian regimes have distrusted jazz, and that jazz has seen itself as a challenge to political authoritarianism is a *cliché*, embodied in the Soviet poster declaring that 'Today you play jazz, tomorrow you betray your country', and conversely in the title of Max Roach's 1960s *Freedom Now Suite* (Johnson 2017C: xvii). We have already glimpsed exemplifications of this configuration in relation to Franco's Spain and Salazar's Portugal, and will do so again in relation to other authoritarian regimes. This extensively documented and mythologised Manichean dynamic does not require concerted documentation here. More useful at this point is a reminder of the flexibility within the antagonism. As everywhere, the relationship between official proscription and actual practice was not uniform. In actual practice 'the attitude of the [Franco] dictatorship towards jazz was far from unitary and unequivocal, ranging from its condemnation as degenerate music, its tolerance as economic sustenance, and its naturalization as mass entertainment' (Iglesias 2013: 102). Nor were the function and status of jazz necessarily static over time; rather, they were bent in response to international winds. Apart from the case of the Soviet bloc, noted elsewhere, under Franco's dictatorship, American popular music passed from being condemned as a threat to national identity, to an anthem of political dissent, and by the 1970s a sign of growing democratic consciousness (Iglesias 2013).

The mythology is of jazz challenging totalitarian regimes with democratic ideals and/or the music of an oppressed community. Certainly jazz has been deployed in the prosecution of this agenda, as in the US State Department tours discussed below. But the relationship is far more ambiguous and complex. Detailed studies of jazz in oppressively authoritarian regimes including the USSR, the Third Reich, apartheid South Africa, Iran and Communist China have disclosed that while official encounters with diasporic jazz are most likely to begin from a position of suspicion or open antipathy, what follows in practice is a process of nuanced negotiations at grass roots level that involve adaptations on both sides (see for example the essays in Pickhan and Ritter 2010; Johnson 2017C, Portugali 2017). In Nazi Germany, contrary to widespread belief, jazz as such was never formally banned (Kater 1992: 33). It was regarded with official suspicion and hedged about with various restrictions partly because it was a music migrating from the US in which, in addition, both blackness and Jewishness offended doctrines of racial superiority. But as documented by Kater it survived in a number of ways, including even by virtue of the tastes of members of the armed forces. Following representations from the Luftwaffe, Goebbels established a radio orchestra, the Deutsche Tanz- und Unterhaltungsorchester (DTU; German Dance and Entertainment Orchestra), that he hoped would keep the pilots from tuning into the BBC but which would also satisfy civilian jazz appetites currently being addressed by broadcasting from outside Germany. Meticulously planned and generously funded, it provided a 'safe haven for jazz musicians and their art' (Kater 1992: 127).

In the Soviet Union, the vast territories made central control very tenuous, so that in Baku, the capital of Azerbaijani, official proscriptions of the 1930s barely registered, and a significant jazz scene was established (Naroditskaya 2016: 103). But in any case, the fortunes of jazz in the USSR varied with the political wind, which at one time understood the music to be the inspirational cry for freedom of an oppressed class, and at others, the demonised product of capitalism, one outcome of which was the development of an approved form of proletarian jazz (Lücke 2010: 88–89); a similar tactic was employed in the Third Reich (see below). These cases exemplify the willingness of oppressive regimes to recognise the 'jazz dilemma': that is, that while the state might disapprove ideologically, even with its brutal coercive powers it could not expunge the popular appetites for various forms of modern American culture, including jazz, leading to a highly dynamic relationship with the music (Starr 1983: especially 79–129). While the convergence of these two forces often led to brutal suppressions, there were also mutual adaptations that produced jazz with local inflections, functions and venues. Paradoxically, operating at different 'cultural spaces of action', these jazz forms could defuse tensions and even become stabilising forces within the state (see for example Ritter 2017; Reimann 2017, 2019; Zaddach 2017). There was also an economic imperative at work in the official attitude to jazz. According to the account of one Prague musician, in Soviet-controlled Czechoslovakia during the 1950s, all band touring outside the country was controlled by the state, which then took a substantial percentage of the band's income upon its return (Johnson 2000, 138–139).

As in the cases of the USSR and Nazi Germany, the reception of jazz was a weather-vane of international as well as domestic politics, but in less theatrical ways the same was true of other countries. Jazz was caught up in the growing urge to modernise throughout the twentieth century, but the image of it carrying all before it with the tide of global modernity overlooks local variations in what the US signified in relation to regional histories (see further Johnson 2017C: 18). These histories were traversed by debates about national identity which were often in tension with modernisation. While in many countries the end of World War Two famously saw a flourishing of jazz cultures (see further below), in Greece, the ensuing civil war was followed by a 'war between popular and European music … the bouzouki and the piano … rebetiko and the modern song'; this turbulence became part of a debate about national identity and anti-US imperialism, by which, by the end of the 1940s, jazz was eclipsed (Anagnostou 2016: 70–71).

Two countries that are geographically and culturally remote from each other – Spain and Iran – provide useful illustrations of the different ways in which relations with the US affected the reception of jazz. The opposition to jazz by the Franco regime that we have noted above gradually shifted to approval, as the country found it increasingly expedient to improve relations with the US during the war, and the post-war US State Department tours accelerated the shift (Martínez and Fouce 2013A: 5; Iglesias 2013: 106). Jazz reflected the policy realignment, with for example the reappearance of Hot Clubs in Barcelona and Madrid (Iglesias 2013: 103), the return of jazz on radio, the music's role in inspiring the work of the Dau al Set (Dice on Seven) avant-gardists in the late 1940s, and in the late 1960s flamenco recordings by jazz saxophonist Pedro Iturralde (Martínez and Fouce 2013A: 7; Iglesias 2013: 103–104). Jazz became pervasive in Spanish culture. By contrast, by the same decade Iran had also received visiting US jazz acts, but apart from a large community of European and US oil workers, 'jazz remained a minority interest' and a rather intellectual middle-class activity (Nooshin 2016: 127). Jazz had first entered Iran in the 1920s (Breyley 2017: 301), but its status in relation to other music genres (art and pop) was a shifting one, a 'floating signifier', partly because Iranian music taxonomies do not correspond with the Western models within which jazz has circulated. To follow the historical arc in Iran, it appears that jazz has not been the same focused target of hostility as it was in the early Franco regime, even though the country has seen periods of stridently anti-US sentiment. And this, it is argued, is because of its evasive status as a somewhat indistinct 'other', which overlaps with art rather than popular music, as understood by the affluent, well-educated urban youth who follow it (Nooshin 2016: 140,141; see also Breyley 2017). As such it is 'a culturally neutral ground on which ideas of universalism and cross-cultural understanding can be played out' (Nooshin 2016: 142).

Performers, Performance Practices and Social Spaces

In the earliest stages of the global jazz migrations there were, unsurprisingly, very heterogeneous understandings of what a jazz performance actually involved. The earliest diasporic practitioners were jobbing musicians seeking to remain abreast of the latest developments in their profession, apprenticed in a range of demotic entertainments, with the closest approach to jazz training being versions of minstrelsy and 'ragging', drawing on a musical vocabulary that was also etched with their own local musical traditions (see further Johnson 2017C: 11–14; for the Australian case, Whiteoak 1999: 83–167). Their first response to this new music, then, was often of bafflement. When Albert de Courville had tried to rehearse local musicians for the American-style revues he presented in London in 1912, they had simply informed him that although 'the syncopated rhythm was effective', this was not music (cited Parsonage 2005: 12; I note in passing that it would have been a fascinating study of the acculturation process to have a recording of the rehearsals *not* getting it quite right, rather than when they finally did). Seven years later, when English musician Lew Davis, later with Lew Stone's band, first heard the ODJB in London 'the music sounded like nothing on earth, but it certainly was exciting' (Parsonage 2005: 131). In New Zealand, pianist Henry Shirley who worked for A. H. Nathan, Columbia Records' NZ agent, recalled listening to the ODJB records while working: 'But no one would buy them. Customers recoiled from this first impact of the hideous noise from New Orleans. To amuse visitors we would sometimes play them "Barnyard Blues" – it was like all the roosters in the world crowing together' (Bourke 2010: 11).

Prior to live or recorded exposure, what jazz meant and what it sounded like, were the subject of considerable variation (see for example Hasse 2012: 208 n. 1). Within the US, in Springfield Ohio ca. 1915, the word was current, but Garvin Bushell and his young fellow musicians 'didn't call the music jazz … except for the final tag of a number. After the cadence was closed there'd be a one bar break, and the second bar was the tag – 5-6-5-1 (sol-la-sol-do) – that was called the jazz' (Bushell 1988: 10). And the farther away from the 'source', the more nebulous the idea of the music became. As a consequence, groups calling themselves jazz bands would be as likely to play what we would not recognise as jazz at all. The Suomi Jazz Orchestra from the 1920s was created as the jazz flagship of Fazer Music, the dominant entrepreneurial force in Finland's music industry. Yet apart from the presence of drums and saxophone, there is virtually no trace of what we would think of as jazz in its recordings, which include waltzes, polkas and jenkkas, and tango. The repertoire is dominated by traditional (often Russian) songs in minor keys, with all vocals in Finnish, sung by semi-operatic performers, as in the case of the minor key waltz called 'Asfalttikukka' ('Asphalt Flowers') one of the biggest selling Finnish recordings of the era (see further Johnson Forthcoming B).[1]

On what grounds did such groups categorise themselves as 'jazz'? In the face of the incomprehension frequently experienced diasporically by interwar exposure, the music was part of a *potpourri* of a generic 'Other' that fascinated post-war Eurocentric cultures, titillated by such highly publicised events as Howard Carter's excavations in Egypt and Lowell Thomas's film presentations of Lawrence in Arabia, and reflected in the phenomenal success of the Rudolph Valentino film *The Sheik* in 1921. Musicians obligingly performed to expectation. When US bandleader Bert Ralton toured New Zealand with his Savoy Havana Band in 1924, hailed as an exemplar of jazz, a review reported that the band set feet tapping 'with a sprightly foxtrot, appealing to the emotions with haunting, mysterious refrains of Eastern origin'. They also played Hawaiian, Scottish and 'plantation airs' (Bourke 2010: 23). Across the Tasman, Scott-Maxwell has explored in Australia a category of jazz that was amalgamated with orientalism, as for example the tour of Sun Moon Lee and his 'Chinese Jazz Band' in 1927, reviewed as 'the real thing in jazz' (Scott-Maxwell 2016: 47) (see Figure 1.1).

FIGURE 1.1 Poster for Sun Moon Lee and his Chinese Jazz Band

Source: Image courtesy of the Queensland State Library

The identification of jazz with all-purpose exotica was still evident in the Greek lyrics of the 1935 'song 'Cuba! Cuba!' which referred to 'jazz and crazy violins / Somewhere far away / In exile / In cabarets // When sailors get drunk / and sing in whisper / an exotic rumba / Softly starts / On an exotic night in Cuba ... Cuba ... / Magic nights with Rumba ... Rumba ... / Sweet nights,

nights in passion / with Hawaiian guitars' (cited and translated Anagnostou 2016: 59–60).

Musically what all this amounted to in the earliest diasporic forms was almost any kind of sonic novelty. The first performances billed as jazz in Australia were in July 1918. A reviewer reported:

> The Jass band consists of a pianist who can jump up and down, or slide from one side to the other while he is playing, a 'Saxie' player who can stand on his ear, a drummer whose right hand never knows what his left hand is doing, a banjo (ka)plunker, an E flat clarinet player, or a fiddler who can dance the bearcat
>
> *Johnson 1987*: 4; see further below in another connection

There were also reports of instrumental farmyard impersonations in live perform-ance, indicating that one of the thrusts of the new fashion was to blur the dis-tinction between instrumental music and trans-special vocalisation. Reviewers also reported the banging of kitchenware with the drummer firing revolvers and throwing his equipment about the stage (all at Johnson 1987: 4; and further, Whiteoak 1999: 170–177). It seems clear that, especially in more distant diasporic sites, the earliest acoustic interpretation of jazz was as sonic chaos; likewise cor-poreal slapstick – the reports above include descriptions of outrageous antics, con-cluding with the pianist standing on his chair 'playing the frenzied melody, while the trombone and saxophone players fell over totally exhausted, gasping for breath' (Johnson 1987: 11). It was also reported that in New Zealand when called on for an encore, Bert Ralton's presented 'the new foxtrot hit, "Horsey, Keep Your Tail Up!" with … [him] … gyrating round the stage mounted on a ridiculous-looking dummy horse' (Bourke 2010: 23).

All this represents a fundamental challenge to the whole idea of 'music', and the ultimate sonic antonyms of music are either silence or noise. But jazz was also the essence of modernity, and the outstanding distinction of the modern sound-scape is not silence, but noise (Johnson and Cloonan 2008: 49–63). It is one of the most distinctive markers of the connection between jazz and the material culture of modernity that the 'music' was so pervasively characterised as 'noise', evoking descriptions like 'general noisy effects', 'general din'. German 'Lärmjazz', with its noisy sound effects was exported to other German-influenced regions like Finland (Johnson 2002A: 43; Johnson 2002B: 96). And sound effects including whistles are still audible on early jazz/vaudeville recordings, such as 'Wild Wild Women' in 1919 by an English band led by US drummer Murray Pilcer.

In the earliest diasporic forms, jazz was widely regarded as incompatible with music, and according to French composer Pierre Ferroud collective improvisation was an impossibility (Goddard 1979: 137). A male entertainment troupe from New Zealand, the Diggers, that emerged from World War One, included cross-dresser Stan Lawson, of whom a reviewer in a 1921 tour wrote, 'Stan cannot sing, but he can put the jazz numbers over with rare vitality' (Bourke 2010: 6). And although Asser Fagerström later became a major participant in the Finnish jazz movement, the pianist was initially suspicious of jazz as 'whatever happens music' (Haavisto 1996: 12). In New Zealand the press reported on the arrival of 'The cacophony of the American Jazz ... eerie effects, and tonal shocks' (Bourke 2010: 11). An Italian song from 1928, called 'Jazzmania', made reference to the 'din', the 'infernal music' to be heard coming from cafes and restaurants, exclaiming 'what a noise!' (Plastino 2016: 318). Notwithstanding the *soi-disant* experimentalism of the later twentieth century, it appears that in this very early diasporic phase of the music, jazz, aligned with the 'noise music' of the Italian futurists and such movements as surrealism and Dada underwent the most radical avant-garde stage of its history.

It did not prevail for long. The shift from the stage vaudeville environment of the earliest jazz performance, to dance halls, restaurants and cabarets, and the arrival of the earliest US visitors led to a more chastened and musically disciplined approach (as in Australia, see Johnson 1987: 3–13; Whiteoak 1999 171–174). As jazz modulated through that process, it established various kinds of accommodation with local musical traditions out of which unique diasporic jazz forms precipitated, as discussed in further detail below. Even so, among those most offended by this American importation the equation of jazz with noise remained durable. Bruce Turner recalled that at the time he saw the 1930 Paul Whiteman sound (and colour) film *The King of Jazz* in Hastings, jazz was understood 'to mean any kind of fast, noisy American music' (Turner 1984: 6). And when pianist Tony Gould was rehearsing fellow Australian Don Banks's 1971 composition *Nexus* for orchestra and jazz quintet, on arriving for their first rehearsal the conductor told the jazz musicians 'to "go away and make your noise" while he rehearsed the orchestra' (Gould 2018: 85).

This profile reflects the musical and social roots of the diasporic forms of the music in demotic entertainments and social spaces (see also Johnson 2017C: 11–12). The canonical jazz narrative makes much of the black/African roots of jazz; in jazz histories an opening account of the dances in Congo Square in New Orleans has long been *de rigueur*. Of this, more below. But most memoirs of US jazz pioneers recall that their often-peripatetic apprenticeships were with touring acts in which, overall, European traditions had been formative and predominant. These included travelling carnivals and circuses, and exposure to brass bands. It is notable how significant a role was played in the formation of twentieth-century vernacular music cultures, including jazz, by the brass band movements – which also relates to jazz instrumentation, in which orchestral 'art music' instruments are so sparsely represented. Most early antipodean jazz performers, including many who would go on to become leaders in the Swing boom from the 1930s, such as Frank Coughlan and his brothers and Melbourne's Freddie Thomas grew up with brass band music in the blood. Both Coughlan and Thomas *pères* were prominent members of the community, Thomas senior was actually banned from further competition because of his relentless success (Stevens 2007: 2007).

It was a music of which John Philip Sousa was a highly influential global ambassador. His turn-of-the-century tours influenced brass band approaches to rhythm in, for example, Austria, and introduced Russians to his repertoire of 'adaptations of black American plantation songs and cakewalk dances' (Wasserberger et al. 2017: 115, 188). In 1937 Polish writer Karel Čapek recalled his pre-World War One exposure to contemporary US popular music as 'step-dancing negroes' but also Sousa, who 'made an impression on us with his quick marches, his noisy brass and drums; finally it was something other than melancholic waltzes or military flamboyance of European music' (Wasserberger et al. 2017: 406, 405). Robert Adams, one of New Zealand's earliest jazz band leaders, recalled the deep impression made on him by Sousa's tour in 1911 (Bourke 2010: 16). In South Africa, as in New Orleans, there was already an institutional structure in place to create a brass band community which provided a platform for an emerging jazz culture, through the church missions where British and German missionaries had introduced the music, 'for the glory of God, the advancement of "civilisation," and the procurement of converts' (Ballantine 2011: 493).

The most ubiquitous public performance space for the very earliest forms of diasporic jazz-inflected music within and beyond the US was the popular vaudeville stage, as confirmed abundantly in memoirs such as Garvin Bushell's, referred to above. Ethel Waters's models as a child were famous vaudeville acts Butterbeans and Susie, the Original Stringbeans and the Whitman Sisters (Waters n.d.: 52). She began her long and extremely successful career signed to vaudeville act managers Braxton and Nugent, and for her debut performance Baltimore in 1917 she sang 'St Louis Blues', modelled on a version she had heard performed by vaudevillian female impersonator Charles Anderson. According to her own recollection Waters was the first woman to perform the song professionally (Waters n.d.: 44, 55). Arnold Shaw (1977: 69, 73) records the survival of vaudevillian acts into the iconic 52nd Street jazz scene. Beyond the US, jazz first appeared on the popular stage. The Chocolate Kiddies tour, Josephine Baker's Blackbirds and the Southern Syncopated Orchestra in Europe were theatre presentations. The ODJB began their UK tours as part of a show *Joy Bells* at London's Hippodrome in March 1919, and with two weeks at the Palladium (Parsonage 2005: 124, 125). Early UK recordings of jazz acts, such as 'Murray Pilcer and His Jazz Band' (Parsonage 2005: 132, 133) are basically novelty vaudeville-type numbers. The first jazz performers in Australia, New Zealand and South Africa worked in vaudeville programmes either on stage or in the pit (see further Whiteoak 1999, 170–174; Bourke 2010: 39; Ballantine 2011, 1993, 2003). It was an association that established the aesthetic and cultural status of jazz in the public imagination. In South Africa, for example, the convergence became ambiguously implicated in the 'hopes and aspirations of the most deeply urbanised sectors of the African working class' (Ballantine 2011: 475). More generally, embedded within the genre of a 'variety act', the early and often outrageous novelty effects often referred to by promoters and reviewers became to some extent naturalised. Much was made

of the strange and primitive aspects of these earliest jazz performances, but vaudeville also framed the music within a safe tradition of 'staged' strangeness and exoticism – of magicians, hypnotists and oriental novelty acts.

It was not long before the music migrated to other venues, including cinemas
(in Brazil, for example; Fléchet 2016: 17), but most frequently in leisure spaces that
also catered for the massive international fashion for social dancing that emerged
from the early twentieth century (see Crease 2002: 73–76). The association was so
close during the 1920s that the diasporic understanding of jazz was as a dance as
well as a music genre. This explains what seems otherwise to be a strange gram-
matical form of the word, as a verb: a woman 'jazzes', in the same way she tangoes,
waltzes, foxtrots. 'The jazz is a dance', reported Australian lifestyle journal *Table
Talk* in August 1919. A New Zealand magazine carried the advertisement:

> **Jazz and be happy!**
> By a remarkable, simple, new method YOU can now master all the latest
> 'Jazz' dances in the seclusion of your own room – without music or partner –
> without anyone knowing you are learning.
> **If you can walk – you can "Jazz"**
>
> *Bourke 2010: 18*

Jazz was a music of literal and metaphorical movement, in the idea of improvisation as opposed to static score and in the often-abandoned animation of the
performers and audiences.

The significance of this identification is profound and multifarious. As
that advertisement implies, dancing is completely democratic. Anyone with a
functioning body can do it, without access to the money to buy an instrument
and years of lessons. The instrumental virtuosity that has become the pre-requisite
of jazz mastery separates the practitioner from 'ordinary' people. But 'if you can
walk, you can jazz', sets up a completely different cultural politics. In addition,
dancing, with vocalising, is the least mediated form of self-expression. There is
the poet and the poem, the painting and the painting, but the dancer *is* the dance.
The alienating distance between producer and consumer is all but dissolved in
the act of dancing, and the dancer is a vigorous producer of culture. Likewise, the
distinction between the mind and the body becomes barely sustainable, and this
will be taken up in further detail below. It has been through its early association
with dancing that, from the beginning, jazz seems to have energised the widest
audiences in terms of numbers and socio-economic range. For the incidental
music to a new era, this is a notable contrast with the high-art music tradition
and its ideology of fixity, as well as to the post-war shift of jazz to a more cerebral regime. People still dance to jazz, but to a generalised disapproval on the part
of its aesthetic custodians. The replacement of that link by the intellectualised
model that evolved over the post-World War Two period is, I believe, the most
profound shift that the music has undergone throughout its history; similarly,

Crease considers it to be 'the most significant single turning point in jazz history' (Crease 2002: 78).

Jazz, often with public dancing, was to be enjoyed in a number of social venues, all of which exchanged meanings with the music. In addition to dancing in the home to the music of radio and recordings, public dancing was also available in the immense *palais de danse* that proliferated from the early years of the century, in restaurants, luxury hotels and clubs of varying social status and in the fashionable cabaret format. In New Zealand, Auckland's first 'large-scale cabaret, the Dixieland' opened on 11 April 1922, promised the smart set, 'You'll hear the latest jazz music as it should be' (Bourke 2010: 18). Parsonage identifies all three categories of dance venue in the case of London: 'performed by dance bands, usually white, at socially exclusive venues such as large hotels and respectable clubs; performed by black music theatre companies, often accompanied by their own ensembles; and performed by small groups of musicians in West End clubs' (2005: 163). This array meant that few members of society would be excluded from the recreation by such considerations as class. 'If you can walk, you can dance' was an economic reality as well as a matter of physical competence. But in every case, the presentation of music for a utilitarian social purpose that was extravagantly corporeal on the part of both performers and audiences, stood in sharp contrast to the art music concert hall dedicated to aesthetic and moral edification. These multi-purposed sites included drinking, eating and socialising, as well as corporeal abandonment – undisciplined noise as opposed to acoustic order. And at the 'lower' end of what was already a lower-order spectrum, the circumstances framing the music conspired to confer upon it an odour of moral and aesthetic transgressiveness, a violation of authorised genteel conduct. The libertarian environment of French and Weimar theatre and cabaret stamped jazz as a heedlessly amoral music. A similar association, but with a more politicised inflection, was established in South Africa where illicit drinking and indoor nocturnal recreation circumvented local street curfews on urban blacks (Ballantine 2011: 476). In Portugal, jazz could also be found in *milieux* associated with gambling, prostitution, drugs and drunkenness (Cravinho 2016: 84). Similarly, in London the West End nightclub ambience established connections between jazz, drugs, suspicious and exotic transients overlapping with the underworld, which 'served to cement a negative image of jazz for the general public, distanced from the music not only geographically but through the pervasive and influential filter of the BBC' (Parsonage 2005: 164). For conservatives, the connection reinforced their disapproval, but for the smart set this latest in cabaret fashion offered a chic experience compounded with the fascination of *nostalgie de la boue*.

A further axis along which early diasporic jazz was identified was instrumentation. In salon dance bands, the violin had most commonly been the lead instrument. But jazz was the music of two closely connected developments that changed this profile. It represented modernity, and one of the distinguishing aspects of modernity was the rising level of constructed sound. These converged in the diversification of instrumentation for dance bands to draw them into the category of jazz. An advertisement in Italy for the 'Partenope Jazz-Band elettrico' listed five musicians doubling on 25 instruments including gypsy violin, 'eccentric piano', 'modern banjo', tenor and alto sax and a 'jazz-band drum set' (Plastino 2016: 322). This kind of ensemble advertises one of the most important changes in the sonic profile of the dance band: increasing volume. The violin that had commonly led a dance band was becoming overwhelmed by the rising noise levels of increasingly capacious indoor urban leisure spaces. Many bandleaders adopted the *stroh* violin in order to remain at a competitive volume, as seen for example in the jazz band footage in the 1926 Australian film *Greenhide*, referred to elsewhere. Similar megaphone devices, such as the 'claritone' for clarinet were being advertised for other instruments (Johnson 2000: 72, 90). But a solution that also proclaimed modernity was the adoption of the saxophone, and among early jazz bands it is notable how many violinists began to double on sax. In Russia, Valentin Parnakh singled out the saxophone as the instrument of jazz dissonances and, for the authorities, to ban the instrument was to virtually extirpate the music (Haavisto 1996: 10; Konttinen 1987: 21; Starr 1983: 46–47, 85, 216). The same synecdoche was made with loathing in the UK (Lawson-Peebles 2013: 27–28), imaged in the 1926 painting *The Breakdown* by J. B. Souter, in which, with distant overtones of Pygmalion and Galatea, a black saxophone player entrances a naked woman so white she almost appears to be marble, coming to life. The scenario was so scandalous that Souter destroyed it after being ordered to remove the work from public exhibition. In Germany the connection created some awkwardness. Initially coded opprobriously as a jazz instrument, the damage then done to German saxophone manufacturing required it to be officially realigned with art composers like Debussy (Kater 1992: 31). In Finland, the use of 'saxophone' in the band name established its status as 'jatsi'. The only sign of why the Suomi Jazz Orchestra, mentioned above, was so named was the inclusion of two instruments that had not previously appeared in dance bands. One of these was the saxophone.

The other was a drum kit. As early reviews of Australian jazz performance have already suggested, banging things very loudly was central to the act (see further Whiteoak 1999: 177–180). Nothing proclaimed the connection between jazz, modernity and noise so clearly as percussion, so much so that the terms jazz and drums were often interchangeable, as in Prague and Paris, and in Portugal where the drummer was also known as the 'jazz-bandista' (Kater 1992: 24; Shepherd et al. 2005: VII: 22; Goddard 1979: 16; Nettelbeck 2004: 106; Guerpin 2012: 77 n. 24; Cravinho 2016: 81; Roxo and Castelo-Branco 2016: 211). In Helsinki at the Konsertti Café in 1923 Hugo Huttunen turned his violin, cello and piano salon orchestra into the country's first 'jazz' band simply by adding a drummer (Johnson 2002A: 43). The prominence of percussion complemented the understanding that flamboyant rhythmic effects were definitive to jazz – a 'hurricane of rhythm', according to Cocteau (Nettelbeck 2004: 106). A report in Portugal in 1926 spoke of jazz as 'rattling snare, restless drumsticks, metallic dry sounds and scatting, horn, bass drum, whistling, shouts and squeals' (Cravinho 2016: 84), and in Brazil it scarcely mattered what repertoire was played, it was jazz if the band included 'American drums' (Fléchet 2016: 19). US drummer Murray Pilcer arrived in the UK in 1916 and formed a jazz band that recorded in 1919. A reviewer declared 'The constituent elements of a Jazz band, consisting mainly of syren [sic], rattle, buzzer, cymbals and drum, make revel in an orgy of cacophony which will rejoice the hearts of all true Jazzites', and in the same year a reviewer in of the Southern Syncopated Orchestra declared in *The Times* that syncopation is associated with 'musical fireworks and jazz drummers who hurl themselves at a dozen instruments in their efforts to extract noise from anything and everything' (Parsonage 2005: 133, 150). When Robert Adams formed his Jazz Band in Auckland, New Zealand, in the early 1920s, it was recalled that the band 'went in heavily for noise'. At the time, the only thing locals knew about jazz was that

> the drummer had to make a din like all hell let loose. So Bob placed himself in the centre of the stage and made a tremendous uproar on a collection of drums, gongs and cymbals and a variety of other articles such as cow bells, motorcar horns and beer bottles'
>
> *Bourke 2010: 16*

Although these accounts are now likely to cause amusement, this sonic profile is no less important than the connection with extravagant dance as a marker of a modernity that, along with blackness, radically threatened the aesthetic and moral foundations of 'civilised' Enlightenment tradition.

The Great Depression

Throughout the 1920s jazz had established itself in the global consciousness with all the cultural alignments we have reviewed. The tensions that marked its relationship with pre-World War One *mores* and musics were now indelible, which helps to account for the sudden disappearance of the word from public discourse with the Wall Street crash in October 1929. The often insolent good-time heedlessness of jazz was inappropriate to the austerities of the deepening Great Depression, largely to be replaced by expressions of yearning for vanished comforts and certitudes. Economic hardship changed leisure practices, increasing the importance of radio, for example, which could be accessed cheaply and without the costs of going out to live venues. With the expansion of transmission services and the availability of cheaper and stronger receivers in the 1930s, a night at home listening to the wireless was a less expensive and bothersome and more varied competitor to public live music. By 1931 in the US 50 per cent of urban families owned radios, and by the end of the decade radio news had overtaken the press as the primary source of information (Cashman 1989: 320, 334). Other contemporary technologies played significant roles in the nature and cultural location of jazz, including the adoption from the early 1930s of the microphone in live performance as a consequence of the increasing size and noise levels of urban entertainment venues from the early twentieth century. The shift from a predominantly rural to an urban demographic recorded in the 1920 US census was driven by the rapid expansion of the northern cities, and musicians migrating to such centres from for example New Orleans were also moving from small to cavernous performance spaces. Pete Lala's in New Orleans, where King Oliver had led a band, was a single-fronted one-storey premises with a dance hall in the rear. New York's Cotton Club was in a two-storey building constructed in 1918, with the dance hall upstairs. By the time it was refurbished after Owney Madden took it over in 1922, it could hold 700 customers, and this was a mere fraction of vast Palais in London, or in Australia where the Sydney Palais could accommodate 3,000 when it opened in 1920. And these were not audiences seated quietly, but dancing, talking, eating and drinking. They presented a challenge to small bands that had previously worked in small spaces, and the solution was to assemble bigger and louder orchestras. This of course drowned out softer instruments, which is why bass players, guitar players and vocalists began experimenting with amplification (and in so doing, developing the technologies and instrumental template for later electrified rock bands).

The outcomes were not limited to simply making existing dance music louder; the character of dance music itself was changed. The heavy emphasis on two beats per bar that had characterised so much jazz in the 1920s was very much an inheritance from unamplified outdoor marching bands. The amplification evolved for huge indoor venues made a different approach to rhythmic pulse possible without physical strain – a greater dynamic range, more supple rhythmic feel spread evenly across the bar and with more subtle effects of syncopation now possible. This affected every aspect of the music that became known as 'Swing', the word beginning to appear on record labels around 1933–1934 (Nicholson 2014): slap-bass virtually disappeared, drummers could free up the kick drum from its rigid foundational beat, guitarists could sustain notes, singers operate in a more conversational, unforced style, and dancing styles reflected the shift away from 2/4 to 4/4. Rudy Vallee took credit for pioneering the singer's microphone in live performance in 1930, and through the early thirties the technology became internationalised. One consequence was the discovery that a singer did not have to 'blast' to fill a large hall, enabling a more intimate performance style which became known as crooning. This in turn transformed the gender politics of jazz singing in radical ways that varied with particular regions, and this will be explored in greater detail later; the point for the moment is that one of the developments associated with the diaspora during the 1930s was the evolution of a new style of live vocal performance (see further below, and Johnson 2000: 81–105).

While sound recordings circulated this new sound, the most important model was distributed by sound films, which could show such performances in action through the spate of musicals which appeared over the 1930s. Their audience reach increased as, in parlous times, the cinema provided a relatively inexpensive alternative recreation to live-music venues. Of course, sound had been matched to 'silent' film from the turn of the century, 'a common form of entertainment in music halls and variety theaters before the First World War'; well over a thousand were made in Germany (Lotz 2012: 161; see more generally Altman 2004). But it was the arrival of the optical sound track in the late 1920s which enabled the standardisation and international distribution of 'talkies', whereas silent film, though often emanating from the US, had undergone some degree of mediation to local cultures by means of the musical accompaniment in regional cinemas. One effect of soundtrack installed at point of origin on the global dispersal of jazz was that the extravagant capering of musicians was no longer necessary to persuade the audiences that they were watching/hearing an up to date hot dance band. This progressive chastening of visual rhetoric paralleled the shift from outrageous noise and novelty effects to more acoustic decorum, and can be traced, for example, in dance scenes in successive Australian films, from *Greenhide* (1926), to what is widely regarded as the country's first 'talkie', *Showgirl's Luck* (1931) to *The Squatter's Daughter* (1933), a trajectory that also runs from the urban milieu of the rebellious flapper, via a film whose plotline is about the making of the country's first sound film, to the re-affirmation of a traditional rural work ethic (see further Johnson 2015).

As well as familiarising global audiences with the sound of what seemed to be class-neutral American speech, sound film also provided audio-visual models of the latest in dance music from the US, which gave further momentum to an international standardisation of practice, as in the example of South Africa (Ballantine 2011: 485). Released in conjunction with the 1933 film of the same name, Australian bandleader Jim Davidson's recording of '42nd Street' became one of his biggest and most influential hits with, for that period, massive sales estimated at 95,000 (Davidson 1983: 30). Finnish band Rytmi-Pojat's 1936 airshot of 'Broadway Rhythm', from *Broadway Melody of 1936* (1935) was one of the few jazz/Swing performances sung in English to that date, incorporating for the first time some of the vocal rasp deployed by US singers (Johnson Forthcoming B).

At the same time, however, the technology deprived musicians of one of the most significant new income streams from the 1920s: accompanying silent film. This in turn impacted on local attitudes to imported US culture. The loss of employment that accompanied the advent of talkies aggravated the long-running hostility of English dance musicians to visiting American musicians, and a dance band section of the Union was formed in August 1930, to tighten restrictions on the entry of foreign musicians (Parsonage 2005: 219). While loss of work to talkies also affected the US, local factors produced distinctive consequences for the diasporic jazz landscapes. In Germany, for example, the foreign musicians who had enriched the jazz culture began to leave as work dried up, their departure accelerated by political conditions (see below). But that alone does not account for the change in mood and leisure habits. It is a signal of a deeper cultural tremor. In his poem 'September 1st, 1939' the poet W. H. Auden looked back on what he called that 'low, dishonest decade'. Subsequent appalling holocaust revelations have discouraged recognition of the interwar strength and pervasiveness of racism, xenophobia and eugenics in countries in the Anglo-Euro-US axis, and the initial level of sympathy for the rise of Fascism in Italy and Germany. The 'bad press' accorded these socio-political movements following World War Two has tended to mask one of the increasingly significant forces of reaction against jazz-inflected dance music during the 1930s. As so often, the nervousness of that decade fostered an inward-looking nationalism and xenophobia and intensified suspicion of the national and cultural 'Other', often finding expression in virulent racism and eugenicism in Anglo-European communities as well as in the obvious case of Germany (Williams 1995: 142–159; Carey 1992: 13–14). The associations established between jazz, blackness and Jewishness, as well as internationalised anarchical modernity threatening local cultures, saw a widespread reversion in popular music to more traditional national narratives and musical structures, from the 'going home' songs celebrating traditional rural values in Australia to the re-emergence of local forms, as in the samba which became Brazil's national music (Johnson 1987: 14; Johnson 2000:13–14; Piedade 2003: 45).

Although the name 'jazz' had by the early 1930s acquired connotations of irresponsibility inappropriate to the new times, and the gaucherie of a fashion that had faded, its musical characteristics were now deeply lodged in the public mind, and gradually resurfaced as weariness with austerity developed, along with some amelioration of the economic hardship. Jazz approaches re-entered popular music under names like 'hot music' and 'Swing'. This term is a continuing point of confusion in jazz commentary, because it refers both to a certain generic musical pulse, but also to a specific style gaining public recognition with the rise of the bands of, for example, Benny Goodman and Artie Shaw during the 1930s. In the former sense, its usage has been traced back to at least as far as Will Marion Cook's pioneering black production *In Dahomey: A Negro Musical Comedy*. It opened in New York in 1903, and later that same year the production came to London (Parsonage 2005: 82). The show opened with the song 'Swing Along' (Parsonage 2005: 90–91), in which the word conveyed a strutting buoyancy that prefigures the general idea of a music that 'swings'. I shall indicate this generic sense with lower case initial. During the 1930s, it was the other sense that defined a new development in jazz-inflected musics; in that instance I shall use upper case initial: Swing.

The arrival of Swing in the US is a story now as well-established as that of the emergence of jazz itself as preserved in the standard accounts. Most pertinent here is how it circulated and was received internationally, and like jazz in the 1920s, modern technologies were the key, now supplemented by sound film. Like the earliest global manifestations of jazz, Swing was the supreme vehicle of the latest in American musical modernity. As in the case of radio and recordings in the 1920s, this coding was amplified by its association with the latest development in film technology. Melbourne's Jim Davidson's recording of '42nd Street' had already capitalised on the new music and its circulation via sound film. The same would be true of Sydney's newest dance venue, whose house band repertoire would draw heavily on material circulated via US movies. That venue was the sumptuous *palais*, the Trocadero, which opened in April 1936. It was a propitious period for symbols of economic recovery and a new modernity. The opening in 1932 of the Sydney Harbour Bridge, which provided much needed employment for thousands, and which literally united the city and bridged urban and sub-urban, had been a sign that technological innovation could lift the country into a new order, superseding the primary industries, which had also been reliant on trade with the 'Old Country', England, but that had failed to protect Australia from economic depression (after Germany, Australia was the hardest hit economically of any Western nation). The aggressive buoyancy of Swing coming from the 'New World', its audio-visual impact intensified by US film musicals, and the months of advance publicity as the new venue was being built, had raised public interest to a peak and represented the venue as summarising a new and more confident era.

The question of who would lead the band for the opening was the subject of lively discussion in both professional and lifestyle media, all shrewdly inflamed by the expatriate Canadian entrepreneur behind the venture, James C. Bendrodt. Frank Coughlan was named, fronting a band would draw on the country's leading dance musicians and vocalists, notably Barbara James (see further below), all of whom had strong jazz-based credentials. Although, like all *palais* orchestras of the time, they could cover the full range of dance music, it was their command of the latest US style that was foregrounded. In the same month that it opened, a radio broadcast from the Trocadero captured the spirit. Interspersed by fanfares an announcer dramatically introduced the orchestra: 'It's new! It's big! It's glamorous! And it swings!' – the last word dragged out. Then, identifying Coughlan as leader, 'the greatest of all Australia's dance band maestros' (fanfare) 'A personality! New! An invigorating personality! And as such he is known in the greatest dance rendez-vous of the world'. Coughlan's credits are then listed – London's Savoy, Claridges, the Palladium, the BBC, Jack Hylton, Ray Noble – then rising to a declamatory climax: 'Frank lives, breathes, and plays [pause] Swing!' (see *The Troc* CD 1991). These (literal) fanfares locate Swing not just as the latest in US music, but as a harbinger of a resurgent modernity after the recent desperate nostalgic retrospection, a cosmopolitanism that pushes against the insular turn that accompanied the Depression. Even this early emphasis on the idea of 'personality' is striking. To a much greater extent than jazz in the 1920s, Swing exported a cult of 'personality' and personal fandom, which made international celebrities of its exponents, most notably the 'King of Swing', Benny Goodman, but also manifested in the cases of Artie Shaw, the Dorseys and Glenn Miller. In the case of singers, notably Frank Sinatra, the sense of engaging with a distinct 'personality' was also strengthened by the more intimate and conversational singing styles that emerged during the 1930s, enabled by technologies of recording and amplification (see further below). It is provocative that, as also in the case of movie stars (the two categories often overlapped), Swing became a site of tension between, but also mutual reinforcement of, competing forces of the twentieth century: mass culture and individualism. 'Personality' carries a significant thrust against the suppression of individual agency that permeated so much of the 1930s (see further below). The centrality of Swing to the constellation of brash new modernities was also proclaimed in the internationally released 1936 Australian movie *The Flying Doctor*, which began with a collage that summarised contemporary Sydney: surfing, night life, the Harbour Bridge, the Trocadero, with scenes set inside and footage of the band in performance, all celebrating an institution, the Flying Doctor, which since its inaugural flight in 1928, in itself embodied the triumph of one of the supreme symbols of modern technology – flight – over the 'tyranny' of Australian rural distance.[2]

Outside totalitarian regimes emerging during the 1930s, the combination of Swing's international popularity and its untrammelled circulation inevitably led to the repetitive exploitation of this immensely marketable music. With over-promotion and increasing staleness, a music that was demonised under repressive regimes ironically came to be identified with an analogous musical dynamic. For dedicated fans of hot music, fascism and commercial Swing were both tropes for the suppression of the individual spirit and cultural impoverishment. This is ironic given the emphasis on 'personality', yet I suggest that it was that emphasis that served to belie the disappearance of the individual within the mass, much as contemporary advertising speciously addresses itself so often to 'your' personal profile.

Arnold Toynbee identified what he called the 'internal proletariat', sections of society characterised by a sense of 'cultural loss'. It is a model that helps to account for the emergence of a more or less youthful international community for whom jazz was the musical enactment of resistance to forces of homogenisation (Johnson 2003: 166–167). This growing objection to the commercialisation of Swing was one of the forces incubating a new interest in what later became known as 'classic' jazz, also enabled by reissue programmes of hitherto obscure 1920s recordings of (especially black) jazz musicians. A new wave of young jazz enthusiasts began to appear internationally, looking back to the earliest examples of the music, as vehicles of folk authenticity, supposedly uncontaminated by vulgar commercialism. As spontaneous expressions of the individual within the collective, their version of 'real' jazz was a 'resistance music', not necessarily in a political, but in a larger cultural sense. Its enemy was stifling regimentation, musically expressed in the most commercial forms of dance music. Bruce Turner recalled that as schoolboys,

> Our attitudes were raw and simplistic. Jazz was 'sincere'. The opposite of this was commercial', a shameful thing for any music to be. Sincere music pitted itself against vested interests and the scurvy businessmen raking in their profits behind the scenes. The 'sincere' jazzman was a heroic figure – not among the common run of men. All this, of course, was partly true but also our naïve simplification of a complex problem. And our conclusions were

hopelessly wide of the mark. Jazz came from somewhere 'out there'. One had to be exceptionally gifted in order to play it, so any outsider who had a go at it was liable to make himself look rather silly. This gave the jazzman a certain glamour.

Turner 1984: 31

Politically this group was likely to align itself against fascism, though there was also a resistance to forms of socialism that were rigidly authoritarian and centralist (Johnson 2003: 159; Newton 1989: 252–274; Kater 1992: 17, 82–85; Gendron 1995: 45–46). Although jazz was thus implicated in political change, in a Fordist world its meaning was broader, the embodiment of a general humanist 'élan vital' (Skvorecky 1989: 83), and a reaction against modern mechanised regimentation. Although not back-to-the-roots purists, at least some of this spirit seems to have informed youth groups like the Hamburg Swing Boys (Kater 1992: 109–110). In Prague, during the brief interval between Nazi occupation and the communist takeover, this coding became central to the ecstatic reception accorded the visiting Australian Graeme Bell band, which represented a brief flash of 'freedom' between two totalitarian episodes and in the context of the tepid Swing that had been hitherto available (Johnson 2000: 136–137).

Internationally, Swing marshalled the full range of modern media both to disperse globally and also to strengthen its coding as the *dernier cri* in popular music. With its sonic occupation of domestic space, as the 'world' moved into another war, radio would prove essential in the process, and at the same time continued to make nonsense of national boundaries, particularly in the form of non-language-specific music. As such, radio represented a powerful political weapon. In 1933 Goebbels declared, 'What the press was to the nineteenth century, radio will be to the twentieth' (Bergmeier and Lotz 1997: 6). By 1941 Hitler's voice would reach an estimated fifty million citizens through the new facility of Volksempfänger, the 'people's radio' (Bergmeier and Lotz 1997: 8–9; Birdsall 2012: especially 103–140). Even the careful management of the soundscape, however, could not constrain the transnational promiscuity of radio waves, nor block their political messages or diminish the appeal of the new American music they carried. Hence, attempts to control the use of radios themselves, a prohibition that certainly made access to Swing difficult but which, like so many top-down measures implemented by authoritarian regimes, could be outwitted in the interstices of everyday life. Guitarist/bassist Frank Mulders recalled his experiences in Holland as a jazz lover:

At home we could play our favourite music (not too loud of course) but since all our radios had been confiscated we lost track of the overseas jazz scene. When the Nazis came door to door with trucks to pinch everybody's radio sets they got a conglomeration of the most outdated junk one could possibly imagine. My father submitted a set that he had built when radio was in its infancy and it had been in the attic for years. The good one with shortwave was carefully hidden under the floor. However we were strictly forbidden to get near it to listen to music on as it was a vital link between the underground and the news broadcasts of Radio Orange from London. Fortunately one of the band members was a radio enthusiast and he managed to build a shortwave set that was hidden in his father's attic. There we could, every now and then amid the pop-crackle and the miserable noises of the Nazi interference-transmitters, listen to the type of music we loved.

Mulders n.d.: 8

World War Two

That recollection was from Nazi occupied Holland. Depending on which country you lived in, the war had broken out some time over the period March 1938 (the Anschluss) to September 1939 (the invasion of Poland). The war had a profound impact on the character, role, dispersal and meaning of jazz outside the US. The general pattern is that it gave impetus to the global spread of American popular culture, but the impact was by no means straightforward or unequivocal, depending on both political alignment and cultural context. In Russia, that alignment shifted with the opening of Germany's 'second front' in June 1941, and US jazz and Swing suddenly enjoyed official favour, especially among the armed services, with even the NKVD putting together its own jazz bands. This brief sunshine period gave Russians a glimpse on film of Glenn Miller (*Sun Valley Serenade*, 1941, and *Orchestra Wives*, 1942), who accordingly established considerable influence before the resumption of austerity and the 'jazz purges' which accompanied the Zhdanov proclamations after the war (Stites 1992: 104–118; Starr 1983: 181–234). Official attitudes to jazz during the conflict were largely divided along allies/axis alliances, but there were also neutral countries in which the absence of any political commitment gave freer rein to how the music was circulated. As a neutral city, Lisbon became a place where representatives of the contesting powers could mingle. Salazar sought to capitalise on this cosmopolitanism by promoting international tourism, which helped to maintain a flow of foreign bands such as the African-American Willie Lewis orchestra in 1941, and with the advance of Allied troops, Swing interest increased further (Cravinho 2016: 98). When he granted the US the use of air bases in the Azores during the war, the military brought jazz with them (Cravinho 2016: 81 and n. 25). The group of Nordic countries provided a spectrum of responses. In occupied Norway jazz was officially underground, unlike Sweden where, although the flow of US visitors dried up (van Kan 2016: 38), the country's neutrality provided an open landscape for a developing local scene that positioned the country to become one of the most active jazz centres in post-war Europe (Wasserberger et al. 2017: 279–280; Martinelli 2018: 204–207; the Swedish/US connection is studied in detail and at length in van Kan 2017). Finland's engagement in the conflict began with an assault by Russia, initiating the Winter War (1939–1940). Hostilities resumed in what was known as the Continuation War (1941–1944), with Finland aided by a strategic alliance with Germany, which meant that it was now technically at war against the allied powers. The development of the country's jazz scene was therefore impeded for multiple reasons. Apart from the diversion of musicians to wartime service, jazz was tainted by its association with the US, especially in a country so richly endowed with its own musical traditions, and in addition public dancing was banned (see further below).

The broad antipathy between jazz and totalitarianism was reinforced in the course of the war, adding impetus to a resurgence of jazz among the allies, signalled in the early stages of the international revivalist movement. Subsequent readings of the 'jazz wars' have been modelled on the traditional/modern binary, but what came to be understood as 'modern jazz' was scarcely part of the diasporic imaginary until after the war. The revivalist movement was initially a reaction to an enervated and commercialised version of Swing, which was losing momentum by the late 1930s. In the earliest stages of the war, outside the US Swing was also submerged under a wave of sympathy for a besieged Britain, projected musically in nostalgic references to English heritage themes and images like the white cliffs of Dover and nightingales in Berkeley Square. This was particularly so within the far-flung Empire, for example in distant New Zealand (Bourke 2010: 97–99). There, as elsewhere, the arrival of the US military brought a change in a public mood of 'King and Country' (during a visit to New Zealand in January 1941, Noël Coward had even been reprimanded publicly for his 'The Stately Homes of England', 'an insult to the homeland' (Bourke 2010: 116). On 12 June 1942 a US flotilla including five troopships arrived in Auckland, the beginning of an invasion of 150,000 servicemen, with 50,000 based in the country at any one time (Bourke 2010: 117), and across the Tasman, Australia experienced its largest 'invasion' ever, with around one million US service personnel passing through a country with a population of only seven million during the conflict (see further Potts and Potts 1985).

The entry of the US into the war reinvested Swing with an appeal that converged with anti-Fascism, generating an appetite for high energy US music. The music was not simply an incidental accompaniment, but one of the main ways of projecting US power and energy internationally. Götz Bergander, a Dresden teenager who, with his family, listened 'avidly' to the BBC, hearing Glenn Miller and Benny Goodman thought, 'People who can make music like this must win the war' (Hastings 2004: 188). From Greenland to Ghana, wherever there were US bases and R&R centres, they took jazz with them and in one way or another stimulated local activity (Shepherd et al. 2005: VII: 202; VI: 140). Their entertainment units included Glenn Miller's Army Air Force band and Artie Shaw's Navy band, both staffed by some of the country's most respected pre-bop jazz musicians. The former was stationed in 1944 the UK, where it unofficially interrupted the union ban on US musicians to stimulating effect (Shepherd et al. 2005: VII: 333). Jazz re-entered London's nightlife through bottle parties, local recordings and events mounted by various kinds of hot music clubs, one of which, the Radio Rhythm Club, led to 'the First English Public Jam Session, 16 November 1941, produced under the auspices of HMV, *Melody Maker* and the BBC', a 'milestone for British jazz' (Studdert 2013: 96).

Even the BBC was forced to change its programming policies when it was discovered that the propaganda broadcasts by Lord Haw-Haw, accompanied by dance music and jazz, were alarmingly popular with BEF troops in France, who tended to tune into the English broadcaster only for the occasional special jazz programme. The wartime conditions had created and disclosed a hitherto overlooked audience demographic: young men who 'listened to the radio in groups. This was an unknown quantity for the BBC, which was used to create programmes for families or for the solitary and concentrated fireside listener' (Studdert 2013: 101). The broadcaster responded with the Special Forces Programme (SFP), launched on 8 June 1940, which presented difficult-to-obtain recordings and had its own band led by Harry Parry and including George Shearing (Studdert 2013: 102). The SFP became the General Forces Programme in 1944 and evolved into the BBC Light Programme from July 1945 (Studdert 2013: 105). These developments advanced the situation of jazz in Britain and the BBC's service area in a number of ways. Apart from increasing the public exposure to jazz, it attuned the broadcaster to the demands of a new generation, preparing the way for similar programmes in the post-war period, in particular the BBC Jazz Club from 1947, and it also conferred a new level of respectability on the music (Studdert 2013: 105).

The boost to jazz with US involvement in the war was paralleled in all allied nations to a greater or lesser extent. Artie Shaw's band played 35 days of concerts and dances in New Zealand from 1 August 1943, open to both US and NZ service personnel and also occasionally to civilian members of the musicians union, who were deeply impressed by the precision and dynamics of the Americans (Bourke 2010: 129–130). New Zealand trumpeter Bobby Griffith was inspired by them, 'Because they blew. Those guys used to blow their heads off. New Zealand was very Mickey Mouse … The Americans really got me' (Bourke 2010: 125). Local pianist Jim Foley was recruited to play with one of the US dance bands because of the unreliability of their own pianist:

> The standard of music was wonderful. I learned over 500 jam tunes, and enjoyed the company of musicians so keen on their musical product that they would never dream of talking when one of their members was taking a solo. … Playing with this band was the biggest thrill I have ever had. My spine used to tingle every night
>
> *Bourke 2010: 126*

In Australia, although supposedly performing only for US service personnel, ingenious locals found ways to hear the Artie Shaw orchestra's official performances. In Sydney, Shaw also issued a personal invitation to members of the Musician's Union to attend his performances (Johnson 2008: 120). Through this exposure, and from unofficial after hours mingling with US service musicians, they gained invaluable experience. In an interview with the author, now held in the Australian Jazz Archives hosted by the National Film and Sound Archive, reed player Maurie Le Doeuff recalled being backstage with a very drunk local trumpet player as a US service band began Miller's 'String of Pearls'. Le Doeuff never forgot the dynamic variation on the repeated two note introduction, so dramatic that in his recollection it instantly sobered up his colleague. The impact of these experiences is strikingly illustrated by surviving airshots enabling us to compare the laboured rhythmic approach of Le Doeuff's Adelaide band before hearing the Americans, whose lighter and more supple style is preserved on a private jam session recording, and the increase in swing imparted to the Adelaide musicians evident on subsequent airshots. Shaw's orchestra included Dixieland trumpeter Max Kaminsky, who recorded with Roger Bell in Melbourne, helping to nurture what would become the internationally influential Australian traditional jazz movement (Johnson 1987: 23–31).

But their influence went beyond musical content; the US presence transformed the New Zealand entertainment culture in areas ranging from stage demeanour to dancing skills to cinema opening hours. There was a boom in nightlife and Saturday matinee dances, as soldiers looked for ways of filling in time during pub closing hours. Their dancing skills were particularly admired and the hit of one Artie Shaw concert in August 1943 was a jitterbug display by black American GIs. When in April 1944 radio station 1ZM was placed under the control of the US forces (Bourke 2010: 118), the more informal style of presentation, increased US content, and format (including the introduction of a US Hit Parade) made it the most popular of the radio stations by the time it passed back to NZ control by December 1944 after most of the US had left for the Pacific (Bourke 2010: 117–125).

All however was not rosy or straightforward in relations with the US garrisons. They had money, glamour and neat attire, even the locally unheard of use of aftershave, and an enthusiastic libidinous attentiveness (Thompson and Macklin 2000: 94–96). Wherever they were posted, local women embraced the Yanks, all too literally for their menfolk, especially for those away on service. In Britain the familiar complaint was that the Yanks were 'over-paid, over-sexed, and over here'. And although the Americans carried a halo of sophistication, they were themselves a heterogeneous community, many of whom were provincial rednecks bringing with them racist attitudes that became a source of friction in countries in which race issues were not overt. Local musicians generally mingled freely, and in the case of jazz performers, eagerly, with black US service men. Many were offended by the segregation that set up separate recreational venues for blacks, such as the American Negro Club in Auckland and Sydney's Booker T. Washington Club, where the music was provided by a local jazz band under Ray Price. It is some measure of Price's own strong feelings on the subject that later, in 1947, he refused to play a Sydney residency that barred blacks (on the Booker T. Washington see the highly informative 1994 memoir by Joan Clarke). In New Zealand at least one outbreak of hostilities was caused by US attitudes to Maoris (Bourke 2010: 127). In Brisbane, which amounted to a US garrison city, tensions between Australian and US servicemen were stoked by a range of inequities, including Macarthur's failure to give adequate recognition to Australian military successes; the fact that the Americans were paid at about twice the rate of the Australians; an entitlement on the part of the former to use Australian service canteen facilities, while the locals were barred from the opulently stocked US American Postal Exchange, aka PX; and Americans-only dances to which local girls ('cuddle bunnies') could be invited to jitterbug wildly to the latest Swing, and be attentively courted (Thompson and Macklin 2000: 158, 186). Fuelled by accumulated resentments and alcohol, and triggered when an Australian soldier intervened in the bullying treatment of a US serviceman by MPs in a street confrontation, a twenty-four hour running fight broke out on America's Thanksgiving Day, 26 November 1942. Eight Australian servicemen suffered gunshot wounds, one of which was fatal, and eleven Americans were injured. Three Australians were later jailed; no US personnel were punished (see Thompson and Macklin 2000).

The incident dramatises a darker side to the US military presence, a reminder that not everyone was uncritically enamoured of or impressed by the visitors and the culture they brought with them. And this rippled into the music, which in a number of regions including the UK, Australia, and by default New Zealand, was the first live exposure since proscriptions had been imposed before the war. Jazz/Swing was now not a music quarantined and cleanly edited within sound and film media, but emanating from flesh and blood performers with whom one could mingle extra-musically. Notwithstanding the unarguable mentorship enjoyed by the locals, there was another side to the responses. The admiration accorded visiting American musicians was not unqualified. A less frequently recorded outcome of the encounter was an increase in local confidence. In both Australia and New Zealand (and probably elsewhere) one of the ways in which the often offensively cocky visiting Americans enhanced their prestige (and sexual allure) was by frequently asking to sit in, claiming to be alumni of the most famous US Swing bands. Although some were impressive, when they got up to play, as reported by local New Zealand bandleader Del Crook, many 'were hopeless' (Bourke 2010: 123). The disparity between their claimed CV and actual competence caused many local musicians to re-assess their own standards. In a notes-taken, but unrecorded conversation with the author, Roger Bell's brother, pianist Graeme recalled them both hearing black and white US service musicians playing their versions of jazz. 'We can do better than that', was Graeme's response, and indeed the wartime experience of live as opposed to tidily recorded and filmed jazz did much to build up the confidence of a cohort of what would become highly influential revivalists.

US (and Australian) military entertainment units also took jazz to the Pacific islands, including Bougainville and Borneo, and in Papua New Guinea jazz left its mark on the bass lines of the local stringbands (Crowdy and Goddard 1999: 50–51). Even in a region as remote from the European and Pacific theatres as South Africa, the war affected the reception and impact of jazz. Ballantine includes wartime inflation and increasingly dense urban black ghettos among the factors which produced a growing 'New Africanism' and associated localised jazz idioms (Ballantine 1993: 54–61).

D-Day was both a military and a musical invasion, reclaiming continental Europe for jazz. Glenn Miller was influential in the establishment of Allied Expeditionary Forces radio service which followed the troops eastward, and which was also picked up by liberated countries and by retreating and captured German troops (Kater 1992: 171–172). But within Axis countries, the story had been even less straightforward. The association of jazz with contamination was of course particularly emphasised in Nazi Germany. Because of the origins of the music and the profile of its earliest performers during the heady libertarian days of the Weimar Republic, jazz was both black American and Jewish. While jazz was never banned by central decree in the Third Reich, the hostility of senior party members like Goebbels ensured that localised harassment of jazz musicians would not be displeasing to the authorities (Kater 1992: 20, 24–26, 29–30, 33, 45). This is not necessarily to suggest armed Gestapo raids; the harassment could take indirect and ingenious forms, as described in the unpublished memoir of Dutch-born jazz musician Frank Mulders, worth quoting in full as a deeply felt personal account:

> At every concert there were always a couple of exponents of the "New Order" sitting in the front row to make sure that there was no "decadent American jazz" played. To make it worse bands were issued with booklets that stated the Do's and Don'ts as far as performances were concerned. It was all too ridiculous for us to comprehend. One was not allowed to use wah wah mutes in trumpets; drum solos for more than four bars were out; hot licks on clarinets were also taboo. In a nutshell, our precious jazz band was doomed.
>
> One memorable experience of those days should be mentioned as it was to be our last stage performance for some time. We had created what we called a "Negro Show" for which we used the St Louis Blues. We had conveniently forgotten on our list to state anything more than "The Holy Blue Louis". The band was dressed in white butchers' vests (the only thing available at the time since one of the members happened to be a butcher), black pants, cardboard top hats and enormous homemade butterflies (bowties). Black stockings with eyeholes and mouth carefully cut out, and placed over our heads, completed the outfits. It brought the house down and the Nazis on our back. They were furious about this outburst of "decadent nigger music". It rained threats of being put to work in Germany, even being sent to a concentration camp etc. After the storm blew over they came to us with a proposal. You had to hand it to the buggers that they always thought of a

propaganda angle in everything. We were to put on the Negro show but the trumpet player was to crawl on his knees over the stage blowing as loud as possible, the drummer had to virtually wreck his kit, we had to scream and shout like madmen and make the whole thing as preposterous as possible. After this we were to go backstage, don "decent" garb and look as clean as we could. Then there was going to be an announcement – "ladies and gentlemen, after this ludicrous outburst of American decadence we shall now listen to some beautiful German dance music". After this episode we all decided to go underground.

Mulders n.d.: 7–8

Such proscriptions were not confined to German occupied territories. The wide open entertainment culture of Shanghai 'withered amid slogans such as "frivolity is the enemy"'. There was a 'domestic dance hall ban' in Japan itself in November 1940, and then the Japanese-owned dance halls in Shanghai were shut down in December 1941, and Japanese musicians were for obvious reasons 'unwelcome in establishments outside of the Japanese concession' (Atkins 2011: 473). Bans were also imposed in Finland, though this only affected jazz collaterally. A week after the outbreak of the Winter War, the government imposed a ban on dancing as an attempt to establish a mood of public austerity. It would remain intermittently in place until September 1948. Penalties for violation ranged from fines, to jail, and in 1944 one person running away from an illegal dance died of a police bullet. With most dance musicians serving in the army, and light music in local broadcasting almost completely replaced by more serious forms, the jazz scene that had developed over the two decades leading up to the war virtually disappeared from public view (Johnson forthcoming B).

In Germany the emigration of musicians, set up a new mini-diaspora that benefited destinations such as Argentina, Australia, Siberia and even the US itself (Kater 1992: 40). Throughout the war jazz was hobbled by various collateral bans, such as on live performance of American music and by the closing down of shows, theatres and cabarets following the attempted assassination of Hitler in 1944. Nor was the music assisted by various constraints on record production and distribution following Goebbels's 'Aryanisation' of the industry from 1938 (Kater 1992: 139, 164). As official opprobrium grew, an enthusiasm for jazz became increasingly by default an anti-Nazi gesture. An attachment to jazz could be added to charges of sedition and various youthful jazz communities, including the Hamburg Swing Boys and the zarzous of Paris, became more conscious of and active in the politics of their musical preferences (Kater 1992: 146–147, 151–160; Nettelbeck 2004: 58). The connection was made explicit by a Gestapo interrogator who declared to a jazz-loving prisoner in 1944, 'Anything that starts with Ellington ends with an assassination attempt on the Führer' (Kater 1992: 194). As a further confirmation of the relationship between jazz and totalitarianism in general, this chimes with the words of a Stalinist poster: 'Today you play jazz, tomorrow you will betray your country' (reported in the *Wordsworth Dictionary of Musical Quotations*, 1993: 284).

Nonetheless, as in all the schematic binaries that set jazz unambiguously against the spirit of totalitarianism, in practice there was considerable nuance and flexibility. As also in the case of Soviet Russia referred to above, Nazi Germany was faced with a 'jazz dilemma'. Although deeply disapproved of by the state, jazz was popular, and the jazz industry was therefore both an economic and propaganda resource. Its popularity embraced the full political spectrum in wartime Germany, including the armed services, the Brownshirts and the SS. Jazz and Swing were still performed live as part of the attempt to maintain morale, including among the troops by official entertainment musicians (Kater 1992: 69, 111, 120). Knowing that Germans were tuning in to foreign jazz broadcasts, Goebbels found it necessary to set up state-controlled Swing groups, including The Golden Seven, which failed to attract any public support (as had also happened with Russia's parallel efforts). A special band was formed to keep the Luftwaffe from tuning into BBC music programmes, but was also regarded as tepid (Kater 1992: 47, 49, 54, 127, 129). One of the strangest responses to the jazz dilemma was the formation of the broadcasting 'propaganda swing' group, Charlie and His Orchestra, which played US and English repertoire with new propaganda lyrics (Kater 1992: 130–131; Bergmeier and Lotz 1997: 136–177). Although it included some outstanding jazz musicians from Italy and Holland, its overall arrangements lacked lustre and to anglophone ears the revised lyrics are risible at best.

As in all combatant nations, Germany also saw gaps in the dance band ranks, partly by enlistment but in Germany exacerbated by the flight of a substantial cohort of Jewish musicians from anti-Semitism. Their place was often taken by musicians from occupied countries that had more advanced jazz competencies and scenes, including Italy, France, Belgium, Holland and Denmark (Kater 1992: 112–116). These were tolerated by Germany as morale builders for its occupation troops, even though certain kinds of circumspection were felt to be advisable, with ambiguous results. In many occupied countries, this 'circumspection' involved inventing new titles for US jazz repertoire. In Norway, 'Stjernestøv' would be announced and listed in a concert programme, and 'Stardust' played (Bergh 1991: [5]). New repertoire was written, some of it based on standard chord sequences, with new melodies and titles. Native traditional repertoire was 'jazzed', as in 'Pål sine høner', by Øvind Berghs Bristolorkester, in November 1941. Frank Mulders recalled the stratagems in The Netherlands:

> When the war broke out on the 10th May 1940 we were just getting in the swing of things. Under Nazi rule 'swing' became a dirty word. Bands were forbidden to perform any works of English, American or Jewish composers, so we had only one tune of Dutch origin left. That was "Blonde Mientje" which we always regarded as a crummy tune anyway. If ever we could play somewhere – even school dances and the like – we had to submit a list of

tunes to the Nazi authorities. As it was useless to put things like "Lady Be Good" or "Honeysuckle Rose" on those stupid lists, we just translated all the titles literally into Dutch and put fictitious Dutch names in the space marked composer. This practice yielded some hilarious results. "St Louis Blues" for instance came over with our rather limited school English as "The Holy Blue Louis"

Mulders n.d.: 7.

The depletion of the professional pool during the war also had long-term benefits. The losses were mostly established dance band musicians whose apprenticeships in the early years of the century were deeply ingrained with pre-jazz thinking. Young performers who had grown up in the 1920s and early 1930s, were internalising and naturalising jazz grammar from their earliest training. They re-invigorated diasporic jazz, and their youthful recruitment into the profession meant that they would sustain a durable post-war jazz scene, as in the case of Finland (Johnson Forthcoming B). In the UK and Australia the vacuum left by enlistments was filled in part by older musicians called out of retirement, but also by promising tyros, bringing with them adventurous energy if not experience, and giving them early professional experience that carried them through careers to the end of the century. In Australia, jazz musicians Terry Wilkinson (piano, born 1931) and Don Burrows (reeds, born 1928), began to take on professional work in their teens, and became highly influential in the Sydney jazz scene, Burrows in particular presenting high profile jazz TV programmes and setting in motion the country's first tertiary jazz education courses from the 1970s (Johnson 1987: 292–293, 123–124).

The Cold War to the 1970s

The war thus continued to activate jazz in its immediate aftermath. Jazz scenes formed themselves around US garrisons in Europe and Japan, as part of what has been called 'coerced Americanisation' (Moore 1998: 265). In Holland Frank Mulders recalled 'Since all the women and girls had gone virtually berserk with the gum-chewing, real cigarette smoking liberators, there was an almost instant market for dance bands' (Mulders n.d.: 10). The US took over Radio Luxembourg from 1945 to 1946 and oriented it to the tastes of occupation troops (Shepherd et al. 2005: VII: 258). The influx of the US military, including black musicians, helped to reawaken jazz activity in France (Shipton 2012: 266). The proximity of US headquarters led to an immensely influential post-war jazz culture in Frankfurt (the 'Frankfurt Sound') from which emerged musicians including Albert Mangelsdorff, and the West German Jazz Federation (Kater 1992: 207–208). In Naples the scene picked up partly because of the presence of Americans and their V Discs (Plastino 2016: 315–316). Returning POWs who had been exposed to the music while in captivity, took their enthusiasm back home and became central to jazz activity, as in the case of Lajos Martiny in Hungary and Hans Koller in Austria (Shepherd et al. 2005: VII: 28, 145). Less often noted, beyond Europe in the years following the war the international dispersal of refugees introduced a multicultural cosmopolitanism that transformed formerly provincial lifestyles and nightlife. When in the 1950s Frank Mulders migrated to what had hitherto been close to an Anglo-Saxon monoculture in Adelaide, South Australia, his memoir records a multi-national nightclub environment that included fellow Dutch and Russian, Italian, Baltic, Slavic and German émigrés, many with recent experience of US music tastes in service bases in their home countries (Mulders n.d.: 29).

During World War Two, the perennial cultural alignment between jazz and the US had become explicitly politicised, and this was intensified with the onset of the Cold War, although the orientations were altered. The USSR was now the enemy rather than Germany, and jazz sympathies were accordingly reconfigured to reset the political bearings. As has been amply documented, in the Soviet Bloc, after a brief period of post-war jazzy euphoria, with the onset of the Cold War in 1946 to the 'Thaw' of the late 1950s, jazz was again officially anathematised as the music of the capitalist enemy (see for example Starr 1983: 204–234; Pickhan and Ritter 2010; Pietraszewski 2014: 48–62; Johnson 2017C: 67–154). As these accounts disclose, as always the music was able to seep into everyday life in various forms and through various means, sometimes through the actual demonisation process. In Azerbaijan during the Cold War, apart from being available illegally on Voice of America and the BBC, jazz could also be heard in Soviet film where it was used to signal 'the entrance of an American spy'. After repeated listenings, jazz enthusiasts would then hurry home to reproduce what they had heard (Naroditskaya 2016: 103). It is important also not to think of the Bloc as a monolith; in Hungary, Ádám Havas has identified a brief 'golden age' of Swing from 1945–1948, after which, during the 1950s, 'official culture politics excluded formerly flourishing jazz – increasingly played by Hungarians and Hungarian gypsies – from both public venues and media, considering it as a trend in 'bourgeois dance music' representing moral decay and imperialism, rather than an autonomous genre' (Havas 2018: 5).

As in the decade following the First World War, the aftermath of the Second witnessed an expansion of US international hegemony, now driven by Cold War strategies and fuelled economically by the rationalisation and co-ordination of US cultural exports from the mid-1950s (Breen 1997: 143–162). In some ways the Cold War disrupted old migratory channels. Dizzy Gillespie was unable to bring Cuban pianist Bebo Valdés into the US to join his band because of the latter's supposedly communist associations (Fernández 2003: 10). In many Middle Eastern, Asian and Latin American regions, suspicion of US (and Soviet) expansionism reinforced nationalist sentiments that resisted imported musics, though, as we shall see, this often fostered local music traditions that would later feed into jazz fusions. More generally, however, an increasing internationalisation of jazz accompanied the expanding global influence of the US.

In 1953, Spain signed an agreement with the US that allowed the installation of US military bases in exchange for recognition and aid (Iglesias 2013: 105). Spain provided a test site for the hypothesis forming within the US government that jazz might be a valuable instrument of foreign policy rather than just as a morale booster for homesick troops. In the face of grim Stalinist totalitarianism, in 1955 the *New York Times*'s Stockholm correspondent, Felix Belair, wrote: 'America's secret weapon is a blue note in a minor key' (von Eschen 2004: 10). Capitalising on the changing mood in Franco's Spain, essays into jazz-based cultural diplomacy included jazz recordings provided by the US embassy to Radio Madrid, officially sponsored concerts of modern US music such as Gershwin and Copland, and then Lionel Hampton's band in Madrid in March 1956 (Iglesias 2013: 105).

Two weeks later a band led by Dizzy Gillespie 'inaugurated the intercontinental jazz tours under the auspices of the State Department' (Iglesias 2013: 106). This was not the first collaboration between the US government and jazz in the field of cultural diplomacy (see Celenza 2019). The *Voice of America* (VOA) radio programme had been inaugurated in 1942 as an information platform for the US, and had passed from the control of the Office of War Information to the State Department at war's end, by which time it was servicing around 40 language communities globally. From January 1955 it included in its programming a daily jazz programme, hosted by Willis Conover, and with some 30 million listeners in 80 countries, it became the most influential broadcaster in the history of jazz (von Eschen 2004: 14). 'Conover received an average of one thousand letters per month' from around the globe. The Egyptian weekly newspaper *Al-Izza* reported that 'Conover's daily 2-hour musical programme has won the United States more friends than any other activity' (cited Jankowsky 2016: 269). Countless jazz musicians from outside the US recall that Conover's broadcasts were essential to their development, playing a particularly important role in more closed regimes, for example in Bulgaria where Milcho Leviev, central to the country's jazz-folk fusion movement, recalls the importance of Conover's programme in his developing jazz consciousness (Levy 2016: 269). During the 1962 Benny Goodman tour in the USSR the impact of Conover's broadcasts was felt in the level of knowledge Russian fans showed about the band members: 'These cats know more about us than we do', said one musician (von Eschen 2004: 111).

Jazz was now not merely musical entertainment, but a strategic weapon in the Cold War. Conover articulated structural features of jazz that pointedly paralleled the idealised US democratic system: 'Jazz musicians agree in advance on what the harmonic progression is going to be, in what key, how fast, and how long, and within that agreement they are free to play anything they want' (von Eschen 2004: 16). The metaphor underpinned the State Department touring jazz packages that formally began with Dizzy Gillespie's tour of the Middle East in 1956, the year, as it happens, that marks the beginning of the Soviet 'Thaw', with Khrushchev's famous denunciation of Stalin at the Twentieth Congress in Moscow and the early Russian counter-offensives in cultural diplomacy (see further Oivi et al. Forthcoming). The major advisor and tour escort for the US State Department tours was eminent jazz spokesman Marshall Stearns (von Eschen 2004: 22). The destinations included Iran (Dizzy Gillespie), Iraq (Dave Brubeck and Duke Ellington), South America (Woody Herman), Thailand (Goodman and later Stan Getz). These reflected the foreign policy agenda driving the project, as they frequently 'mapped onto the geographies of Eisenhower's defensive perimeter from Afghanistan to Turkey', including essential sources for US oil and other current political flashpoints such as the Suez (Jankowsky 2016: 272; von Eschen 2004: 32–33, 146). In terms of the jazz diaspora, however, they also established the primary contact with live US jazz in, for example India, whose modernist pioneer, Goan saxophonist Braz Gonsalves, met and informally studied with Sam Most in Bombay. Gonsalves, who went on to perform elsewhere in Asia and Europe, was also involved in the post-concert restaurant jamming during Duke Ellington's visit to Bombay in the early 1960s, sessions which continued for another five years (Pinckney 2003: 62, 63).

In diplomatic terms the tours were a great success. An editorial in a Pakistani newspaper declared after one of the tours 'The language of diplomacy … ought to be translated into the score for a bop trumpet' (von Eschen 2004: 33). Burt Korall wrote in *Billboard*:

> Jazz has succeeded where American diplomats have foundered. It has created a meeting ground, been something that made for a deeper understanding of the American way of life, for to be interested in jazz is to be interested in things American
>
> *von Eschen 2004: 18*

However, as with the USSR's cultural diplomacy projects, the agenda of the state was not always under its control. Musicians met, had discussions and formed attachments, and made stage announcements that had nothing to do with official diplomacy (von Eschen 2004: 25). The tours became the site of some of the deeper contradictions that traversed the jazz diaspora in general. Chief among these was the tangled issue of jazz and blackness. Part of the reason for the choice of Dizzy Gillespie for the inaugural tour was the government's wish to promulgate an integrationist message – black musicians representing the US. Gillespie was sharp enough to understand this, as well as the hypocrisy of the gesture especially in the context of the Civil Rights campaigns taking place in the US over the same period (von Eschen 2004: 3); he 'didn't hesitate to defy the State Department and local convention, promoting his own vision of America, which was considerably more democratic than that of the State Department' (von Eschen 2004: 35). In November 1955 Louis Armstrong had been an early choice for such a tour, but refused specifically because of the Civil Rights issues (von Eschen 2004: 58). Following his diplomatically successful tour of Ghana, plans were made for him to tour the USSR and South America in 1957, but Armstrong pulled out when in September Governor Orval Faubus used the National Guard to block entry by black students to Central High School in Little Rock, Arkansas. 'The way they are treating my people in the South ... the Government can go to hell' (von Eschen 2004: 63).

The reference to 'my people' is the clue to a central contradiction not just in the State Department tours, but in jazz itself: especially when outside the US, whom does a black American jazz musician represent? And one of the ironies in these international tours is that while intended to internationalise US values, much of the time they in fact helped to internationalise a black African community. Touring in Brazil, Gillespie reported that they found 'a lot of brothers, Africans – and their music is African' (von Eschen 2004: 40). In Ghana Louis Armstrong was struck by a resemblance between one of the African women dancing and his mother: 'I know it now. I came from here, way back. At least my people did. Now I know this is my country too ... After all, my ancestors came from here and I still have African blood in me' (von Eschen 2004: 61). Ironically then, a political project intended to glorify the US often served instead to foster a pan-Africanism that many Americans regarded as a threat. Dave and Iola Brubeck collaborated with Armstrong to write and produce a satirical musical called *The Real Ambassadors* over 1961–62, performed to much praise at the Monterey Jazz Festival of September 1962. It 'brilliantly captured the often complex (and contradictory) politics of the State Department tours at the intersection of the Cold War, African and Asian nation building, and the U.S. civil rights struggle' (von Eschen 2004: 79).

Brubeck had been one of the white Americans to undertake a State Department tour, as also was Benny Goodman, which brings us to one of the richest ironies in this international exercise in jazz diplomacy. It was Soviet officials themselves who were 'crucial' in sending Goodman. They did not want a black bandleader, partly because it might undermine their case of racism against the US (von Eschen 2004: 102, 103, 104). So, although the USSR at certain times favoured jazz as the folk form of a suppressed community, and opposed US racism, they found the idea of a black-led jazz ensemble unpalatable both because it undermined their anti-US case and of course because the USSR itself was not free of racism. At the same time while the US was enduring violent internal ructions because of systemic racism (including within the State Department), it wanted integrated bands as an advertisement for democratic integration.

This cultural diplomacy programme was crucial in disclosing the paradoxes in jazz and its internationalisation: the centrality of blackness to the global perception of jazz, but against the reality of black rights in the US; the tension between jazz as representing universal aesthetic values, yet as the bearer of race particularism. In the debates over jazz and Africanism, this has been the perennial centre of gravity. Apart from conflicted agenda, along with VOA this programme was the most sustained institutionalised and institutionalising diasporic project in the music's history, continuing to resonate for the rest of the century. In 1987, jazz was declared by Congress a 'national treasure' and 'America's classical music' in a resolution that listed six reasons that the music should be accorded institutional status (Jankowsky 2016: 278). The resolution begins: 'Whereas jazz has achieved pre-eminence throughout the world as an indigenous American music and art form, bringing to this country and the world a uniquely American synthesis and culture through the African-American experience'; Jankowsky quotes in full the six reasons, in which all the contradictions discussed are implicit. In 1998, at a major White House function, Hillary Clinton called jazz 'an American metaphor', 'the quintessential voice of America', 'while honoured guest Vaclav Havel briefly narrated a Czech history in which "freedom was identified with jazz" until the Nazis and the subsequent communist regimes suppressed both' (Jankowsky 2016: 279).

The touring programme coincided with and certainly helped in the increasing artistic legitimisation of jazz from the 1950s (Van Eschen 2004: 17–18). The sacralisation of jazz was also given a boost by the arrival of a new low-rent music which shouldered much of the odium of its predecessor. Rock now embodied vulgarity, corporeal excess and youthful defiance of moral standards; in many places, including Australasia and the UK, it was a working class music at a time when the middle classes were appropriating jazz as a music, a lifestyle accessory, an advertising motif. And in the rush to distinguish their music from rock, jazz followers and spokespersons constructed a discourse based on high art that would frame the evolving canon and all its corollaries (see further below). Ironically, this was happening at exactly the same moment that the State Department tours were demonstrating that the fate of jazz, in both its geographical and cross-class migrations, was politically rather than aesthetically driven. I would argue that this programme, in conjunction with the changing relationship between jazz and dance, represented the most important transformation in the cultural status and understanding of jazz in the post-war era, including creating the framework for the construction of the canon-based history.

The major stylistic development to be internationalised following World War Two was bop. The post-war black American consciousness was very different from that of the 1920s. Regarding the war itself, the US service personnel were engaged for nearly four years, compared with twenty months in the earlier conflict, and extending over a much greater geographical and cultural space, from Europe into the Pacific, including Australasia. In the later conflict the broader range of attitudes they encountered included a respect that they had not enjoyed at home, and they brought back with them a less submissive consciousness. This reverberated into jazz developments, particularly in the sense of the ownership of post-war developments. A more aggressive assertion of black identity reverberated diasporically, and this was reflected in attitudes to bop, intensified by a hiatus in exposure to its evolution during the war. One of the reasons for that hiatus underscores again the importance of recording technology, which was reaffirmed in two very distinct ways in the decade or so following the war. The first of these was to do with the revolutionary impact of bop. Its development had taken place during the war years, but it only now receives mention here, for the simple reason that it was scarcely known outside the US until after the war. One of the main reasons for this was because access to the most up to date US jazz developments was blocked by, among other circumstances, a lack of recordings brought about by diversion of the raw materials to war purposes, and the recording embargo imposed by the American Federation of Musicians. Bop only began to be heard outside the US through the late 1940s. In Australia, for example, the first reports are from 1946, in the UK from 1948 (Bisset 1987: 88; Johnson 1987: 37–39; McKay 2005: 98). In the absence of access to successive stages in its evolution, the style was therefore virtually incomprehensible as having any connection with jazz (Johnson 2000, 17–18). In some relatively low-population centres, such as New Zealand, although it attracted the close attention of musicians dedicated to the latest developments, the audience was too small to generate a significant market, particularly where the connection between jazz and dancing had remained important (Bourke 2010: 212–213)

One consequence of the emergence of post-war progressive styles was the formation of a 'modern/traditional' divide. In the US, the 'first shot' in the confrontation has been dated at 1942 with Barry Ulanov's attack on the purism of the revivalists' anathematisation of commercial Swing, but bop raised the stakes (Gendron 1995: 32). This was even more so outside the US in countries where the wartime elision of stylistic developments made the contrast so much more stark. When Bruce Turner finished his military service, he found that in England 'the music of a thousand styles had now been whittled down to only two – New Orleans and modern progressive. If you didn't happen to conform to either of these stereotypes, you just didn't have anywhere you could go and play' (Turner 1984:76). He also made the point that this situation was less the creation of the musicians than of 'the pundits, expounding their well-publicized theories and calling the tune' (Turner 1984: 77). In many cases this division defined the jazz scene for the rest of the century, and even to the present among older generation 'mouldie fygges' (traditional enthusiasts). For others, as they gradually came to join the dots between bop and its predecessors, it came to appear that bop was actually an 'end-point' of historical logic, beyond which no clear direction seemed to be indicated (see further below).

One of the directions taken by jazz from the beginnings of its global migrations was towards its increasing differentiation from other forms of popular music, such as vaudeville and dance. The purism of the revivalist movement was one manifestation, but was anchored in the past, still complicit for example with dance. In some cases, and particularly on display in the stage concerts that became a major jazz format in the antipodes in the 1950s, 'dixieland' was sustained by older musicians still bearing traces of comedy vaudeville roots. New Zealand saw a number of 'Dixieland' revivals, the strongest in the mid-1950s. Among the earliest, in the early 1950s, was the Dixielanders led by Nolan Rafferty, who had been with Epi Shalfoon for nearly fifteen years (Bourke 2010: 206). Among a newer generation from the late 1950s, the reliance on slapstick by Merv Thomas and his Dixielanders tended to reinforce the disdain directed towards 'dixieland' by the more progressive jazz musicians like bopper Bart Stokes (Bourke 2010: 207–208). Even the Bell band in Australia, pillar of revivalism, were not above comedy and even blackface as in their presentation 'Coons on Parade' (see Bell 1988: 53). Bop on the other hand was the acme of jazz as 'pure' music, marking the zenith of its trajectory in what were seen as evolutionary terms, an absolute form of jazz that could be confused with nothing else.

Developments in sound recording technology played a further role in the global penetration of jazz as a distinctive and autonomous form of music during the post-war decades. The Long Playing (LP) record was introduced by Columbia in 1948 but did not gain ground until after some jostling for various standard formats (Gellatt, 1976: 290–297. The LP recording enlarged and consolidated the emerging canon. Its systematic jazz series, complete sessions, alternate takes, sleeve notes and booklets, all conferred scholarly gravitas upon jazz 'texts', and far more effectively standardised jazz practices and discourses than was possible with the more discrete two track format of earlier three minute seventy-eight rpm recordings. The result both circulated a canonical history and inclined the music towards international homogeneity, closing the gap between source and diasporic sounds.

The process was also accelerated by the advent of rock, the first distinctly new youth music since the arrival of jazz around 35 years earlier. Initially there was in some regions a degree of synergy between jazz and rock, with both genres often billed together in popular music venues, radio and TV youth programmes and film, in the UK and the antipodes. Apart from the UK programme *Six-Five Special* (see BFI Screenonline) at www.screenonline.org.uk/tv/id/561782/index. html, accessed 17 January 2019), English director Richard Lester's first film, *It's Trad Dad* (1962) featured both traditional jazz bands and rock performers; early Australian and New Zealand live and TV rock presentations covered both genres (Johnson 1987: 50–51; Giuffre 2016 – to whom thanks for additional information; Bourke 2010: 268, 275). Indeed, as in the 1920s, many professional musicians maintained their livelihood by commuting comfortably back and forth between the older and the new fashions; this was especially so in centres with a small pool of local popular stylists, like Tasmania (Johnson 1987: 277). By default, New Zealand's earliest rock functions were dominated by older musicians, from vaudeville, jazz, country and Hawaiian musics (Bourke 2010: 279). The band for the 'first rock'n'roll dance' in Auckland, on 5 October 1956, a week after *Rock Around The Clock* opened, was Frank Gibson's All Star Rock'n'Rollers – made up entirely of jazz musicians (Bourke 2010: 276). It was this band that established a venue The Jive Centre, 'as New Zealand's leading rock'n'roll dance hall' (Bourke 2010: 278).

More generally, however, and as 'moral panic' US movies like *Blackboard Jungle* (1955) internationally circulated the image of the delinquent teenager, in the public mind rock became the new and threatening musical 'Other', against which the increasingly comprehensible mainstream and traditional forms of jazz could be defined, and in consequence come to seem palatable, tractable, orderly, both musically and in terms of associated lifestyles. Rock foregrounded the teenager as the new threat from within, while the followers of jazz, however youthful, were walking in well-defined parental footprints.

In a dynamic rarely noted, the early adjacency of rock and the established jazz scenes in such regions, and then the growing dubiousness of the former, contributed to a weakening of the link between jazz and dance. In New Zealand the Wellington Festivals of Jazz concerts evolved into Rock'n'Roll Jamborees by early 1957, and this in turn led to some musicians establishing a 'Jazz for Listening' series of presentations, in which dancing was discouraged. (Bourke 2010: 282). The transition of jazz from a dancing to a listening music is most often attributed to the 'undanceability' of bop, from the 1940s. That is, jazz is conceived of as, so to speak, a closed system, aesthetically self-regulating. But the factor in this case was a collective reaction by jazz musicians (including even those who were gaining employment from rock), against the rowdy and physically extravagant audience responses to rock and the reduction of performance to loud and formulaic clichés. This in turn strengthened the hand of a jazz style so unequivocally different from rock as bop. The divorce between rock and jazz would be made absolute by the advent of The Beatles and full electrification, waiting until the emergence of jazz/rock fusion for a *rapprochement*. But now, in the words of veteran New Zealand musician Ken Avery, many of his colleagues 'put away their saxophones and trumpets during the guitar band craze and unfortunately never got them out again' (Bourke 2010: 348).

All the developments in the post-war decade that have been noted combined to open a major new stage in the global jazz scene: the 'ascent' of jazz as distinct and aesthetically valid, and its establishment as a musical Esperanto. By the 1960s, it was increasingly difficult to distinguish whether jazz was being played by someone from within or outside the US, and the two categories could comfortably intermingle. During the final US State Department tour in the late 1970s, Clark Terry put together a 'Festival Big Band' to celebrate the internationalisation of jazz; it included musicians from the US, Poland, Portugal, Sweden, Japan, West Germany, India, Denmark, UK, Puerto Rico and Norway (von Eschen 2004: 248–249). By the late 1950s jazz was now fully reconciled with the mainstream media – it was 'owned' by the media industries, by entrepreneurs, publishers, record companies, film and TV, and it had become fully codified. In the absence of anything else, it had been still a slightly 'outlaw' music as compared with the high art tradition, but with the rising tide of rock many jazz practitioners and commentators fled to the higher ground of art music (see further Johnson 2002B, 107–112). Through the 1960s jazz came to be more or less uniformly understood internationally as a fully coherent musical tradition. Apart from the LP recording, jazz codifications and canonisations were conducted through books, histories, discographies, memoirs, documentaries, international jazz festivals, specialist radio/TV programmes, and the arrival of Fake Books and standard chord charts, licks lexicons, *Music minus One* records, jazz theory and formal education programmes.

Jazz had been incorporated in various *ad hoc* ways into educational projects as far back as the 1920s and 1930s in, for example, Germany, Denmark, Finland

and France (Kater, 1992: 17; Shepherd et al. 2005: VII: 156; Johnson 2002A: 47; Nettelbeck 2004: 52; see further below). But from the 1960s these became increasingly common and standardised adjuncts to conservatorium programmes in, by way of a sample, Hungary in the 1960s

> As a consequence of the softening cultural politics, the growing scientific attention towards popular music … and the autonomy claims of jazz musicians, the first jazz department of the socialist block was founded in Hungary in 1965. The growing number of jazz musicians holding prestigious national awards and the expanding media coverage are also reliable indicators of jazz music's increasing cultural legitimacy, whose boundaries gradually became institutionally codified
>
> *Havas 2018: 5–6*

Formal tertiary jazz education programmes were established from Australia to India in the 1970s, and in prestigious art music bastions like the Paris Conservatoire and Finland's Sibelius Academy in the 1980s (Shepherd et al. 2005: VII: 29, 166; Johnson 1987: 61; Pinckney 2003: 68; Nettelbeck 2004: 90). These processes resulted in an international codification of jazz practices, including performance and deportment, lifestyle and image. In late Elizabethan England, one sign that the sonnet had gone to seed was the appearance of what were called 'legislative rhetorics', books which listed phrases to describe the lover's lips, or hair, or eyes, the strength of passion, and so on. Sonnet 'licks'. The bebop grammar books signify, in a parallel way, the formularisation of a placeless and depersonalised jazz grammar: rhythmic approaches (the triplet or 12/8 foundation), harmonic foundations, especially the 6,2,5,1 pattern, and the choice of notes (flattened and raised 9ths). The result is a highly codified bop grammar in which the only routes for further development and individualisation are tempo and range. It is a situation that produces widespread dismay. Veteran Garvin Bushell, himself a highly literate musician, wrote of formal training jazz courses, 'The musicians of today are so well trained technically, and able to read, that they don't depend on creativity, they depend on what you put on paper for them. The educational process is making fantastic imitators out of young players' (Bushell 1988: 122; see a recent general overview in Prouty 2019).

Of course, there are equivalent codifications for other styles such as Swing and classic jazz, but as an endpoint of mainstream jazz logic, bop enjoys the most convincing international accreditation of jazz competency. Anything less is underdeveloped, anything other risks straying from the path. The traditional-to-bop body of jazz is increasingly regarded as a kind of fully completed *oeuvre*, with significant individualisation (personal and collective, regional and national) only possible outside that field. The objective of reproducing the canonical styles of the source was largely achieved by the late 1960s, and often then modulated into an unchallenging facility. Film, TV and advertising manifested the point globally.

Since the 1930s, jazz had been a sometime *subject* of films, from *St Louis Blues* (1929), through *Cabin in the Sky* (1943), *Young Man with a Horn* (1950) and *Pete Kelly's Blues* (1955). As such, it was part of a continuing enquiry into and construction of the history and character of jazz and its mythologies, working out an alignment between jazz and the values of Middle America. Through biopics like *The Glenn Miller Story* (1953), *The Benny Goodman Story* (1955) and *The Five Pennies* (1959), jazz was becoming cinematically wholesome.

For reasons adumbrated above, by the late 1950s it had become a semiotically secure *component* of film and TV, then advertising, because the character and affective repertoire of its various styles were so fully established that jazz could be relied upon to carry agreed meanings to an international 'interpretive community'. In *Anatomy of a Murder* (1959) Duke Ellington's friendship and piano duet with the protagonist, the cosily provincial attorney and amateur jazz pianist Paul Biegler (James Stewart), was an internationally circulated message about a US lifestyle with which jazz was finding a secure accommodation within – even if only just within, or straddling (Cooke 2008: 211–224) – the borders of respectability. Internationally, Henry Mancini's film and television music was significant. In *Peter Gunn* and *A Touch of Evil* (both from 1958) it was the music of those who patrolled and secured the borders (literally so in the latter), modulating to his work for *Pink Panther* (1963), where jazz was now understood as a coolly decorative frame for a good-natured narrative, and available for appropriation by commodity capitalism through advertising.

Fin de Siècle

The trajectory of global jazz development over the twentieth century can be mapped through numerous parallel arcs, defined by such forces as race, gender, economics, politics, nation and, of course, stylistics. The following inventorial sketch is intended to illustrate a trend that will be explored in more detail later in this study. It reverses the pattern among jazz musicians up to the late twentieth century. For decades a primary objective of jazz musicians outside the US was to implement what Atkins explored in relation to Japan, 'strategies of authentication': the closest possible approximation to US models (Atkins 2001). The objective was to consolidate jazz as a completely distinctive and unique form, defined by the US. As an attempt to split jazz off from other modern musics, this process could be described as 'jazz fission', in order to schematically distinguish it from a reverse shift from the 1960s towards jazz fusions. The closer the jazz 'mainstream' formally and semiotically approached global standardisation based on canonised US models, the more important it became for increasing numbers of musicians to preserve a sense of innovation through reaction against US-centred homogenisation. To avoid a misleading idealist model of change simply driven by aesthetics, it is important to emphasise that it was also generated by material and socio-economic forces such as global geo-politics, including anti-US sentiments arising from the aggressive hegemony proclaimed, for example, in the war in Vietnam (Jost 2012: 278; Nicholson 2014: 142).

Gathering critical mass and validation from the 1960s, there was a challenge to US templates, with their increasingly formularised harmonic sequences, rhythmic rhetoric, repertoire and performance format. A point was reached at which the music was often less arresting than the political discourses framing it. Various aspects of this reaction are addressed at greater length and in more detail later in this study, but the following summary overview provides orientation in relation to the present chronicle. The reaction pushed in several directions, most notably towards the more open structures of Free Jazz, generic and stylistic fusions, and self-consciously eclectic experiments in syncretisms between jazz and regional forms, moving along the road towards World Music. All three incorporated convergence with musical practices imported from outside the established understanding of jazz. Such 'hybridisations' (problems with such terms are noted elsewhere) in various forms and permutations have been woven into the diasporic jazz tapestry since its beginnings. Early regional manifestations of jazz bore audible traces of local musical traditions, such as *chanson* in French jazz (Nettelbeck 2004: 88). Even the form and function of Free Jazz may be found in prototype in the very earliest anarchical versions of diasporic jazz, though at that time the reaction was against received local understandings of music, and towards what was imagined as jazz.

Various versions of 'Free Jazz' emerged within the US, but they gained insufficient following to sustain a significant and durable scene. By the end of the 1960s, European musicians had developed a distinctive form of Free Jazz with its own aesthetic (Jost 2012: 277, 296–297). From the late 1960s, a much more commercially successful extension of the standard jazz parameters was developed by a crossover with contemporary forms of rock, which by now had itself achieved a gravitas that was commensurate with the rising aesthetic trajectory of jazz. Like Free Jazz, 'jazz-rock' found its most fertile soil outside the US, and particularly the UK (Arndt 2012: 343).

From the later twentieth century there was a growing momentum in fusions between jazz and local musical traditions. From the 1930s to the late 1950s an international compulsion to authenticate regional jazz led in most quarters to attempts to erase compromising 'local accents'. At various times these accented jazz forms have disappeared behind the weave, overlaid by other patterns of development, but in the late twentieth century they emerged as major designs (in both senses) in formal innovation in jazz. US musicians have always participated actively in these movements, from Jelly Roll Morton's 'Spanish tinge' in the 1920s, through Dizzy Gillespie's Afro-Cuban jazz and Stan Getz's involvement in Bossa Nova in the 1950s and 1960s. The dynamic has altered since then, however, as increasingly decisive musical contributions have also come from musicians from outside the US. An overview of experimentation in what may be called 'ethno-jazz' since the 1960s embraces Lithuania, Bulgaria, Macedonia, Serbia, Finland, Norway, Greece, Scotland, Italy and France (Shepherd et al. 2005: VII: 13, 106, 125, 134, 163, 276,

286, 117, 347; Zenni 2003: 115–125; Nettelbeck 2004: 88–89). Various forms of African jazz fusions are found in Lesotho, Benin, Sudan, the Congo, Sierra Leone, Ghana, Nigeria (Shepherd et al. 2005: VI: 88, 123, 62, 28, 178, 137, 160). One of the most successful of such fusions has been Afrobeat, from the late 1960s, in which Nigerians Fela Kuti and drummer Tony Allen were central and internationally influential (Simpson 2007; Feld 2012; see further below).

These shifts in direction have moved the centre of gravity of the international jazz world away from the US, as argued forcefully especially in studies by Nicholson (2005; 2014: 89–154), and indeed the concept of a 'centre' is dissolving or being replaced by the idea of a global pan-African model that informs World Music. Von Eschen (2004: 233) cites Val Wilmer: 'The Western world deceives itself when they talk of Jazz – the only original American art form. What they should be saying and saying loud – is that Black Music is the beat to which the whole world is dancing'. So radically has the force field shifted that musicians from 'the margins' are often finding themselves forced to resist coercion towards an exaggerated postcardism, posing in musical national dress. Especially in the case of regional musicians sponsored from a 'centre' (as in some of Joachim-Ernst Berendt's projects, such as 'Sakura Sakura' and 'Noon in Tunisia'), there often appears to be the same paternalistic pressure to exoticise their jazz as is found in the politics of World Music, into which much jazz-fusion activity has been absorbed (Hurley 2006, 2008 and 2009: 186–192; Brusila 2003: 89–220). While in the early twentieth century, as jazz was globally migrating and negotiating with local ethnic forms, it was merged with 'modern dance', it is now increasingly conflated with (post)modern World Music.

A further exemplification of the shift is that in these recent developments most of the discursive and industrial infrastructures and working 'colleges' have emerged outside the US, including such communities and musical associations such as Instant Composers' Pool in Holland and the Brotherhood of Breath (inaugurated in England by South African expatriates), both formed in the mid-1960s (Bakriges 2003: 104–107; McKay 2005: 180–186). Current festival forums for eclectic jazz performances are prolific outside the US, including Sardinia's Berchidda Festival and the Etnofestival in San Marino (Shepherd et al. 2005: VII: 235, 287), and jazz musicians regularly appear with folk-fusion groups in the massive folk-oriented festivals in Woodford in Australia and Kaustinen in Finland.

For freer improvisational jazz-based musicians, recording opportunities are provided by a remarkable proliferation of specialist labels in Europe since the 1960s, one of the most eminent of which has developed such a distinctive house style that the term 'ECM jazz' is internationally recognised (Bakriges 2003: 102; Piedade 2003: 50). The developments under review in this section are most actively fostered outside the national 'home' of jazz. Indeed, so evidently has this been the case that in addition to the Free Music scene mentioned above, many US jazz musicians have found more congenial bases outside their homeland for pursuing such developments through collegial communities, performance and recording opportunities. Leading US figures such as Archie Shepp, Albert Ayler, Don Cherry and Cecil Taylor overwhelmingly found a more nurturing environment outside their homeland, enjoying extended sabbaticals and even settling in Europe, where they participated in concert, touring and recording activity at a level unavailable at home (McKay 2005: 180; Bakriges 2003). These migrations in search of inspirational replenishment, have led to such developments as Indo-Jazz fusions drawing on the music of India (Pinckney 2003: 65–70). A 'return' to Africa (and Islam) resulted not only in musical change, but also the emergence of what amounted to a separate internal political nationalism within the US itself, as also in the case of Free Jazz.

All these developments have enjoyed a high profile in discourses intent on identifying and promoting the idea of jazz innovation, the dubious teleology of the 'cutting edge', but as we conclude this survey, a cautionary perspective is required. For all these highly publicised developments, when events carry a specifically jazz billing, in quantitative terms the dominant style remains US-centric. Various forms of fusion have enjoyed great success when presented within the framework of World Music. But to frequent a 'jazz' pub, club, festival or concert, is most often to be presented with jazz lying somewhere on the spectrum of styles that crystallised from the 1920s through to the late twentieth century. And although US jazz musicians find most of their performance opportunities away from home, one reason is their continuing drawing power because they are American, as documented by Picaud in the case of France, which demonstrates 'the dominant position of the United States and the opposition between the Western world and the global South' (Picaud 2016: 126).

Conclusions

This review has identified some general features of jazz outside the US. Perhaps most significant among these are the move from being a provincial music in a semi-rural political economy to one of metropolitan modernity, and the development into a technologically mediated expressive form, with all that follows regarding conditions of performance and reception, cultural coding and social functions (see further Johnson 2002A: 34, 41–42). Taking New Orleans as its point of origin, we see of course the same process within the US, but the way in which conditions elsewhere intersected produced significant differences in the character and cultural location of the music. Broadly speaking, and notwithstanding the incorporation of Afro-primitivism, jazz was an urban music seen as aligned with the technologies and politics of global modernity. This appears to be a major differentiating force in its local reception. Where modernisation was embraced, there was a hospitable reception for jazz, unless of course modernisation was also identified with local nationalism.

Such differences turn our attention to a range of questions awaiting further enquiry. Why did jazz lodge so deeply in some regions but not in others? Overt political suppression has clearly been one factor, but also appears to be a passing gust in the larger twentieth-century context. Jazz has a stronger presence in Germany, Russia and former Eastern Bloc countries than in Spain and Greece where it never endured the same levels of proscription. The quasi-romantic stereotypes that this might prompt, about Mediterranean versus Nordic temperaments, come to grief on, among other things, the cases of Italy and Southern France (Marseilles in particular), where there have been durable jazz scenes. Arguments that the strength of local folk music traditions impeded jazz development in Greece, for example, are confounded by the cases of Scandinavia and Russia, and, to break out of a nation-based taxonomy, by the gypsy Django Reinhardt. This takes us to internal national differentiations. Jazz is music of cities, but which cities, and even where in the city, depends on such questions as public transport, class and ethnic profile, function (as we have seen, ports are likely to be stronger jazz centres than inland cities) and local entertainment laws. In Australia, the differing state-by-state restrictions on hotel trading hours and gambling have been crucial in the local development of jazz scenes. Material conditions are decisive, including climate. Jazz performance is more sensitive to locality, often favouring outdoor venues, than concert-hall sheltered art music. In Scandinavia the outdoor jazz festival season lasts for only a few months. In Australia it spreads itself across most of the year, though to varying extents in different climatic regions from Brisbane to Hobart.

The recent developments reviewed above position us to reflect on the contribution made to the jazz tradition from outside the US. The most obvious statistic would be a review of the enormous number of US-immigrant musicians who became key figures in the music's history. Any attempt at a sample would only diminish the magnitude of the category; a casual perusal of places of birth listed in standard reference works makes the point more tellingly. In many ways more striking are those who made significant impact without moving to the US, often by cultivating approaches to the music that are distinguished by their departure from the US template. I take these up in the next chapter.

Notes

1 Before we become too precious about our superior discrimination of 'true' jazz as compared with the 1920s – who had been exposed too far less of it - it is worth noting the contents of the 2014 CD compilation *The Very Best of Jazz – 50 Unforgettable Tracks* (see at www.youtube.com/watch?v=9f6V-QehbU4, accessed 8 November 2017). It includes Ray Charles, 'Hit the Road Jack'; Frank Sinatra, 'I've Got You Under My Skin'; Nat King Cole, 'Unforgettable'; Louis Prima, 'Just a Gigolo'; Dean Martin, 'Sway'; Doris Day, 'Let's Keep Smiling'; Judy Garland, 'Over the Rainbow'; Perry Como, 'Papa Loves Mambo'; Marilyn Monroe, 'I Wanna Be Loved By You' and 'My Heart Belongs to Daddy'.
2 The influential term 'The Tyranny of Distance' was coined by Australian historian Geoffrey Blainey as the main title of his 1966 study, subtitled *How Distance Shaped Australia's History*.

PART 2

Second Eight

Products of the Diaspora

2

DISCOURSES AND INFRASTRUCTURES

The foregoing chronological summary already indicates that the jazz diaspora involved a great deal more than simply the global export of a music fully formed in its region or country of origin. This chapter will survey the extent to which jazz discourses and infrastructures were created as part of the diasporic process itself, both beyond the supposed fountainhead of New Orleans and beyond the US. Clearly, the style typologies that frame the canon largely correspond with diasporic movements: Chicago, New York, Kansas City and the West Coast (Johnson 2002A: 33). 'One of the supreme ironies of the history of New Orleans jazz is that so much of it took place in Chicago. By the early 1920s, the center of the jazz world had clearly shifted northward' (Gioia 2011: 43). Thus, the first significant development in the history of jazz was a function of the diaspora; without it for example, there would be no canon ('only those who departed made major reputations' (Gioia 2011: 43)), which is the essential basis of the jazz narrative.

The Name 'Jazz'

We can begin with the name itself: jazz. In its earliest manifestations in its putative city of origin, the music which became known as jazz was extremely ill-defined as such in the terms we now take for granted. Nick La Rocca famously declared that the word 'jazz' became attached to the music in Chicago; 'I never heard the word in New Orleans' (Shipton 2001: 96). A personal agenda operating here might well have generated a strategic recollection, but nonetheless, the earliest use of the word in New Orleans was generally recalled as being highly unstable. For Louis Armstrong and many of his colleagues, jazz, hot music, gut bucket, blues, ragtime were all much the same (Gendron 1995: 35). Jelly Roll Morton identified the music of bandleaders now associated with early jazz, including Buddy Bolden, as ragtime, and spoke of ad-libbing in ragtime by 'spasm bands' (Lomax 1950: 13, 61). Beyond New Orleans, these shifting distinctions relating to music from the south were reflected in the sheet music of 'Dallas Blues' by white bandleader Hart Wood, published in 1912, and described as a 'Southern Rag' (Mawer 2014: 20). The understanding of 'jazz' prior to around 1920 'might more accurately be considered a type of instrumental ragtime from New Orleans, one with a distinctly regional flavour lent by that city's unique musical culture' (Taylor 2000: 43).

Apart from its stylistic sub-sets, the printed record indicates that the word jazz itself seems to have been a polysemic formation derived from outside New Orleans. Originally it had no connection to music, but evidently referred to energetic activity in general, often with sexual overtones (Braggs 2016: 22). Its probable origins in oral culture invite a broad range of speculations about its origins, including particular individuals (for example an energetic dancing slave called Jasper), African language sources, jasmine (a particularly stimulating perfume), and the French 'jaser', to gossip or chat (Braggs 2016: 22; Bushell 1988: 13; Mawer 2014: 101; see further for example Gabbard 2002). The earliest printed reference is usually cited as an article in *The San Francisco Bulletin* in 1913, where it was used to characterise a particular energy in modern dance, and later the same year in the same newspaper, referred to in relation to sport (Merriam and Garner 1998; Taylor 2000: 43; Shipton 2001: 1). The word was evidently being used in relation to African-American bands as early as 1914, not however in New Orleans but on the West Coast, and although Jelly Roll Morton claimed to have started using the word in 1902 'to show people the difference between jazz and ragtime', the written record suggests that it was not applied to the music in the sense now understood until Tom Brown's band opened in Chicago in 1915 (Lomax 1950: 62; Shipton 2001: 109, 100). Cugny also cites an article from the *Chicago Daily Tribune*, 11 July 1915, by Gordon Seagrove, called 'Blues is Jazz and Jazz is Blues' which identified the 'blue note', a 'sour note ... a discord, a harmonic discord... The trade name for them is "jazz"' (Cugny 2012: 306). In summary, the etymology of 'jazz' as a musical descriptor is highly contested, but it seems to have become stabilised in the diasporic process.

Discourses

It is now largely taken for granted that forms of popular music are framed by their own distinctive discourses. This however is a relatively recent development, largely the outcome of the German *Volkslied* movement and its attempt to harness traditional song to national heritage (see further Scott 2001: 98, 174–177). Jazz, however, was arguably the first new popular style to generate its own discourse that conferred intelligibility on the music: 'a fully fledged art world with a community of critics, articulate musicians, and avid readers producing an unprecedentedly rich popular music discourse in books, magazines, newspapers, and mimeographs

(or what would later be called "fanzines")' (Brennan 2017: 6). And this community largely emerged from outside the US. From the 1930s, a shared discourse
was emerging from international networks of connoisseurship through critical
writing, obsessive historiographical and discographical projects, mythologisations,
the sharing of private collections and establishment of small specialist record labels,
broadcasting and the formation of amateur jazz bands.

'Some of the most searching jazz criticism has been written by citizens of countries other than the United States' (Gennari 2006: 16). In his 'Introduction' to the
1945 English translation of Belgian writer Robert Goffin's *Jazz: From the Congo to
the Metropolitan*, editor of *Esquire* Arnold Gingrich ruefully acknowledged that it
took 'this Belgian, Goffin, and the two Frenchmen Panassié and Delaunay, to get
us Americans to sit down and listen to jazz' (Goffin 1945: ix). Gennari reports a
discussion between a group of famous jazz musicians and critics as late as 1961, at
which, upon being asked by Horace Silver about the kinds of qualifications needed
by a jazz critic, Martin Williams replied (as paraphrased by Gennari): 'while there
are a number of Europeans with the requisite musical knowledge, here in the
United States there were only a handful, notably Williams and Gunther Schuller'
(Gennari 2006: 205). The critical mass of these 'authenticating narratives' was
largely developed by European, and especially French writers (Braggs 2016: 27).

Although there were scattered early US writers on jazz, such as Roger Pryor
Dodge (see further Welburn 2000: 748), they did not generate the same coherent
community of interest as emerged in Europe, where it was primarily through this
discursive network that jazz was gradually elevated to the status of art. 'European
music critics in the 1920s, mostly French and English, woke Americans up to
the value of jazz beyond its American contexts. They put a Western high-cultural
stamp of approval on the music qua Western music' (Heffley 2005: 5; see further
for example Gioia 1988: 24–32; Parsonage 2005: 53–57; Cugny 2012; Nicholson
2014: 179–185). Swiss conductor Ernest Ansermet's early recognition of the
deeper cultural significance of jazz in an appreciation of Sidney Bechet's performance with Will Marion Cook's Southern Syncopated Orchestra in 1919 has been
often cited (see for example Cerchiari 2012A: xii).

It was this diasporic community that generated a body of early jazz litera-
ture, including F. W. Koebner's *Jazz and Shimmy: Brevier der neuesten Tänze* (1921),
Heinz Pollack's Die Revolution des Gesellschaftstanzes (1922), Alfred Baresel's *Das
Neue Jazzbuch* (1925) (Nicholson 2014: 182–183, who lists sixteen such books just
from the 1920s). From the UK came R. W. S Mendl's *The Appeal of Jazz* (1927),
Stanley Nelson's *All About Jazz* (1934), Constant Lambert's *Music Ho!* (1934) and
Adorno's 'On Jazz', written while he was based in England in 1936 (Parsonage
2005: 36). It was through such publications that central and durable assumptions
became established, in particular the gradual effacement of any origins to jazz
other than blackness. In *Le Jazz* (1927) Arthur Hoérée declared that 'Jazz is, for
the most part, characterised by its rhythmic elements of specifically Negro origin'
(Cugny 2012: 314). The running title of Goffin's book, above, does away with the

implication 'for the most part', as does the title of his opening chapter: 'Tom-Tom in New Orleans' (1–21). His first publication on jazz was an article *Le Disque Vert* as early as 1919 (Goffin 1945: 1–2). In his *Aux frontières du jazz* (1932), he evoked a romanticised 'down South' origin for the music: 'It has the Edenic innocence of days we have not lived; it is as naïve as the Negro slaves' singing in the Southern plantation, it is the expression of an oppressed people without a fatherland and the cry of deliverance for Negroes and Jews, instilled with their inexhaustible loneliness and devastating depression' (Cugny 2012: 319). Among the most influential proponents of jazz as essentially a black music was French writer Hugues Panassié, whose *Le Jazz Hot*, 1934, was published in the US as *Hot Jazz: The Guide to Swing Music* in 1936 (Cugny 2012: 318). In *The Real Jazz*, which had gone through nine editions by 2007, he declared unconditionally that 'jazz is a music created by the black race', and that 'the spirit of the Negro jazz musicians … is the only real jazz spirit' (Panassié 1944: vii, 81).

The evocations of Africa echoed other post-World War One perspectives that looked beyond the enlightenment tradition for cultural re-invigoration. In this endeavour, jazz provided a Janus face as both a music derived from a primitive people and, as noted earlier, at the same time a revolutionary music of the future. It was through the diaspora that jazz gained its meaning as the music of modernity. Czech writer and Prague Conservatory graduate Emil Burian, in *Jazz* (1928) acknowledged both the African origins of jazz but also its potential to rejuvenate an enervated European art music tradition (Cugny 2012: 316). What needs to be emphasised just here is that this coding was very much established in the diasporic process. 'Louis Armstrong might have *made* music of the twentieth century, but it was not he who *made it* the music of the twentieth century' (Johnson 2002A: 50). The most admirably detailed general account of the relationship between jazz and modernism is provided by Stuart Nicholson (2014: 155–252). He notes the paradox that while the US was the source of the music that came to be regarded as the quintessence of modernity, the Americans were at the same time slow to take up modernism in the visual arts (Nicholson 2014: 185–187). The same disjunction was the case in other regions, including as it happens in Australia, and I suggest that the paradox becomes less puzzling if we make careful distinctions between modernism and modernity. Nicholson describes jazz consumers of the 1950s as 'engaging with "the state of being modern"' (Nicholson 2014: 243), which I think can also be described as engaging with 'modernity'. This is not necessarily the same as being a modernist (the distinction is elaborated at length in Johnson 2000: 31–53). The experience of twentieth-century modernity was shared by the entire Anglo/European/US axis, but 'modernism' was only one response to that experience. It is useful to invoke Philip Morgan's concept of 'alternative modernities', which recognises that 'engaging' with ubiquitous modernity takes many and often contradictory forms (Morgan 2003: 192). Opposition to jazz is thus an 'alternative modernity', not an alternative *to* modernity. Jazz and totalitarianism, which seem to be at odds, were alternative modernities (see further

Johnson 2017C: 7–10). And while jazz was generally a manifestation of modernity as it dispersed across the globe, its convergence with modernism was largely part of an 'alternative modernity' primarily to be found during the interwar period outside the US. By the early 1920s jazz was attracting the attention of modernists in Europe: Stravinsky, Milhaud, Hindemith, the Bauhaus, and most of the authors of the jazz monographs referred to above. Clive Bell referred to T. S. Eliot and Stravinsky as 'supreme practitioners of jazz in their respective media' Rasula 2002: 58; see further Johnson 2002A: 41–42).

Infrastructures

Collectors, Hot Clubs, Magazines

The material supporting mechanisms of any cultural form largely evolve in association with its discourses, and accordingly a great many of the jazz infrastructures also developed outside the US. Gennari writes of the emergence of 'an aestheticized discourse of jazz' in the 1930s and 1940s 'carried out in collectors' "hot clubs" and in the Modernism-inspired "little magazines" attached to them', that 'defined the very idea of jazz – down to our time' (Gennari 2006: 65). The United Hot Clubs of America was actually a record label founded by Milt Gabler in 1936, originally selling by subscription (Kernfeld 1988 II: 565). But the obsessive jazz connoisseurship described by Gennari that began documenting details of the early primary texts, clustered in European 'hot clubs' and their specialist jazz journals that were already forming throughout the 1930s in for example Belgium, France, the UK, Sweden, Germany, Finland and Denmark (Shepherd et al. 2005: VII: 152, 332, 316; Kater 1992: 70; Johnson 2002A: 35; Stendahl 2007: 3). The most enduringly influential early jazz chroniclers were French activists Charles Delaunay, who in 1936 produced the first of the jazz discographies that underpinned the formation of 'the canon', and the prolific Hugues Panassié, who also founded the Hot Club of France in 1932, which at its peak, boasted some 5,000 members (Welburn 2000: 752; Nettelbeck 2004: 46–47; Perchard 2015: 41; 12), and inspired other 'Hot Clubs' throughout Europe. The first of these was in Germany in 1934, founded by Dietrich Schultz, aka Dietrich Schulz-Köhn, who later, as a Luftwaffe lieutenant-colonel based in occupied Paris, assisted Delaunay with the second edition of the discography and who became the most authoritative of Germany's pioneering jazz mediators (Kater 1992: 70–74; Wasserberger et al. 2017: xxvi, xx, 174–175).

These clubs often provided the framework for the production of jazz magazines and bulletins. When jazz was the *dernier cri* in dance music, however, it is not easy to declare which was the first jazz journal, as opposed to one for the up to date popular musician, as seems to be the case with the Swedish journal from 1929 *Estrad* (Nicholson 2014: 185), which presumably is a reference to 'estrada', a term applied to what could be called popular 'variety' music. The earliest listed by Nicholson is the French *Le Magazine du Jazz*, from 1924, followed by *Melody*

Maker from 1926 which, along with *The Gramophone* began to carry jazz reviews in the mid-1920s (Nicholson 2014: 185; Welburn 2000: 748). Others from the 1920s include the French *Revue de Jazz* from 1929 followed by others in the early 1930s including the Dutch *De Jazzwereld*, the *Czech Prehled Rozhlasu* and the Swiss *Jazz* (Welburn 2000: 748; Harris 2003: 113; Nicholson 2014: 185). The earliest of the journals included Sweden's *Orkester Journalen* (1933), identified by Gioia as the first jazz magazine (Gioia 2011: 159). Finland's *Rytmi* was launched in 1934, its first issue largely given over to Swing and jazz related material (Johnson Forthcoming B). But *Le Jazz Hot*, 'the first magazine avowedly dedicated totally to jazz', was launched on 21 February 1935 (Harris 2003: 113; see further Johnson 2002A: 35; Perchard 2015: 13).

Jazz Festivals

One of the primary sources of income for today's jazz musicians, especially in the northern hemisphere, is the jazz festival. The 1988 edition of *The New Grove Dictionary of Jazz* lists around 350 annual jazz festivals globally, most of them in Europe and the US, where relatively manageable distances make them accessible to musicians (Kernfeld 1988 I: 372–374). The experience of expatriate Australian trombonist Max Collie exemplifies the point. When he relocated to the UK he formed his own band, the Rhythm Aces, in 1966. Although active in residencies, it was during the European and US jazz festival seasons that he enjoyed the highest level of success and recognition, including winning a 'world championship' in traditional jazz in the US in 1975. The festival circuit was also his best source of income, including through record and other cross-marketing sales (this is based on numerous conversations with Max with whom I shared accommodation in Bromley Kent for some months, and his compulsive conversations about the band). Festival engagements also provide a focal point for other gigs in the region, as in the case of ex-Mingus trumpeter Ted Curson, who framed his annual Pori Jazz Festival appearances in Finland with a residency in Turku's Vaakahuone pub (source: gig conversations with Curson in Vaakahuone).

These mainstays of so much jazz activity were diasporic creations. Most frequently cited as the world's first, the Nice Jazz Festival, organised by Panassié, was in 1948, six years before the US Newport Festival, and during that interval France had developed a thriving jazz festival scene (Nettelbeck 2004: 66–67; Gennari 2006: 211; McKay 2018: 708, 717). Less well known, though noted in Grove as 'the first fully-fledged jazz festival' (Kernfeld 1988 I: 361) is the even earlier annual festival, the Australian Jazz Convention, for most of its history, held in different towns or cities each year. This was inaugurated in 1946 and in the lead-up to the seventy-fourth in 2019, is the world's longest running jazz festival, and the most durable rallying point for traditional jazz in Australia (Johnson 2003: 152–157). Even that, however, was preceded by nearly 30 years in 1919 in the one-off 'Sydney Jazz Week', the poster for which announced 'Jazz dances, jazz music, jazz movies', including in this last category a locally made movie *Does the Jazz Lead to Destruction?*, alas, now lost (the poster is reproduced below, p.144). The answer to its question was apparently a cheerful 'Yes!' to judge from a subsequent poster, and the event proved so popular that it was extended by public demand (Johnson 2016: 7–8).

Jazz Education

Along with the LP recording, the proliferation of secondary and tertiary education programmes is probably the most powerful force for the global standardisation of canonical jazz practice, dominated as they are by the objectives of technical mastery of an established vocabulary and grammar (Nicholson 2014: 30; similarly Ake 2002: 133). At the outset, however, jazz 'education' was informal mentorship or, in New Orleans for example, tuition in music by teachers imbued with a black music culture, as in the case of the Tio family, especially Lorenzo Tio, whose students included Barney Bigard, Albert Nicholas, Johnny Dodds and Jimmie Noone (Beale 2000: 757). Early attempts to formalise jazz training include books and articles in professional journals that explain particular aspects of execution; the former include a 1919 publication by Henry Fillmore on trombone smears (Prouty 2019: 46). Lawrence Gushee has documented the spate of 'How to' books published under the names of high profile jazz musicians including Miff Mole and Red Nichols (cited by Prouty 2019: 46), with titles like Rube Blooms's 1926 *100 Jazz Breaks for Piano* (Johnson 1987: 7). Black educational institutions that also taught music were important training grounds. The Jenkins Orphanage, established in 1892 by Rev Daniel J. Jenkins in Charleston, South Carolina, formed its own brass band as a fund-raising body, and this became a *de facto* training ground for many jazz musicians-to-be including Jabbo Smith and Cat Anderson (Chilton 1980: 2, 13; for a full list see 52–60). The Bama State Collegians from Alabama State University undertook successful tours that included New York in 1934, and was where Erskine Hawkins served his apprenticeship (Prouty 2019: 47).

More usually, however, the idea of including jazz in US music programmes was regarded as anathema. A 1940 textbook on teaching music in high schools warned against the 'fleshly' character of Swing and its inability to 'yield abiding satisfaction' (Ake 2002: 118). The famous US jazz courses such as those at Berklee College of Music or University of North Texas date from the 1950s and 1960s; the latter offered what is generally believed to be the first college level degree in jazz studies in 1946 (see further Beale 2000: 759; Ake 2002: 198–199; Nicholson 2014: 105; Prouty 2019: 47). In a music sector in decline in the US, these proliferating programmes are extraordinarily successful, 'The one area of the jazz economy that does make real profits … an industry that has quadrupled over the last twenty years' (Nicholson 2014: 12; see also Prouty 2019: 49).

In his survey of jazz education, Prouty makes only brief reference to such programmes outside the US – Canada, Britain and Australia (Prouty 2019: 49) – but in fact the institutionalisation of jazz education, including its incorporation into conservatoria, was very much a diasporic initiative, especially in Europe, as far back as the 1920s. Shortly after arriving in Finland from the US in 1926, as a member of the ship's jazz orchestra on the 'Andania', reed player Wilfred 'Tommy' Tuomikoski, who was born in the US of Finnish parents, founded a saxophone school and published a saxophone tutor (Haavisto 1996: 13; Jalkanen 1996: 211). The first jazz curriculum presented in a conservatory was not in the US, but in Weimar Germany, where Bernard Sekles established a programme in jazz interpretation in the Hoch Conservatoire in Frankfurt am Main, 1928 (Jankowsky 2016: 262; Wasserberger et al. 2017: 144). One of the world's most transformatively influential jazz education programmes had its beginnings in South Africa in 1930, where jazz pianist Wilfred Sentso spoke of the importance of developing 'the theatrical music of our people ... dreams of a scientifically organised education of our Bantu people as well in Music'. In 1937 he set up a school of performing arts in Johannesburg, which was a major academy of jazz for non-whites. His 'Synco Schools' provided a training ground for South Africa's most important performers including members of the Broadway Stars, the Merry Blackbirds, the Jazz Maniacs, and the Synco Beats, which, as reported in a contemporary source, 'have performed in European Night Clubs, theatres, halls, open-air Stadiums' (Ballantine 2011: 497). 'European' in this context means local venues owned and largely patronised by whites. The timing of Sentso's educational initiatives was crucial in that it enabled cross-racial transmission of black culture

> more than a decade before the National Government came to power, and even more years before the promulgation of legislation prohibiting the sharing of certain facilities by mixed (black-and-white) patrons. In the late 1930s, white-owned venues could still be attended by blacks, and, more to the point, black bands (like Sentso's) could still be hired to perform in them.
> *Personal communication from Ballantine, 22 March 2018*

Sentso's initiative appears to have been the most influential single jazz education programme in the history of the music. And, most relevant to this study, like so many of the pioneering formal jazz education programmes, it was not in the US, but in a diasporic site.

3

LOCAL FORMS AND SYNCRETISMS

Introduction

Much of the international diaspora has been characterised by the attempt to reproduce US models, and in doing so to produce a music that is distinctively 'jazz', to
erase all traces of local contamination (Jost 2012: 276). Arguably, this process was
completed by the late 1950s and early 1960s, by which time it became increasingly
difficult to distinguish between jazz played in the US and outside it; the music had
reached a kind of teleological endpoint in the international mastery of bop. That
stream remains active, fully codified and commercially accommodated, its main
challenge to delight audiences with a heightened, even freakish reproduction of
US models, most spectacularly in the form of a bop style that achieves maximum
facility and speed (see for example at www.youtube.com/watch?v=yf2cuIG6b1E,
accessed 14 November 2018). We can usefully think of this as the ultimate stage
of the 'fission' model in the globalisation of the music to which I referred above,
in the sense of cultivating a formation that is unmistakeably distinct from all other
contemporary musics.

'Fission' provides a platform on which to invoke 'fusion', the development of
syncretisms between a now fully defined jazz formation and other music genres,
a stream which from the late twentieth century flowed into the broader deltas of
World Music. Several stages in that process can be identified as a platform for further discussion. First, on first contact, the attempt to occlude local musical traditions
by US sourced material, leading over time to the standardisation of the jazz *lingua
franca*; this has been followed by the deliberate embarking upon fusions between
a now fully defined understanding of 'jazz' and other genres or local musics, mer-
ging into World Music. These stages have overlapped. Currently, for example,
fusion experiments are conducted in one sector of the global jazz community

while elsewhere steroidal bop packages as well as 'heritage' jazz projects attract large enthusiastic and, it appears, mainly older middle class audiences. What I am calling the 'heritage' category extends from high profile concert performances such as those conducted under the aegis of the Rockefeller Centre/Marsalis axis, to the less evangelical residencies in local pubs and other recreational sites, the bread-and-butter of the journeyman jazz performer. These embrace the full range of music advertised as jazz: revivalist through to self-styled avant-garde.

At every point in its global peregrinations, however, jazz had to enter into negotiations with specific local musical and cultural traditions. As we have seen, in some cases those negotiations were characterised by a protective anxiety for the preservation of the native musical fauna, and at other times by mutual adaptations, leading to new jazz formations and colorations that might range from a local 'accent', through a 'style', to a new jazz sub-genre (Johnson 2002A: 42–49). There are many terms by which this process can be described, each foregrounding different aspects of the process. They have included such terms as 'globalisation', 'transnationalism', 'diasporism', 'hybridisation', 'acculturation', 'syncretism', 'fusion' (for various ways of modelling these processes specifically in relation to jazz, see Nicholson 2014: 89–109; or more briefly Higgins 2016: 360 n. 10). Each of these terms offers only a partial insight into the process, but for present purposes 'glocalisation' is a useful point of departure for the following discussion: 'globally transmitted culture is broken down into a series of individual encounters, each explained in terms of local, social, and cultural context and how it interacts with the global' (Nicholson 2014: 96–97). Glocalisation has also resulted in local jazz forms, social meanings, functions, and instrumentations (for a useful summary of attempts to identify such forms, see Meehan 2017: 161).

Most of this attention has been directed at Europe, the source of some of the most celebrated local jazz formations, including the 'Manouche jazz' centred on Django Reinhardt's mainly interwar activity, and the 'Nordic Sound' associated with Jan Garbarek and Manfred Eicher's ECM record label founded in 1969. Free jazz, 'the beginning of an alternate jazz universe' (Heffley 2005: 169), has also been the major site over which this dynamic has played. 'Jazz in Europe, significantly more than in the United States, has found itself in a continuing process of differentiation brought on by the revolution sparked by free jazz in the 1960s' (Hellhund 2012: 433). All these exemplify 'jazz styles that have evolved outside the United States that do not necessarily follow the way that jazz is played inside the United States' (Nicholson 2005: 172).

Free Jazz

Of the three examples mentioned above, it was free jazz that enjoyed the widest general diffusion, ranging as far as, for example, New Zealand's Primitive Art Group in the 1970s and 1980s (Meehan: 167), and the work of the group Free Kata in Sydney led by pianist Serge Ermoll. But these were very much minority subcategories (and ones that were indifferent to if not sceptical of commercial appeal), in what was already a minority niche market (jazz in general), in relatively small populations where active networking was hampered by distance, and as such failed to gain durable traction. After leading Free Kata, Sermoll returned to a more accessible, if still explosive style. The fact that, apart from the band's Australian members (including drummer Louis Burdett), the leader was Shanghai-born and the saxophonist Eddie Bronson Russian, suggests that the cosmopolitanism of the group helped to open it to the possibilities of taking the music so far from the established US models.

This tends to be confirmed by the fact that the primary locus of the movement was the Anglo-European region, and habitually involved transnational collaborations. While there were initiatives in the direction of free jazz in the US, as in the work of late Coltrane, and of Albert Ayler, it was largely a European phenomenon, with an aesthetic that was in clear contrast with similar ventures in the US, producing a distinctively European approach (Jost 2012: 277; see also 296–297 and Perchard 2015: 158). Through the 1960s, each stage in the evolution of this distinctive formation was marked by a more radical rejection of US models, in some cases, as in the collaborations between Dutch performers Misha Mengelberg and Han Bennink, the movement was an attempt to 'abrogate all valid tools of aesthetic evaluation, all a priori principles' (Jost 2012: 294) (rather like, it is worth noting, Dada and some of the earliest forms of diasporic jazz).

Although the free jazz movement was pan-European, there was nonetheless a sense of national inflections (Jost 2012: 293). To underline the distinctiveness of free jazz in France, in 1967 Barney Wilen proposed the term *nouveau jazz* (Perchard 2015: 170). It also appears that free jazz in the UK was marked by a more extensive participation of women vocalists, and a more ecstatic as opposed to an ascetic spirit (Jost 2012: 291, 292). In any event, it was a movement that was self-consciously aware of its independence from the US. By 1972, German musician Peter Kowald reflected that the movement demonstrated that 'our generation could well do without the musical influence of most Americans' (Jost: 2012: 282), and the German press referred to 'Europe's *Emanzipation* from American jazz' (Heffley 2005: 3).

Regional Styles

The other two formations referred to above, 'Manouche' and the 'Nordic sound' both raise instructive questions about jazz typologies that are distinctive to the diaspora. A number of musicians have produced a style marked by an accent or approach that is significant by virtue of being distinct from US models. Few in this category approach the stature of guitarist Django Reinhardt. It was not simply his virtuosity, but his distinctiveness that signifies here. US trumpeter Doc Cheatham summarised it in the compliment that Reinhardt 'wasn't playing American jazz, but he was swinging' (Goddard 1979: 247). Cheatham's admiration was internationally shared, including by such luminaries as Coleman Hawkins, and evidently English band-leader Jack Hylton was among those who sought to recruit the guitarist as early as 1928 (Zwerin 1985: 111–112). He is the most imitated jazz musician from outside the US, and the most recognisably imitated of all guitarists. His influence can be heard from the 1930s and 1940s in, for example the Norwegian bands led by Freddie Valier and Frank Ottersen, the latter featuring the uncannily Django-like Robert Normann. Cheatham claimed he inspired US guitarist Johnny Mitchell, and other US players from blues, country, rock/pop and fusion, from Les Paul through B. B. King to John McLaughlin, have cited him as a model and inspiration. (Givan 2003: 20; Goddard 1979: 247). More recently he has become voguish, with young groups like Sweden's Blue Suede recreating the 'Hot Club of France' sound in which he was central. Woody Allen's 1999 film *Sweet and Lowdown*, pervaded by the Django sound, was followed by tribute events in New York, including the city's first Django Reinhardt Festival in 2001 (Givan 2003: 19–20).

Manouche jazz is, however, only one of many distinctive diasporic jazz formations. The UK, for example, has made significant contributions in terms of both jazz formations and individual musicians, but these are largely ignored in the US-centred canonical narrative, as observed tartly by Bruce Turner in relation to English tenor player Chas Birchall: 'He is treated by our critics as if he didn't exist. If the latter ever decide to wrench their gaze away from the Americans … they might notice this array of local talent which lies under their noses'; more generally, 'We must get rid of the fiction that British jazz is nothing more than American jazz played by Britons. This simply isn't true any more' (Turner 1984: 210, 211). Parsonage argues that by the mid-1930s, a distinctively British jazz was audible (Parsonage 2005: xiv, 260), and regarding later stylistic developments, pianist and educator Michael Garrick also identifies 'an upsurge of originality in British jazz (cited Nicholson 2005: 181; see also Arndt 2012: 343).

There were several directions from which the British contribution to new jazz formations emerged, ranging across the whole stylistic spectrum. The 'Trad Boom' from the late 1950s marked the last period to date that a form of traditional jazz occupied international hit parades on a large scale, accompanied by a new wave of recruitment of youthful musicians. It was brought to an abrupt halt by the advent of the Beatles and the 'Mersey Sound', which effectively drew off the largely middle class audiences that had hitherto disdained rock. Trad was an English phenomenon, as recalled by one if its leaders, Chris Barber: 'We were getting up and suddenly we'd established traditional jazz an art form, an English/ British art form, in its British style, not that different to the basics we knew, and became very popular with the public' (Barber 2013: 4). Barber was also one of the figures involved in an offshoot of the 'Boom' called skiffle, largely kicked off by his guitarist/banjoist/singer Lonnie Donegan. A melding of jazz, folk, country, blues and even music hall, it also attracted young practitioners for its DIY appeal, including for its cheap and often improvised instrumentation.

Barber's eclectic tastes prompted his split in the mid-1950s from the more-New Orleans purist bandleader Ken Colyer, and led him towards the electric rhythm and blues revival involving, among others, Alexis Korner and Graham Bond. Out of this movement emerged the jazz-rock fusion of which Barber himself became an exponent, and bands like Soft Machine and Cream ('it was really a jazz band, there was so much improvising' recalled bassist/singer Jack Bruce, cited by Arndt 2012: 349). 'The first moves towards jazz-rock began not in the United States but in Britain' (Shipton 2001: 851), although in a conversation with the author in London ca. late 1969, Barber mentioned Chicago Transit Authority as an important influence on the direction he was taking. But it was this largely UK-led movement that provided the launching pad for the 'British Invasion' of the US in the 1960s (Arndt 2012: 343). A later, but more short-lived jazz-based phenomenon which came out of England in the mid-1980s and spread across Europe and beyond was the sub-genre referred to as 'Acid Jazz' (Gioia 2011: 333).

In light of research leading to 'encyclopaedic' publications (Wasserberger et al. 2017; Martinelli 2018; van der Leur Forthcoming), it would be gratuitous to undertake a European country-by-country inventory here. This is especially so given the rapidly developing library of publications devoted to particular continental nations, such as forthcoming studies on jazz exchanges between Sweden and the US (van Kan, building on his 2016 article and his 2017 doctoral dissertation), and free jazz in Hungary (Havas 2018, developing his published work in Hungarian). It would also be rather beside the point of this study, which is to seek to tease out patterns that exemplify the general importance of the diaspora in understanding the history of jazz. That is, here I am less focused on regional/national jazz histories for their own sake, where that history is largely one of the progressive assimilation of US sources, than on what these diasporic sites have contributed to the jazz narrative beyond those sources.

Recent research into the late twentieth-century European jazz scenes, already cited, amply demonstrates that the region has evolved in directions that are independent of the US models that had hitherto been the template for jazz practice. From Scandinavia and Russia, from the UK to East Germany, jazz performers have begun 'to forge improvisational and compositional styles and voices rooted in Europe rather than America, and/or to shift the compositional platforms from American blues, show tunes and standards to other folk and concert material closer to their homes' (Heffley 2005: 67; for an overview see 68–73). Over that post-war period, these new jazz formations have often been the outcome of a conscious reaction against US hegemony. The following comments are from interviews included in Benedikt 2006:

Albert Mangelsdorff (Germany): I realized at an early stage that it doesn't make much sense to copy American models, that you should go your own way. (42'20"–42'50")

Till Brönner (Germany): Quite early in I was confronted with not only the Americans' opinion that Germans couldn't be trusted to play authentically ... What are my own roots then? While I was grappling with this question I discovered my real German roots and at some point I asked myself: Must I be black and American to be allowed to play jazz? Or is jazz by now a language, or vehicle, a vocabulary which is accessible for everyone and which we should just use to orient ourselves in the direction we actually come from? (44'20"–45'20")

Enrico Rava (Italy): I've never had this complex that many European jazz musicians during those years towards jazz: 'Jazz is American and we Europeans should play like them.' I never had that complex. (50'10"–50'30")

Klaus Schulz reports that when Attila Zoller (Austria) shared an apartment in Lennox with Don Cherry and Ornette Coleman,

They made him realize that he'd never be able to play like Wes Montgomery or Kenny Burrell. And then the penny dropped, so to speak, and he realized that he shouldn't deny his own roots. He'd never be able to play the blues like a black man. That was very important. It greatly enriched the international language of jazz (48"30"–49'05")

In 1963 Albert Mangelsdorff made his first album as a leader into something of a manifesto on the theme, writing in the cover notes:

Every art form is an expression of its time and a reflection of its world. The jazz musician in Europe should therefore not play forever like a black musician in New York or Chicago, he shouldn't try to and one shouldn't expect him to because his problems are simply different and his life's sphere subject to different forces (cited in Heffley 2005: 32).

Similar sentiments are recorded by drummer Günter Sommer and Norwegian singer Silje Nergaard (Heffley 2005: 212; Nicholson 2005: 93). Nicholson cites Swedish pianist Bobo Stenson:

We have other traditions here, more from classical music and folk music and stuff, and I guess we put that into the thing more than 'traditional American jazz'. More important, we don't need to play the American way, we can leave that and come back to it. It allows you to take the music in new directions.

Nicholson 2005: 175

Jerome Harris finds examples of localised jazz identities across Holland, France, Russia and Japan (Harris 2003: 129 n. 40). From the 1950s there was a concerted effort to cultivate a national jazz in France, with the inauguration of the Académie du Jazz, which sought to recognise the 'best French jazz musicians' with the annual Prix Django Reinhardt (Perchard 2015: 193; the irony in the fact that Reinhardt was a Belgian-born Romany points forward to a discussion below of the problematics of nation-based conceptions of jazz).

Many of the new Anglo-European developments discussed above, such as the oft-disdained 'Trad' movement, had few if any exemplars in the US. Moving outside Europe, however, the case is altogether different regarding Latin jazz, which remains a distinctive presence in the US canon. At opposite extremes in the category are the high-energy Cubop (or Cubana-Bop) and the suave West Coast inflected Bossa Nova. The politics of this – as with other US/diasporic fusions and their naming – are recognised by Clifford Hill Korman, who seeks a term that describes the syncretism of jazz and Brazilian music, but which requires 'a descriptive label that is more nuanced, and … more based on an equivalency of contribution than the American-centric "Brazilian jazz"' (Korman 2016: 153). He proposes the term 'Popular instrumental improvised music' (PIIM) to describe a music that emerged in Brazil during the 1970s, as represented in the recordings of Paulo Moura (Korman 2016: 154).

Research into this relationship is almost exclusively devoted to the post-1958 period. But Fléchet argues that the history of Brazilian jazz in the first half of the century 'is key to understanding the emergence of the bossa nova' (Fléchet 2016: 15). Latin accents have a long history in US jazz, fed by Cuba and other Caribbean countries like Puerto Rico and the Dominican Republic. Morton frequently exploited the habanera, likewise W. C. Handy in the perennial 'St Louis Blues'. Fusions with local musical traditions have produced distinctive jazz styles in Latin America and the Caribbean: *Avanzada* in Paraguay, *Candombe*-jazz in Uruguay, Voodoo-jazz in Haiti (Shepherd et al. 2005: III: 324, 348, 57). What Korman calls Brazilian PIIM is in part the outcome of Brazilian/US popular music encounters dating back to the early twentieth century. These include the work of Pixinguinha (the nickname for flautist/saxophonist Akfredo da Rocha Viana Fiho) and his band in 1922, which 'brought *choro* and *samba* to Paris and encountered American jazzbands (Korman 2016: 157). Cubans brought aspects of the tradition into the US in the 1930s, as in the hit song 'The Peanut Vendor', by Cuban composer Moisés Simon. Havana-born trumpeter Mario Bauzá, who came through the orchestras of Chic Webb and Don Redman, emerged in the 1950s as a major broker for Afro-Cuban jazz from the 1950s. It was he who introduced his compatriot Chano Pozo to Dizzy Gillespie, a partnership that consolidated the genre (Fernández 2003). Cuban musician/composer Pérez Prado introduced the mambo craze in the 1950s (Garcia 2017:221–267), Brazilian music also fed the stream with what became its national music, the samba, and other rhythms were introduced by Brazilians like Airto Moreira and Flora Purim, but it was the convergence of Antonio Carlos Jobim, Joao Gilberto and Stan Getz that made Bossa Nova a massively popular and enduring thread in the tapestry of US jazz (Piedade 2003).

Africa

The case of Latin fusions with jazz signals a common source, since much of the former arises from the same geo-cultural traditions as jazz: African influences migrating across the Atlantic through the slave trade. This historical circumstance gives a unique cultural and musical resonance to the reception of jazz in Africa, which thus warrants particular attention. The entrenched mythology of jazz history has been constructed on reductive geo-cultural simplifications, but no region has suffered more from this process than the vast region called Africa. This infinitely complex and heterogeneous continent has largely been reduced to simply functioning as the beginning of the story of jazz, after which it drops out of the narrative, frozen in time while jazz sails on with dynamic energy and growing sophistication. In the context of this chapter what matters is the energetic and continuing transactions between 'Africa' and jazz, resulting in prolific, diverse and influential new formations. Its jazz culture is so rich, however, that in this context we can do little more than illustrate by sample that the new formations discussed in this chapter are not to be seen simply as reactive responses to jazz, but as proactive engagements with the music. Because Africa has so often been consigned to historical inertia following its contribution to the origins of jazz, it is more than usually important to emphasise the fact that the new formations discussed here are reflections of continuing creative transactions and two-way exchanges.

These exchanges include both African musicians working in the US, and vice versa, in situations of collaboration, mutual instruction and mentoring. This kind of international two way traffic has been particularly evident in the case of the genre usually known as Afrobeat, of which Nigerian Fela Kuti was a significant pioneer, and which he saw as growing out of a jazz-Highlife fusion 'reconciled through modal harmonies found in traditional Yoruba genres', and 'heavily inflected by African-American culture', involving affinities with the modal jazz of Miles Davis, John Coltrane, Archie Shepp, and sounds 'common among people of the bush' (von Eschen 2004: 233). When B. B. King toured under State Department auspices he performed in Lagos with Fela Kuti, and listened to concerts by local musicians, from all of which he reported on his return to the US reported that he had 'learned lots' (von Eschen 2004: 235). There were similar reciprocities with James Brown who played in Nigeria in 1970 (von Eschen 2004: 234).

Also involved in the development of Afrojazz and Afrobeat was the extraordinary drummer Guy Warren, born Warren Gamaliel Akwai, and aka Ghanaba. Warren's career, documented in detail in Feld 2012, invites some discussion as an illustration of the inadequacy of the simplistic model of jazz globalisation as a steady one way traffic of influence from the US, and it is all the more significant for coming out of Africa. He first visited the US as trainee for the Office of Strategic Services in 1943, and also spent time in London, where he played in Kenny Graham's Afro-Cubists. In 1950 he lived in Monrovia, Liberia working as a journalist, DJ and drummer, then moved back to the US in 1953, first to

Chicago and then New York, where he 'introduced African drums to American jazz musicians, specifically the under-arm pressure "talking" drum odonno' (Feld 2012: 39). He was 'the first African to have a composition covered by American jazz artists' when Art Blakey recorded Warren's composition 'Love, the Mystery of ...', which Randy Weston then took as his theme song. The title of Warren's first album, in 1957, makes one of the points emerging here: *Africa Speaks, America Answers* (Feld 2012: 40). Africa did not fall passively silent after seeding jazz. Nonetheless, Warren barely registers, if at all, in histories of jazz, because he simply doesn't fit the *schema*. Max Roach said of him that he 'was too African for bebop and too early for free jazz' (Feld 2012: 33). He returned to Africa in the mid-1960s, settling in Ghana where he undertook such implausible projects as recording (for which Feld was enlisted) a talking drums version of Handel's 'Hallelujah' chorus, which emerges 'as a mixture of African, Christian, Buddhist, and Islamic ritual together with a formal European concert performance and Ghanaian ceremony' (Feld 2012: 35). Apart from US visitors mentioned above, Warren also attracted the UK drummer and Cream alumnus Ginger Baker, who set up a recording studio in Lagos where Warren recorded the song 'Blood Brothers 69' for Baker's album *Stratavarious* which also included Fela Kuti and Nigerian drummer Tony Allen, and which 'became the point of enunciation for Warren as the spiritual father of Afro-jazz' (Feld: 2012:74). It is notable that it was a musician publicly associated with rock who gave early exposure to the importance of Warren in the world music genre of Afro-jazz.

But distinctive music exchanges with US and other international influences did not have to wait until the formal arrival of World Music in 1987 and African engagement with it (Brusila 2003: 43; Brusila's study is an invaluable analysis of that engagement). 'Highlife', which also went into the Afrobeat mix, was a local music particularly associated with South Africa, going back to the late nineteenth century, but taking on aspects of jazz when the music began entering the region. In South Africa Ballantine also identifies two imported genres, spirituals and jazz, as being of special significance in the Concert and Dance phenomenon (Ballantine 2011: 486). 'Concert and Dance' was an indoor vaudeville style entertainment followed by a dance conducted nocturnally over such hours as to work around curfew laws and poor public transport. It was held in venues ranging from 'ramshackle halls in the black townships, to fashionable centres such as Johannesburg's Bantu Men's Social Centre (BMSC), or the Ritz Palais de Dance' (Ballantine 2011: 476). Concert and Dance was of particular importance in preserving African traditions during a period of European colonialism that threatened the native culture, and it also united Africans across class divisions (Ballantine 2011: 487). The repertoire of these entertainments was derived mainly from the US, and local sources, the latter of which in turn drew on marabi, a ghetto music developing since the early twentieth century (Ballantine 2011: 488). Fusions between South Africa's Bantu music and jazz produced mbaqanga, majuba and msakazo, in which the local marabi form and repertoire are conspicuous (Coplan

1985: 161).[1] Marabi was 'primarily a keyboard, banjo or guitar style based on a cyclic harmonic pattern, much as the blues was' (Ballantine 2011: 489). It was later disdained for its associations with alcohol, sex, illegality, and working class ghetto low life, and so it went unrecorded and little written of, but it was an important element in the music of the Concert and Dance movement, as in the case of the band the Jazz Maniacs (Ballantine 2011: 490–491). It was 'the crucible in which the black South African jazz tradition was forged between the twenties and the early forties' and also a musical vehicle for the preservation of a threatened local culture (Ballantine 2011: 497).

Rather like Fela Kuti and Afrojazz, Ethiopia produced a jazz formation largely originating from one musician, vibraphonist and percussionist Mulatu Astatke, or Astaqé, regarded as the father of what has become known as Ethio-jazz, partly fed by a range of musics he assimilated during music studies in England, where he played with calypso musicians as well as the Latin band of Edmondo Ross, then went on to further studies in New York where he formed his Ethiopian Quartet (von Eschen 2004: 231). On returning to Ethiopia he found conditions that were favourable for the cultivation of a local jazz formation. One of these conditions was a shift away from the native traditions of instrumental performance either solo or accompanying a singer, a shift associated with the emergence of a brass band movement from the 1920s (Shelemay 2016: 242–243). His Ethio-jazz pulled together the influences he had absorbed during his sojourns in the UK and the US, with various local forms ranging from native traditions to Ethiopian church music (Shelemay 2016: 248). During Duke Ellington's tour of Ethiopia in 1973, the two became good friends (von Eschen 2004: 231) and Astatke's eminence was such that they performed together.

In the words of Shelemay, the origin of Ethio-jazz 'unsettles the standard jazz narrative', particularly in that it is at no point a story driven by inter-racial tensions, and takes us beyond Gilroy's authoritative model of the Black Atlantic (Shelemay 2016: 252–253). It is also a further reminder of the inadequacies of attempting to engage with jazz on exclusively music(ologic)al terms. While many self-consciously engineered syncretisms are overtly conducted simply as exercises in musical form, these new diasporic formations give particular force to the complicity between musical form and material culture, in this case the availability of a pool of brass instruments (Shelemay 2016: 242).

Local Instrumental Traditions

Instrumentation has been one site for the growth of local jazz forms outside the US, affecting not simply the sound, but the politics of the music. Finland's longest surviving dance band, Dallapé was founded in 1925, and apart from a hiatus from 1955 to 1960, has continued to be active to the present. It exemplifies and is largely responsible for the Finnish category of 'accordion jazz' (it is named after an Italian brand of accordion with which early members equipped themselves).

The accordion carried particular connotations of local workers' movements and rusticity, on which the expensive imported instruments conferred an up-to-date sophistication, thus reconciling Finland's rural folk traditions with modernity (Johnson Forthcoming B). East German drummer Günter Sommer had to assemble his own drum kits from pre- and non-jazz percussion. Initially anxious about using these on an international gig, he discovered that it filled his American peers with 'wonder and delight': 'this was my way to be unique, to sound different and have a different melody in my playing to distinguish me from all the others. From then on I was quite proud of my old-fashioned stuff' (Heffley 2005: 211).

In Africa, in particular, local instrumentation has played a major role in the evolving jazz aesthetic, made more distinctive and conspicuous by the culturally eclectic deployment of instruments, including those improvised from *objets trouvés*, strikingly illustrated in Feld's study of Ghanaian jazz. He describes the ashiwa bass box, from the Congo via Santo Domingo, Cuba and Jamaica (Feld 2012: 27), and notes that Ghanaba's colleague Nii Noi's 'soprano afrifone' is assembled as an exercise in jazz cosmopolitanism (Feld 2012: 91–92). It also serves to reset the politics of jazz/Ghanaian fusions: in the words of Nii Noi, the afrifone 'makes our music more African than African American … and that's what I want, like Ghanaba, not to be an African playing what people think of as jazz on standard jazz instruments, but playing African music on African instruments that are informed by the history of jazz and especially the spirit of Coltrane, and the politics of those times' (Feld 2012: 105). Ghanaian musicians have also incorporated jazz influences into por por bands, using electric car horns as musical instruments. Their music and stage deportment are modelled on big US Swing bands like those of Count Basie, and their performance in the funerals of transport workers is inspired by traditional New Orleans funerals, including second line dancers (Feld 2012: 43, 44). Jazz is also consciously woven into the work of Ghanaian guitarist Koo Nimo, who seeks

> to marry the traditional highlife guitar with Spanish and Latin American music; an Afro-Spanish style using traditional rhythms with arpeggio. I always use finger-picking, never the plectrum. Also I want to develop an Afro-jazz and use Wes Montgomery and Charlie Christian type chords in it
> *Feld 2012: 57*

Even this very partial African overview reinforces the idea of a narrative of global jazz not as a development from African and European music – in which model, African music has been of interest mainly as a place whence something more important emerged – but evolving music of the continuing African diaspora, a 'Black Atlantic' in Gilroy's words, among which is to be found a great many hybrids including jazz, which happened to enjoy the benefit of appearing at a time and place which enabled its sudden globalisation. And as a corollary, this model also 'rescues' so-called developing regions including Africa from a demeaning static pre-modernity.

Local Cultural Traditions

South Africa's Concert and Dance tradition also illustrates another axis along which distinctive local jazz identities can form. It is not simply the kind of music being played, but the nature and history of the events and venues in which they are experienced. The case of public dances in Finland where, like African Concert and Dance, means had to be found to circumvent entertainment prohibitions, is a case in point, and is reviewed later, but the example of New Zealand is also illustrative. Of course, the 'text', the nature of the actual music played, is also essential to these discussions and we must avoid the danger of the specificity of musical practice disappearing behind a cultural thesis. There have been studied engagements with musical form that have cast valuable light on the character of New Zealand jazz both nationally and regionally. Dan Bendrups and Robert Burns, for example, have reflected on the ideas shaping their own Dunedin jazz fusion band Subject2Change, and that it is not simply based on US models, but also on local attitudes to music and other international influences (Bendrups and Burns 2011). A similar balance was sought by New Zealand bassist Paul Dyne, who felt that while the US provides an essential foundation, his work as a composer also reflects his national identity. Similarly, compatriot drummer Anthony Donaldson, working since the late 1970s, sees his free jazz work in the in the Primitive Art Group as drawing on US and European influences, but producing also 'something new' (Meehan 2017: 166, 167). Norman Meehan's interviews with New Zealand musicians led him to two conclusions: that original composition was felt to be the site from which 'a distinctly local music emerges', and that eclecticism is an essential component in that process (Meehan 2017: 167). The importance of international and especially US models is of course a ubiquitous feature of diasporic jazz, but in addressing the local culture Meehan takes us in the direction of a distinctive profile, defined, sometimes ambiguously, by the participation of the Maori community and its musical traditions in the New Zealand jazz scene (Meehan 2016: 171 n. 3; see also Hardie and Thomas 2009: 88–98). One of the features of this community is a strong tradition of collective public and domestic music making (Brown 2011), and this turns our attention towards one of the distinctive forces in the formation of jazz in New Zealand.

Research by Aleisha Ward suggests that the jam session was a major site of the country's jazz development, but, more particularly, that the New Zealand version was distinctive if not unique. From the 1920s New Zealand jazz enjoyed strongly supportive fan bases that were highly proactive; the earliest jazz fan club, the Christchurch Jazz Club, was established in 1920, and used its dances to raise money for local charities (Ward 2017: 186 n. 1). They also created jazz infrastructures including from the late 1930s what were called 'official jam sessions' (which, incidentally moved the music away from a dancing to a listening practice; see Ward 2017: 180). These sessions were by invitation only, though there was no entry charge: invitation/admission depended on one's recognised status as a devoted and well-informed fan (Ward 2017: 180).They were held either in private houses or a hired church or community hall (Ward 2017: 178), though the former were preferred because there were no constraints on time and noise levels. Unlike commercial gigs, these events abolished the barrier between audiences and performers and, publicised in club journals and local press, were decisive in the formation of local jazz scenes (Ward 2017: 182, 183). Fans and musicians produced the specialist magazine *Swing!* in Wellington, from September 1941 until terminated by wartime paper and personnel shortages in August 1942, then later, from August 1947 to April 1947, and *Jukebox* in Auckland (Ward 2017: 187).While individual features of these fan activities and the jam sessions were evident internationally, the particular combination of three of them seems to have been unique to the New Zealand jazz scene: 'fan activities (record recital, analysis, presentations, discussions and games), private gig (fans as an invited, private audience) and the traditional musicians' jam session' (Ward 2017: 185).

One reason that these 'official jam sessions' could thrive in New Zealand as compared with its antipodean neighbour is a simple economic one: in 1938 the Australian Professional Musicians Union 'moved to enforce a ban on unpaid work because of the prevalence of jam sessions' (John Whiteoak 2009: 26–27). But in seeking some explanation for both of these phenomena we are taken back to the work by Michael Brown, from which, in conjunction with Ward's research, I believe we can extrapolate a provocative hypothesis. Brown has conducted extensive study of the history of vernacular music in New Zealand (Brown 2008, 2011, 2012, 2013, 2017), and has traced at length a strikingly strong tradition of active community music participation well into the jazz era, ranging from tramping songs to Maori music (Brown 2012). Bourke also documents examples of the ubiquity of 'home-made' music in Maori life (Bourke 2010: 331, 334, 335) and it is paralleled in the European settler (Pākehā) population. How far this might be a matter of exchange between the two is unclear. While there have been and still are racial tensions at work in New Zealand society, it is a matter of relativities, and certainly compared with the shamefully egregious history of settler/indigenous relations across the Tasman in Australia, the balance of power, respect and harmonious inter-relationships in New Zealand is far more equitable, and in particular, members of the Maori community have been an essential presence in jazz in New Zealand. Other factors likely to have encouraged this form of entertainment arising from local conditions and history include the urban/rural demographic, the relative lack of other public amenities and media, the persistence of six o' clock hotel closing, and a high level of outdoor/campfire life.

Bourke records the rise of the 'Community Singing' movement beginning in Wellington in 1922, and growing through the 1930s, in theatres, halls and even via radio. During the war this movement was harnessed as a very effective fundraiser (Bourke 2010: 115). In his study of the level of domestic piano ownership in New Zealand, Brown cites figures that 'contribute powerful evidence for a New Zealand music history centred not around composers, musicians and canonical

works, but rather on musical practices which were the domain of the majority',
and by the early twentieth-century piano sing-alongs in the home were 'well-
nigh universal' in the sample he studied (Brown 2017: 27, 38). It seems to me
reasonable to suppose that the particular form of jam session identified by Ward,
in which in one way or another both musicians and fans were active participants,
was another manifestation of these various forms of local live music practice. In
addition to factors already cited, I suspect that what matters here is a distinctive
array of local conditions that also include metropolitan centres large enough to
produce a community of jazz fans at that particular historical moment, but not
large enough to generate a viable separate fan-base, or enough jazz gigs and jam
sessions. In early twentieth-century New Zealand we have a community that is
metropolitan enough to be alert to international developments in popular music
via modern media, but provincial enough to generate a collective participatory
culture.

Notwithstanding such examples as this, the main focus of research into
'glocalisations', for want of a better word, has been from the late twentieth century, in the wake of the international standardisation of jazz along the lines of US
models. Discussing the Manouche jazz of Django Reinhardt, Gioia (2011: 382)
declared that to find further examples of non-US jazz musicians drawing on their
own local traditions we must then 'fast forward to the jazz scene of the twenty-
first century'. But as many of the foregoing examples suggest, diasporic jazz has
been drawing on local traditions from the beginning, and in ways that are deeply
instructive as part of the process of its still coming into being as a global modern
music. Staying for a moment with France: Jeffrey Jackson identifies 'the first widely
famous French jazz band leader' as a flamboyant Armenian immigrant Grégor,
who, ca. 1927, promoted his jazz as a distinctively national French music, even
though it was evidently a highly cosmopolitan *potpourri* (Jackson 2011: 451). From
the late 1920s French bandleader Ray Ventura, with his 'jazzing' of French songs,
gained the reputation for having produced a 'French jazz' (Jackson: 2011: 452).
'The late 1920s and early 1930s were the years when a new, self-consciously
French jazz community emerged in Paris. Musicians fashioned for themselves an
identity not simply as jazz players, but as French jazz players' (Jackson 2011: 460).

Spain has a history of jazz interacting with the local culture, particularly in
fusions with flamenco from the 1960s in the work of Pedro Iturralde (Iglesias
2013: 108–109). But already in the 1920s, jazz was entering the culture via a range
of performance sites that brought it into co-existence with '*pasodobles, concertantes,*
waltzes, tangos, romanzas, *chotis*, marches, polkas and mazurkas' (Iglesias 2013: 81).
In Italy, and in particular Naples, jazz did not displace local musics, but entered
into a productive relationship with them, as surveyed by Plastino (2016: 328–332).
Plastino illustrates the point through a particular examination of the 1934 song
'Tammuriata Americana'; 'Tammuriata' is a folk dance, and the music combines US
with Neapolitan references (Plastino 2016: 322). In Germany Ralph Benatzky's
work known in English as *The White Horse Inn*, which premiered in 1930 in Berlin,

incorporated a wide range of musical forms and traditions including jazz, identified by Plastino and Bohlman as a major moment in 'world jazz', as also in the case of Kurt Weill's *The Threepenny Opera*, and *Rise and Fall of the City of Mahagonny* (Plastino and Bohlman 2016: 15–16).

The jazz that emerged in these early cases was of course affected by the character of the musical traditions it encountered in each case. German martial music encouraged a strong stress on the first beat of each bar, and later its version of Swing incurred the charge of a rigidity and lack of suppleness (Kater 1992: 14, 59, 116). French jazz pioneer Léo Vauchant felt that the national predominance of the time signatures 3/4 and 2/4 impeded the 'swing' of local jazz musicians (Goddard 1979: 18). In other cases the encounter became a creative reciprocity, as in the working-class 'accordion jazz' of Finland's Dallapé band referred to above (Haavisto 1996: 15; Jalkanen 1989: 393). Jazz could thus be drawn into attempts to preserve and modernise local national musics, exemplified in its layering over folk forms and repertoire in Sweden, in titles like 'The Troll Jazz' (Fornäs 2003: 216). From Estonia to Colombia, regions with folk music traditions that remained active in community life produced distinctive jazz colorations (Shepherd et al. 2005: VII: 4; III: 29).

On aural evidence, such distinctive fusions seem to be especially powerful when jazz encountered robust local, and especially non-Anglophone, narrative and musical traditions. Bulgarian musician/composer Milcho Leviev found productive affinities between jazz and his local folk traditions that enabled him to bridge rural and urban cultures (Levy 2016: 79). Similarly Azerbaijani jazz drew on native musical and instrumental traditions, notably mugham, to produce an early example of a distinctive ethno-jazz fusion (Naroditskaya 2016). Where such affinities did not exist, however, the strength of such traditions could present barely penetrable barriers to the early jazz that had, so to speak, almost exhausted itself in its cultural journey, as has been argued in the case of India and eastern Yugoslavia (Pinckney 2003: 94; Shepherd et al. 2005: VII: 140). It is reasonable to relate the unevenness of the penetration of jazz in Latin America during this first phase to the robustness of non-Anglo/US local music traditions, in combination with the distance of its various countries from the US.

One of the central lessons in all this is how often and early have been the transactions between jazz and local vernacular musics. In many cases these have become markers of regional identities, a process that has at the same time generated misleading over-simplifications. A closer analysis of some particular case studies will disclose further ambiguities and complexities in the formation of these local jazz formations. Consider first the so-called 'Nordic Sound' or 'Nordic Tone' and the ECM record label, referred to above. This has achieved such strong definition that it is one of the few diasporic forms that is given recognition in mainstream US-centric jazz histories, as in the case of Gioia: 'the first major jazz label to rely heavily on non-U.S. talent, and this commitment to broadening the geographical base of the music would prove as important as the distinctive sounds associated with the company's imprimatur' (Gioia 2011: 339). Nicholson provides a useful overview of its situation within jazz discourse (Nicholson 2005: 195–222; see also Hellhund 2012: 442–444), and cites Ian Carr's assessment of ECM that it has fostered music included 'one of the finest groups in jazz history' (Nicholson 2005: 207). Internationally ECM has come to represent 'a distinctively Nordic sound' (Shand 2009: 7), and has been praised hyperbolically as solving 'for the very first time the question of jazz and its relationship with other kinds of music … by creating a new and unique sound' (Cappelletti 2012: 125).

Beyond serving to identify the 'house style' of a particular record label, the characterisation 'Nordic Sound' is misleading, however, and for a number of reasons. First, it generalises the sounds produced by a single studio into the sounds that characterise a very large and diverse transnational culture. The Nordic region of which ECM is 'the sound' is usually understood as encompassing Denmark, Finland, Iceland, Norway and Sweden, as well as island groups that include Åland (central to the 20,000-island archipelago between Sweden and Finland) and the Faroes, and Greenland. This is a culturally heterogeneous array with not even a shared language group – Finnish is Finno-Ugric, its nearest linguistic kin being Estonian and Hungarian. Their political and social histories are very dissimilar, even in the century of jazz. During World war two, for example, Sweden was neutral, Denmark was occupied by the Germans, and Finland was allied with Germany. Iceland has the world's oldest parliament (the Althing), and Finland only came into being as a sovereign entity in 1917, to be followed by a civil war, unique in the modern Nordic zone, that cast a long shadow over the whole culture. Topographically and climatically the region is much more varied than the cliché of 'icy blasts and beautiful fjords' conjured in the word 'Nordic' (Shand 2009: 8).

As is attested in relevant entries in, for example, Wasserberger et al. 2017 and Martinelli 2018, as well as specialist studies such as van Kan on Sweden, Haavisto on Finland, Rastrick on Iceland, the heterogeneity elided by the term 'Nordic Sound' is equally reflected in their respective jazz traditions, beginning with the access to US sources enjoyed by Sweden and Denmark through touring circuits that gave exposure to black US musicians, while Finland and, as Rastrick observes, Iceland had virtually no contact with racial difference (Rastrick Forthcoming). Finland's main early jazz conduit was Germany, and its popular music deeply inflected by Russian traditions. Jazz in the Nordic region has engaged with the heterogeneous popular and folk traditions of each country since its arrival, producing syncretisms that are both cultural and musical – Finland's earliest jazz, for example, is deeply infused with a minor key Russian melancholy, or modelled on German 'Lärmjazz', as well as using conscious adaptations of its own folk music and folk culture. Widely regarded as Finland's first jazz recordings, 'Isoo-Antti' and 'Raatikkoon Blues' of 1929 are both based on Finnish folk material (Johnson Forthcoming B). Even these 'national styles' break down into smaller units defined by region; so for example the importance of port cities, by which Copenhagen and Stockholm developed jazz with far more mutual affinity than with remote rural jazz scenes in their own countries. The term 'Nordic Sound' implicitly assigns cultural and musical meanings to a multi-national region that are deeply misleading and stereotyping; 'ECM Sound' would be more appropriate.

What is 'Local Identity'?

US jazz geography is constructed in sub-national terms like New Orleans, Chicago and New York, and even smaller territorial units. Storyville in New Orleans is ubiquitous in the mythology, but so is, for example, New York's 52nd Street (Shaw 1977) or particular venues such as Mintons and its coterie and individual musicians in New York (DeVeaux 2000: 219–227). But the pattern for diasporic jazz has been predominantly nation-based, as in the recent surveys of European jazz by Wasserberger et al. 2017 and Martinelli 2018 (and in my own work including Johnson 1987 and Johnson 2000). While this is the obvious starting point, the more closely we explore the path of diasporic jazz, the less satisfactory does this approach appear to be, rather like trying to identify a street in Łodz by looking at a map of Poland. I mentioned above that Acid Jazz came out of England, but it would be more accurate to say that it came out of London; I know of no evidence, nor imagine much likelihood, of Acid Jazz clubs being part of the entertainment life for Isle of Skye crofters or dairy farmers in Devon.

Perchard argues that much of the jazz activity in France through the 1970s was 'part of a much broader renewal of interest and faith in the country's provincial cultures' (Perchard 2015: 203). That is, the centrifugal movement of jazz was not just to diasporic national and metropolitan centres, but more localised than the term France or Paris can disclose. This raises a range of questions surrounding the relationship between musical and geo-cultural context in jazz mythologisation, and how the understanding of that relationship might differ inside and outside the US. The relationship between what might be called figure and ground – individual and national culture – tends to shift when the spotlight moves beyond the US. So, for example, is Argentinian guitarist Oscar Alemán (who bears a striking similarity to Reinhardt) an outstanding musician in a particular jazz tradition or a gifted medium of a distinctive national dance music? When the highly individual Australian musician Ade Monsbourgh was heard in England with the Graeme Bell band in the late 1940s, his (and the band) sound was declared to be 'Australian', though even in Australia he was distinctive enough to have inspired conscious imitators (Johnson 2000, 160–161; see further below).

It should be noted that musical tributes to Django Reinhardt are also recreations of the totality of the Quintet of the Hot Club of France: we need to hear those other rhythm guitars and a violin for an 'authentic' Django experience. Nor should Reinhardt's individual virtuosity distract from the fact that he was also carrying into jazz (and being carried by) a local musical tradition which does not correspond simplistically to a national model, a gypsy Manouche style. While this is generally acknowledged, Reinhardt's case highlights the over-simplified way this relationship is usually articulated. The importance of that context is suggested in the fact that some of his most convincing 'imitators' like Bireli Lagrene are also from Romany backgrounds. The 'Django' style thrives among Western European gypsy musical communities, many of whom gather annually in Samois-sur-Seine in France for a commemorative festival (Givan 2003: 20). Going beyond France and Belgium, a notable proportion of Hungarian jazz musicians also came from gypsy backgrounds (Shepherd et al. 2005: VII: 38; Havas 2018). All this is not to take a position on the relationship between individual musician and context, but to suggest that in the case of jazz, it is a relationship configured outside the US with differing emphases on the components figure/ground, individual/place. Reinhardt contributed to, but was also the conduit of, a jazz style that is not a function of 'nation' in the political sense.

Reference to Australian Ade Monsbourgh above evokes yet another case where the idea of a 'national style' takes on the character of a mirage as we approach it more closely. The sense of an 'Australian' jazz was projected early in the history of the music, in the name of one of the country's earliest jazz exports to seek to capitalise on national identity. In 1924 a band from Melbourne embarked on what would become nine years of successful touring in the UK and the US. Originally called Ross's Jazz Band, for the tour they changed their name to the Three Australian Boys, and as such played prestigious venues and recorded 14 tracks for English Parlophone (Sutcliffe 1989: 2). How far they actively 'performed' to the idea of Australian-ness is not known, but it seems likely that this might well have been in the eye/ear of the international audiences: that is, an inclination to imagine a connection between the known origin of the band, its name, and the character of the music played. This suspicion is fortified by the case of Australian bandleader Cec Morrison who travelled extensively internationally in the early 1930s. In the US he presented a radio broadcast of what was advertised as 'Kangaroo Jazz', received with great enthusiasm even to the extent of prompting a musician in Chicago to declare that this converted him to jazz, and that Morrison should remain in the States to 'educate' its jazz musicians. (Johnson 2000: 146–147). It is difficult to imagine what musical qualities specifically might have evoked kangaroos (the music evidently consisted of his own orchestral arrangements), and it seems most likely that simply knowing of Morrison's nationality persuaded listeners that something of this was actually audible in his music, rather as later writers 'hear' fjords in ECM.

The proposition that there is something distinctive about Australian jazz has remained durable. In their 1987 encyclopaedia format international overview, Carr et al. (1987: 17) described the Australian jazz scene as arguably producing 'the most stimulating music of any outside America'. It has been demonstrated that the work of seminal Australian jazz modernists Frank Smith and Bryce Rohde cannot be understood simply in terms of US models (Ralph Whiteoak 2016: 215–228; Seguin 2016: 229–247). Australian pianist/composer/educator Tony Gould argues that many Australian jazz musicians, as for example Brian Brown, have taken jazz beyond the US models (Gould 2018: 76, 79). In her study of the currently active jazz-based and internationally acclaimed improvisational Sydney band The Necks, Jane Galbraith cites English jazz writer John Walters's description of the group as 'Entirely new and entirely now … teaching us to listen in a new way … a whole new world of music' (Galbraith 2016: 267). He judged them to be 'one of the most extraordinary groups on the planet', and 'a revolutionary consortium redefining music for the new century' (cited Johnson 2008B: 125–126). In formal terms, this is audible in the unusual circumstance of a group of virtuosi jazz musicians foreswearing displays of virtuosity and solo flights.

The relationship between jazz and Australian identity shifted between the interwar and post-war period. As discussed in further detail below, one profound change was in the gendering of the music. Through the 1920s, jazz was a feminised, emasculating urban music, a cautionary contrast to the manly values of rural Australia. In film, publicity material and even to a surprising extent in instrumental profile, jazz was seen to enter the culture through women, in particular the 'New Woman'. In the wake of the Second World War it was masculinised so thoroughly that its earlier gendering has all but been erased. This happened also in conjunction with events that are inextricably bound up in what I see as a feedback relationship with the most enduring model of an 'Australian' jazz. These events primarily involved metropolitan centres in south-east Australia: Adelaide (South Australia), Hobart and Launceston (Tasmania), and centrally Melbourne (Victoria). Apart from the fact that Melbourne was geographically central to this axis as a recreational destination, jazz-interested representatives from each of these were thrown into contact partly by wartime mobilisations. From Hobart, reed player Tom Pickering and pianist (and for a time trumpet player) Ian Pearce; from Launceston the musicians associated with a band calling itself the Jazzmanians, led by trumpeter/guitarist/bassist Ted Herron. Central to the Adelaide group was pianist/trombonist/composer Dave Dallwitz, with reed player Bruce Gray and trumpeter Bill Munro also major musicians. The Melbourne group centred on the Bell brothers, trumpet/washboard/player Roger and pianist Graeme, and multi-instrumentalist – but especially reed player – Ade Monsbourgh, whose contributions to the band sound were described by Carr et al. as 'almost disturbingly original' (1987: 17). All of those listed also composed to varying levels of prolixity. Together all these musicians were pillars of the emerging national revivalist movement which crystallised dramatically with the inaugural Australian Jazz Convention, held in Melbourne at the end of 1946, alluded to above.

The emergence of this community has been extensively documented (for back ground on the musicians see for example Bisset 1987: 114–139, relevant individual and regional sections in Johnson 1987, and memoirs/biographies of some of the participants including Graeme Bell, Tom Pickering and Ian Pearce (Bell 1988; Kuplis and Pickering 2012; Kuplis 2015). And it was this movement that incubated what has been called the 'Australian' jazz style. The evolution of that style, and its connections with a wave of Australian modernism and radicalism in politics, painting and literature, have been studied and debated at length from the level of anecdote through local jazz journals to scholarly research in Australian cultural history, the latter beginning with Clunies-Ross (1979; writing later as Ross 2016), and including Bisset 1987: 114–139; Johnson 2000: 147–163; Martin 2000; Boden 2016). I don't propose to rehearse all those details here, extraordinary though they are, but I do want to extrapolate some material that bears on the problematic relationship between diasporic jazz and national identity.

In a carefully considered overview of the Australian jazz narrative, Peter Martin argues for the connection with a fine grasp of its balance between assimilating the US models and the formation of a local 'colour', an understanding that what doesn't exactly fit the US model might in fact represent a credit rather than a deficit. He finds in Australian jazz in the post-war period 'a joy of liberation and swing all its own' (Martin 2000: 580). In the development of this 'accent' his roster ranges from the growth of the traditionalist movement, to a spirit that continues into the 'self-invented' character of the work of altoist Bernie McGann, the 'innovative' drums of Lou[is] Burdett (Martin 2000: 581), the 'local tang' of tenor saxophonist Mark Simmonds and trumpeter Scott Tinkler, a 'creative eclecticism' and 'ockerish disrespect for stylistic boundaries' in the work of composer, percussionist, vibraphonist, trumpeter John Sangster, and a pervasive eccentricity (Martin 2000: 581–582; on McGann's style see also Evans 2016). In his analysis of this 'distinctive sound' Matthew Boden (2016: 109) touches on similar attributes, including an *ad hoc* 'piecemeal' style thrown together at a great distance from the US models and before the international codification of the music (Boden 2016: 124). The result is a carefree, extroverted eclecticism and a certain 'larrikin' roughness around the edges (Boden 2016: 123, 125), as well as 'the ability to not take oneself too seriously' (Boden 2016: 117) for which the preponderance of amateur status is also responsible (Boden 2016: 124).

These relatively recent assessments continue themes also sounded in Clunies-Ross, Bisset and Johnson as cited above, and that were articulated in the earliest identifications of the 'Australian' style, which, it is important to note, originated *outside* Australia. In particular, they were part of the responses by English commentators to the first of the immensely influential international tours undertaken by the Graeme Bell band in 1947–48. Writers and musicians in the UK were startled by the aggressively confident sound and demeanour of the Australians, who showed no signs of the deference to be expected of colonials in the 'mother country'. They also had the effrontery to violate the established formats of jazz appreciation clubs with their fixation on matrix numbers, record sessions and historical disquisitions, by opening their own club in Leicester Square advertising jazz for dancing, thus changing both the music's then social role and the audience demographic, as vast crowds of youth found a space to let off steam in the drab austerity of post-war London. The swaggering 'larrikin' virility associated with Australians was reinforced by the concurrent cricketing tour of Don Bradman's 'Invincibles' as well as the Australian tennis doubles victory at Wimbledon by

Frank Sedgeman and John Bromwich during the band's tour, all leading to press announcements of an 'Australian Invasion' (see further Johnson 2000: 152–157).

It was this tour that laid down the template for 'The Australian Sound'. The relevant point in this context is that it was constructed by English writers, who, from a distance, generalised and essentialised the Graeme Bell band in terms of national character. But in the history of jazz in Australia there have been thousands of musicians whose work cannot be characterised in the same terms as the Bell band. What English writers declared to be 'Australian' was in fact largely the work of the small coteries described above, initially centred on the Bells and Monsbourgh and then running through the bands of Frank Johnson and the Barnard brothers, Bob and Len, from the 1950s, and the Red Onions Jazz Band (mentored by Monsbourgh) from the 1960s, each generation having a significant effect on the next. It is a fascinating musical tradition, but not a national one.

They also, especially the 'founding fathers', shared a particular culture of time and place, which is worth an extended study in itself. Its features include a kickback against the rather conservative Melbourne culture of the 1930s–1940s. The reaction manifested itself partly in the very active social, artistic and political alliances between the jazz musicians and modernist movements in literature and painting, and it was one of the leaders of those movements, Max Harris, who was among the first to grasp the importance of the Bells' role in both Australian modernism and the international perception of an Australian jazz style (see Johnson 2000: 25–26, 158–159). The lightly carried cultural literacy of this community continued to be manifest in memoirs and particularly the urbane cover note commentaries by, among others, Len Barnard, of 1970s LP reissue compilations on the Swaggie label of their early recordings. What is equally striking in terms of the cultural history and 'character' of Australian jazz, however, is the extent to which all this was belied by a social veneer of vernacular blokiness that sometimes had as its darker side a tendency to misogyny. It was a calculated air of football-and-pies matey down-to-earthness: no bullshit, a strong 'insider' group-think that deployed its private nicknames like a Masonic handshake, that developed its own argot and shared insider jokes, supremely exemplified in the memoir by John Sangster (1988), whose calculated sunny ockerism puts into shadow a disturbing and often dark psychological complexity proclaimed by his extraordinary compositional *oeuvre* (Johnson Forthcoming C).

I believe that we can say that this jazz profile represents a particular aspect of Australian culture: a self-assured pragmatism that can improvise 'she'll-be-right' solutions from whatever is to be found lying around and a valorisation of male 'mateship', all traceable to a masculinist pioneer settler history based on solid and straightforward values and virtues. Peer-groups and the broader social context have favoured the formation of such sodalites. The Bells and their circle were of a time and place that encouraged that form of self-performance, and it was a style that was emulated and probably exaggerated by admiring disciples. And for historical reasons, they became the most influential pioneer standard-bearers of 'Australian' jazz internationally. Without resorting to national stereotyping, I think a detailed micro-study would reveal the historical connections between a particular *mythos* about Australian character, and the founding fathers of the Australian jazz sound, and why those connections were so strong in that place and time. But it is not necessary to defend such cultural generalisation here. What matters is that while this was the image that defined the perennial 'Australian' jazz style, it was in fact the outgrowth of a highly localised sub-culture and of a very specific moment.

Conclusion

The foregoing overview of diasporic jazz formations identifies several provisional categories. One distinction which has traversed the field is between spontaneous and engineered experiments, Manouche jazz and the 'Australian' style exemplifying the former, and free jazz and the fusions undertaken by, for example, Joachim-Ernst Berendt, referred to earlier and documented in fine detail by Hurley (2009), representing the latter. Roughly corresponding to this, another line of demarcation is between cultural and formal musical intersections. There are other ways of categorising the processes of diasporic jazz formations, and they can all be manipulated in relation to each like a Venn Diagram, and are in any case highly schematic. To distinguish between music as form and music as culture is to invoke a model of autonomous music that has been convincingly discredited (see for example Tagg and Clarida 2003: 3–92). As we have seen, even the emergence of the apparently abstract formalism of some free jazz experiments is framed by politics, such as the European reaction to the US presence in in Vietnam. Each of the categorisations I have invoked is simply a provisional way of casting a slightly different kind of light. More broadly, to give attention to these formations is to challenge an imperialist centre/margins model of cultural diffusion and to respect all attempts to play 'jazz', no matter how geographically or historically marginalised (see further Johnson Forthcoming B). These counter-narratives to the US canon-centred version yield specific kinds of insights into the story of jazz as the global phenomenon on which its importance rests.

Note

1 It is well to remember that such generic and stylistic discriminators are often politically sensitive, as Ballantine's body of work pervasively makes clear, and of course they are also porous. For South African jazz scholar Jonathan Eato, terms such as 'mbaqanga, majuba and msakazo are often very confused and are applied to such a wide variety of music that I wonder about their usefulness as genre markers' (personal communication 12 May 2014), and his study of South African jazz under apartheid also discloses the complicity of politics in the country's jazz discourses (Eato 2017), likewise Duby's study of jazz education and state control (Duby 2017).

PART 3
Bridge

4
ANOMALIES

The foregoing discussions disclose the range of jazz forms and discourses that fall within and, in many cases, originate in the diasporic process, and therefore some of the limitations imposed upon jazz scholarship by narratives that confine themselves largely to the US. But as we have traced the diaspora we have also had frequent glimpses of not just lacunae but also contradictions in the standard canonical model, and these reflexively compromise the narrative even as it concerns the US as well as beyond. This is not simply about the well-documented problem of which individuals or communities might be excluded from the canon, but the categorisations and material forces that are explicitly and implicitly deployed to structure the jazz story. As a bridge to the next section, I provide a brief exemplification of the limitations of four of the load bearers of jazz discourses, including one that identifies this study itself.

Diaspora

One point clearly emerging from the discussion is the underlying fragility of the conceptualisations deployed with such confidence in jazz discourses. Even while the use of the term 'diaspora' here provides the most succinct way of informing potential readers as to the subject of this study, placed under some self-reflexive scrutiny its outlines blur. It implies a straightforward *ab ovo* myth (fertilised mainly by Africa) with a subsequent migration flowing unilaterally from a single source, as in the Stanley Crouch model (Gennari 2006: 357). That is, as we have seen, tenuous at best, ignoring 'the unforeseen detours and new arrivals that, in turn, release new political and cultural possibilities' (Gilroy 1999: 86). Feld's study of jazz in Ghana (2012) is an extended case study in the complex reciprocities of the jazz diaspora. We have reviewed the emergence of local formations, and these could become implicated in international networks that bypassed the music's source. The international influence of Django Reinhardt is the best-known example (Shipton 2002: 391). Terry Martin identifies the Australian Graeme Bell band's 1947–48 tour as the 'spark' for the revivalist movement in Europe and the UK (Martin 2000: 580). Czechs declared that the tour was the first 'really pure' jazz they had heard (Johnson 2000: 150). Later, English trombonist Chris Barber's band 'became one of the most influential and widely imitated bands in the history of the traditional revival anywhere in the world' (Shipton 2012: 262). According to Barber's own recollection, it even appears that his tours of the US, ca. 1959/ 1960 were for many audiences their first exposure to jazz (Barber 2013: 12). In interwar Brazil, France was the major mediator of the music (Fléchet 2016: 15). The Philippines produced a pool of jazz musicians who were highly influential in Japan and Shanghai (Atkins 2003: xv). Haitians and Guadeloupeans returning from Paris contributed to the formation of local jazz bands (Shepherd et al. 2005: III: 56, 52). From the 1930s jazz-influenced musicians from Burma and Nepal recorded in India (Pinckney 2003: 62), and Russian musicians took their version of jazz into the Chinese hinterland from Shanghai. One of the earliest jazz bands to tour Japan was the Dixie Minstrels from Hawaii (Jones 2003: 231– 232; Atkins 2001: 60).

As also in the case of many US musicians, diasporic performers and scenes were fed from non-US sources. The enormously influential Australian saxophonist Frank Smith found a number of pathways to his individual voice, not least of which was the decidedly non-US-jazz model Paul Hindemith (Ralph Whiteoak 2016). There were also instances of reverse flow, of influences feeding back into the US from, for example, European sources. Garvin Bushell was inspired by gypsy music in Budapest, 'the greatest and most creative musicians in the world' (1988: 61), Quincy Jones by Turkish musician Arif Mardin, and Dave Brubeck by musicians from India (von Eschen 2004: 37, 52). Ellington's encounter in 1933 with the 'highbrow' attitude to jazz in Europe inspired him to undertake more ambitious projects (Rasula 2002: 65), and through an analysis of recordings Perchard identifies aspects of Django Reinhardt's playing that fed into Coleman Hawkins's influential proto-bop experiments (Perchard 2015: 59). On such 'reverse flows' from Europe to the US see further, in chronological order, Shipton 2001: 834–836; Nicholson 2005: 142, 830; Mawer 2014: 220; Cugny 2016: 253 n. 12; Plastino 2016: 316).

While the trope of 'diaspora' provides a platform on which to build a study of global jazz routes, the word itself and its origins in the Jewish experience, set up a 'centre/margins' flow that imposes the very politics that are under challenge, and, in recognition of its inadequacies, other terms have been proposed to define the movement of the music, including 'frontier', 'exchange', 'cross-pollination', 'diffusion', and my own neologism 'polyspora' (Atkins 2011: 465, 466; Johnson 2002A: 52). In any event, the word must yield to the practice.

Jazz Exceptionalism

The other major term in the title of this book, 'jazz', is also profoundly unstable. It is unnecessary to document a debate over a question that has pervaded the entire history of the music: 'What is jazz?' The understanding of jazz has been so protean that today much of what was categorised as jazz practice up to a century ago would not now be recognised as such. This underscores the fact that what distinguishes jazz, what constitutes its 'exceptionalism', is itself culturally and historically evasive. Nonetheless, the canon identifies certain essences as distinctively constitutive of jazz. But writers who look beyond the black/US axis discover practices of which jazz has 'taken ownership' but which are in fact outgrowths of pre-existing local traditions; examples include the Hungarian Rezso Lavotta, who 'identified a parallel between American jazz and Hungarian folk music' and Czech writer Bohumil Karásek who described jazz as a folk art analogous to Moravian dances (Jankowsky 2016: 265). One of the features that have at various stages of its history been held as distinctive to jazz is its physically compelling rhythmic character, a confirmation of its African sources. It has therefore been a source of puzzlement to discover similar effects in white European musics, such as the syncopated implications of the Scottish Snap (Garcia 2017: 44, 45; for a revelatory history of the Scottish Snap see Tagg 2015).

In his 1927 monograph *The Appeal of Jazz*, R. W. S. Mendl discussed minstrel show plantation presentations and identified the foot-tapping of the banjo player as a marker of the primitive Negro. Hovering over this is the European art music tradition, while in fact such corporeal gestures appear to be universal among folk or vernacular musicians. But the formal feature of jazz which is now most pervasively identified by Euro/US writers as its distinctive character is the central role of improvisation. Although the repertoire of the Southern Syncopated was wide-ranging, reviews from 1920 foregrounded jazz content and the ability to improvise, with particular mention of Sidney Bechet (Parsonage 2005: 154, 156, 159). In his 1927 monograph mentioned above, Mendl had recognised one of the features that distinguished jazz from classical music: 'the jazz players will introduce actually unrehearsed effects into the performance', and enjoy 'the privilege of changing the notes' (cited in Parsonage 2005: 55). Through the music's historiography, improvisation has continued to be the much-vaunted discriminator of jazz practice (see for example throughout Berliner 1994). Yet among the early practitioners, the rote memorising of parts was more common, with improvisation a way of filling sections that could not be recalled (Raeburn 2011: **7**, 34); the site of the jazz genius simply grew out of what could be called musical mumbling.

But the most powerful argument against this identification of jazz exceptionalism is the simple fact that improvisation is not the sole prerogative of jazz. Bulgarian writer Vladimir Gadzhev noted that critical commentary on jazz tends to ignore improvisational practices in other musics (cited Levy 2016: 93). The Manouche tradition that informed Reinhardt's work is perhaps the best-known example, but in France it can also be heard in French *Chanson* (as in the accordion backing to Edith Piaf's 'L'accordeoniste', at www.youtube.com/watch?v=Vhu-0IBZm5s, accessed 2 January 2019). While improvisation is definitive to jazz, it is not distinctive to it. Bohlman and Plastino point out that improvisation is practised in Portuguese fado and Indian fusion and Naroditskaya argues that the strong improvisational component in Aijerbaijan mugham 'endows native musicians with an intimate understanding of jazz' (Bohlman and Plastino 2016A: 6; Naroditskaya 2016: 100). The following descriptions could be from a romanticised history of jazz: the 'music does not tolerate notation. If you play music from notation, what then do you need a soul for?', and the musicians are 'autodidacts and ear players, performing a vast repertoire of songs and dances by heart and by ear, improvising while playing, spontaneously, from the soul and heart'. But they are describing contemporary Serbian brass band musicians (Gligorijević 2019: 30th page of unpaginated draft of chapter 3). Luca Cherchiari suggests that the tradition of improvisation is so strong in Europe that we could reasonably infer that this was its source in jazz (Cherchiari 2012A: x). Far from being surprised by these affinities, we should expect them, given that, in the words of Derek Bailey, 'Improvisation enjoys the curious distinction of being both the most widely practised of all music activities and the least acknowledged and understood' (Bailey 1992: ix; see further Nettl and Russell 1998). In contrast to Western art music's sacralisation of the written score, improvised music is often valued more highly than pre-composed, as for example in the Middle East (Nettl and Russell 1998: 7–8).

In the context of such observations, we begin to understand that classically, conservatoire-trained musicians are historically not the norm but the aberration. Gunther Schuller wrote that 'African native music and early American jazz both originate in a total vision of life, in which music, unlike the "art music" of Europe, is not a separate, autonomous social domain' (cited Hersch 2008: 21–22, n. 8). As Elsdon argues, the reference point for the exceptionalism of jazz remains Western art music (Elsdon 2019). The problem is created by maintaining this as the reference point, the standard against which other musics are found to be deviant. But it is this standard which is deviant in the larger historical picture. In most societies, including pre-Enlightenment European, the musical norm has been as part of a 'total vision of life', in relation to which it is European art music that is the 'Other'. Much might well be learned about jazz by, instead of fencing it off, locating it as part of that larger historical tradition occupied by non-jazz popular music traditions.

Authenticity

One of the major ways in which jazz is 'fenced off' is by the idea of 'authenticity', deployed so blandly by jazz writers, particularly those with a deep investment in the canonisation process. Of course jazz is not the only form of music to fall under its shadow (see further Allan Moore 2002), but it set the template for modern popular music. As early as 1919, a reviewer in *The Daily Herald* wrote of the visiting Will Marion Cook Orchestra 'At last we have the real thing. They had come straight from the cotton-fields of Georgia' (Parsonage 2005: 146). And already cracks are visible in the criterion of 'the real thing', since the band was in fact formed in New York, Cook himself was born in Washington DC (where his father was the Dean of the School of Law at Howard University), and he studied with Dvořák. Particularly under the influence of Panassié, authenticity has continued to be articulated as such (Cherchiari 2012A: xvi) and through such terms as 'the real thing' (John Lucas, cited Parsonage 2005: 36; Zwerin 2000: 537); 'genuine' (Morgenstern 2000: 767); 'sincere' (Turner 1984: 31); 'true' (Ielmini 2012: 201). Authenticity has resided in many qualities, but most perennially in 'blackness', which is why Morgenstern finds it 'ironic' that the first recordings of 'genuine' jazz were by an all-white band, the ODJB. The irony is of course self-generating, because it entirely depends on the *a priori* assessment 'genuine', or to put it simply, on a 'theory' that has remained obdurate in spite of the evidence – and evidence there is aplenty in for example Sudhalter's 1999 monumental history of white jazz musicians 1915–45 (see further below). The magnetic field of blackness can weaken with cultural distance; Havas explores a shift in Hungarian jazz from a race-based criterion of authenticity to an aesthetic/political one (Havas 2018: 11), but in whatever form, authenticity has been a ubiquitous weapon in the various jazz battles.

Yet, as the foregoing examples indicate, it is a quality that is conferred, not inherent (Moore 2002: 212) and as such is tenuous in the face of the evidence of actual practices. Garcia's 2017 *Listening for Africa* demonstrates abundantly how often even the best intentioned scientific researchers in search of the authentic heard what they wanted rather than what was there. In his interwar lecture/concerts, anthropologist Fernando Ortiz made much of we would call 'authenticity', presenting his field recordings of Yoruba, Bantu, Calabari Ganga and Dahomey Negroes in Cuba as being uncontaminated by any outside, modern, influences, 'conserved pure and orthodox' (Garcia 2017: 90). But the ideology underpinning the project was a further tactic of 'othering', of excluding that community and its culture from modernity, and in vain, since, as Garcia notes even in 'out-of-the-way' Cuba, people bought 78 rpm records, watched Mexican films, listened to the radio, and indeed often 'incorporated some of these tunes into their performances for anthropologists, folklorists and comparative musicologists' (Garcia 2017: 115). Feld's participant/observer ethnography in Ghana provides a detailed confirmation of the paradoxes and complexities of assigning 'authenticity' to tradition in order to distinguish it from modernity, by 'custodians of an invariant, anti-historical notion of black particularity to which they alone somehow maintain privileged access' (Gilroy 1999: 91). In his study of the revival of the Byzantine musical tradition, Tore Lind argues that the quasi-positivist distinction between modernity and the past is itself a feature of modernity (Lind 2012: 19).

There is a profound irony in the stridency of the 'jazz border patrol' regarding a music that, itself, could not have come into existence without completely unregulated borders. The earnest purists who arbitrate on what constitutes jazz and not jazz, who condemn its contaminations based on genre, race, ethnicity, place, gender, instrumentation, either singly or in permutations, are defending the static standards of purity and authenticity in a music that is inherently mongrel and in constant transition. The history of jazz, including the one authorised by the guardians of its borders, is a history of fusions, hybridities, syncretisms and generic violations. These processes are *constitutive* of the music and its history. As Brusila has argued in relation to World Music, hybridity itself has become a new marker of authenticity (Brusila 2003: 13–21). There is some warrant for referring to an art music performance as authentic if by that is meant its fidelity to the score, but simply transferring that criterion to a jazz performance is clearly inapposite. In jazz studies, the more prominently the criterion of authenticity is displayed, the more threadbare it looks.

Blackness

Of all the issues woven into the idea of authenticity, none has been a more vivid and ubiquitous motif than race, 'jazz any-and-everywhere is about the place of race in musical history' (Feld 2012: 6). From the earliest diasporic reports of the music, it has been recognised that it is marked by black African influences. The resonance of that influence deepened as black aesthetics were increasingly politicised after World War Two, and echoes still in bitter exchanges over the ownership and provenance of the music. The issue remains the subject of high profile public debate: when the 2016 film *La La Land* was being canvassed as an Oscar favourite in early 2017, it became the subject of virulent attack because, in the words of Ira Madison of *MTV News*, 'If you're gonna make a film about an artist staying true to the roots of jazz against the odds and against modern reinventions of the genre … you'd think that artist would be black' ('The La La Land Backlash: Why Have Critics Turned on the Oscar Favorite?', *The Guardian* 6 February 2017 online at www.theguardian.com/film/2017/feb/06/la-la-land-criticism-race-gender-jazz-awards, accessed 7 February 2017). This echoes the extreme position of a statement by Gunther Schuller who declared of jazz that 'every musical element … is essentially African in background and derivation' (cited Youngren 2000: 20). At the opposite pole, Richard Sudhalter's 1999 study of the contribution made by white musicians to jazz in the first half of the twentieth-century documents in intimidating detail the tenuousness of the black/white binary, including through a continuous process of shared innovation, mutual exchange and admiration.

There are abundant overviews of the issues and the literature in which the subject of blackness and African sources is set out, including the following highly selective sample of work just in the twenty-first century: Horn 2002; Gennari 2006; Tucker 2011; Garcia 2017; Burke 2019. These, and the body of literature of which they are representative, demonstrate unequivocally that while blackness (which itself takes various forms) is central to the discourses of jazz in the US, what is at stake changes from place to place and from time to time, generating all manner of paradoxes and strange bedfellows. The 'blackness' of jazz could be deployed to confirm the primitivity of African-Americans, their exclusion from the cultural commonwealth, from the superior refinement of white America. But at the same time, it could represent the purchase which African-Americans had in the most powerful musical emblem of US modernity. Very broadly speaking, in historical terms, although both positions were evident at any moment, the trajectory was from the former to the latter, corresponding to the increasing artistic legitimation of the music. US African nationalists made it a political as well as a cultural and aesthetic issue (Gennari 2006: 251–298). At other times black US musicians including Ellington, Max Roach, Roland Kirk, Miles Davis and Yusef Lateef have had reason to disassociate themselves from the word (Bohlman and Plastino 2016B: xiii–xiv; Heffley 2012: 391). The strategic paradox at the heart of all this is that the jazz narrative simultaneously ennobles black American jazz musicians by an account of this 'progress', yet at the same time roots them in a genesis myth of primitivity, of ancestral Africanism from which it is difficult ever to liberate themselves. Garcia amply documents the inescapable dilemma by which black American musicians trained to the highest levels of Western art music were obliged instead to undertake careers in which they 'performed' African-ness, a dilemma re-enacted in the controversial 2018 film *The Green Book*.

African origins and African-Americans have been as strong a presence in discourses outside the US, but while the term 'blackness' has been freely exported, like the term 'jazz' itself, what it signifies is as protean as in the US, each local force field generating different semiotic charges. It has received attention within the general terms of the black diaspora and the pan-African movement (for example Gilroy 1999; Born and Hesmondhalgh 2000B; Monson 2003; von Eschen 2004; Feld 2012; Garcia 2017). Specific regional/national studies confirm in detail the problematic status of blackness, as we have seen for example in the way it affected the receptions of the music in the USSR and in the Third Reich. In the UK, in contrast to the US, because of the comparative sparseness of a black population in the UK during the nineteenth century, jazz often found itself haloed by an appealingly exotic aura of a 'Black Harlem' transposed to London clubs (Parsonage 2005: 5; Studdert 2013). The case of France has attracted considerable attention (see among many examples, Nettelbeck 2004; Jackson 2011; Braggs 2016), and its much vaunted hospitality to the idea of blackness was not shared throughout Europe. Hitler's Third Reich was by no means the only site of eugenics, which was in fact far more widespread than post-war sensibilities found convenient. In Sweden, in 1921 was founded the Swedish State Institute of Racial Biology with a mission 'to protect the Swedish race from contamination from inferior races' (van Kan 2016: 39). As we have seen, the migration of jazz was also the migration of the idea of blackness, and one could not be discussed without the other. Recent discussions can be found in Burke (2019), who refers to the cases of Shanghai, Brazil and South Africa, and the last of these has also been explored in detail in the work of Ballantine (1993, 2003, 2011, 2019; see similarly Duby 2017; Eato 2017).

Such studies document the self-evident generalisation that displacement from the US material and intellectual environment produces a radically different perspective on the race issue in jazz historiography. Studies of South Africa disclose the incandescent convergence between a music coded as 'black' and a local tradition of deeply racialised power relations. But compare this with, for example, a national community perceiving itself as being a white mono-culture for which jazz was actually its introduction to the concept of race, as in the case of Iceland (Rastrick Forthcoming: 19th page of pre-publication draft). In turn, however, compare both South Africa and Iceland to Australia, where the 'White Australia' policy survived into the late 1970s, and to its trans-Tasman neighbour New Zealand. Unlike the case with many South African musicians, even though Maori musicians were an essential and harmonised presence in the development of the local jazz culture, Bourke (2010) discloses no particular attempt on their part to exercise political leverage by declaring common cause with black Americans. Indigenous Australians on the other hand have been seen, as a group, as negligible participants in the country's jazz history. The country has its own egregious record in the treatment of its 'First Peoples', but the balance of power has always been so overwhelmingly white that the issue, simply (and disgracefully) has not held attention in any way comparable to the equivalent situation in the US. In spite of a pre-existing indigenous cul-ture, jazz in Australia has been almost exclusively a white narrative. Two indi-genous women who achieved recognition in a jazz context were sisters Heather and Dulcie Pitt, the latter aka Georgia Lee. Both enjoyed national fame, and Dulcie also international success including singing with Geraldo (Neuenfeldt 2016: 201). Although she was juxtaposed with Billie Holiday in promotional publicity, Neuenfeldt's 2016 essay on her career is a study in the distinctive ways in which an Australian version of 'blackness' in jazz was negotiated. The very low profile of aboriginal participation in Australian jazz puts the issue of race into a perspective in which so many other forces are in play: the local history of race relations, of colonial dynamics, of local indigenous music traditions. Aesthetically/politically (the two so overlap that the distinction is tenuous) driven attempts to essentialise 'blackness', or 'non-whiteness' as a key to understanding jazz have clear and understandable purchase in the US, but much less so, or at least are more ambiguous, as soon as we move beyond its shores. It is not black and white.

In the coming chapter, I explore some of these problematic categorisations in greater detail.

5

PROBLEMATICS

With the possible exception of 'diaspora', which is specific to this study, the categories identified in the foregoing bridging section have received extensive critical attention throughout jazz historiography. I now want to turn in more detail to some others which have generally managed to camouflage their problematics or simply to conceal themselves from scrutiny, but which come under a stronger spotlight from the diasporic perspective.

Mediations: Sound Recordings

It has been one of the truisms of jazz history that that the dissemination of the music was enabled by modern media, particularly sound recordings, generally perceived as functioning to 'sonically capture the performance with as little interference with the music as possible, while also keeping it as close to the aesthetic of a live performance as the recording process will allow' (Bierman 2019: 209). As Bierman notes, however, like all mediations, as we have glimpsed above in the case of radio, we should not imagine this one as a clear conduit through which jazz unproblematically flowed from the source to the ears of its listeners, producing a 'pure' sonic image of the original. This is the status implicitly accorded the primary canonical text, the Smithsonian collection assembled by Martin Williams. Recording, like all mediations, was by no means a transparent and frictionless conduit. Jed Rasula asks the question 'What is the epistemological status of a technologically primitive artefact like a 1923 acoustic recording of King Oliver's Jazz Band? Is it a conduit, an acoustic window giving access to how the music really sounded, or is it an obstacle?' (Rasula 1995: 135). Media technology in general was both channel and filter. It is not enough to construct an account of the dispersal of jazz going in at one end of the media and simply coming out at the other.

These media, for example, determined which forms and examples of jazz would be disseminated, depending on access to record production, marketing, distribution, and also playback availability. Recordings made on the old 'hill and dale' system, for example, vanished from the archive with the dominance of lateral grooving. The selectivity of jazz dissemination because of the politics of the mass media set up definitions of the music which only became contested by later revelations. France was broadly representative in that available recordings gave primary exposure to white jazz bands before disclosing the work of their black models (Nettelbeck 2004: 37). Paul Whiteman's record sales made him a major influence on the perception of what 'jazz' meant, occluding the New Orleans and classic styles during the 1920s (Kernfeld 1988: I: 587). Because of what was available on record, one of the most important figures in Russian jazz, Leonid Utesov, took white vaudevillian Ted Lewis as his model. Perhaps the most celebrated case of the interventionist role of recordings was the late emergence of bop outside its seminal centre, New York, because of the infamous Petrillo-led union recording ban and shortages of raw materials diverted to the wartime effort, as noted above. Less noted, it was not only bop that was thus eclipsed, but highly progressive tendencies coming out of Swing (Nicholson 2014: 228–230)

Dynamics within the burgeoning media industries also determined whose work gained exposure and whose did not. In some cases, this affected not just individual performers, but entire regional communities. Like many others, the case of New Zealand demonstrates even further the inadequacy of the image of recordings as a straightforward mediator of the music being performed in any given time and place. Although exposed to imported dance and jazz recordings since the early days of jazz, 'the real birth of New Zealand's indigenous recording industry' (Bourke 2010: 155) had to wait until post-World War Two, since prior to that the monopoly on local recording was held by HMV who had no interest in local performers. Attempts to enter the industry by local players, notably the Radio Corporation of New Zealand, even into the 1950s, were stymied by HMV's control of supply, technology and pricing, threatening retailers with higher wholesale costs, and even a total embargo, if they carried recordings by emerging local labels Tanza, founded 1949, and Stebbing, founded 1950 (Bourke 2010: 155–164). The structure and politics of the glocal recording industry thus determined what jazz got recorded – it opened channels to the latest US sources, but not in a way that was evenly distributed internationally, nationally and intranationally; it affected the extent to which local musics were circulated.

Recording technology affected not only who was heard, but what was heard. This applies to sound balance and microphone types and placements (see further Corbett 1995: 237; Bierman 2019), but also, especially in early jazz recordings, instrumentation. The constraints recording placed upon percussion are well known, with a consequent effect on the way in which early recordings shaped the understanding of what jazz drumming was. Similarly, the banjo was popular in the recording studio because of its 'restricted frequency range and percussive penetration, especially when compared to the piano' (Parsonage 2005: 116).

What was heard was also a matter of repertoire and style, and in this, the recording company policies as well as technologies played a major role. Ronald Radano has traced the way in which the Arista record label shaped not only Anthony Braxton's image, but even his compositional aesthetics, including encouraging him to 'prepare short, accessible works for his first albums, highlighting his quartet music', which would encourage airtime (Radano 1995: 199). More generally, during the interwar period especially, by controlling repertoire record companies participated in a feedback loop that amplified the perception that only black musicians could play jazz, and that black musicians could play only jazz. Elijah Wald documents the pressures brought to bear on black bands to record only 'hot' material, as in the case of Fletcher Henderson's orchestra, even though in live performance their presentation of sweet and soft non-jazz material attracted great applause. Henderson was reportedly 'very disappointed at not being permitted to record his famous *Rose* medley', a medley of waltzes with 'Rose' in the titles (Wald 2007: 135).

While the tyrannies of the profit-driven record industry executives are very much part of the jazz mythology, less often noted is the collaboration in the racialisation of jazz by scientifically driven recording projects. Pekka Gronow has documented the massive ethnomusicological archive generated from the early days of sound recording. Germany's International Talking Machine Co (producers of Odeon Records), and Beka-Record, for example, both established in 1903, sent agents throughout the world to record artists. Beka recorded 1400 titles in Turkey, Egypt, India, Burma, Thailand, Java, Singapore, China, and the company was advertising material from these countries in its 1906 catalogues. ITM followed in 1906, its activity including a 10,000 franc contract to a 'Sheikh' in Egypt, reportedly at that time the highest price ever paid to a recording artist (Gronow 1996: 96). This kind of ethnographic enterprise had a sufficiently high public profile to be the subject of an article in *Time* magazine in 1937, reporting that 'using the same weapon as the phonograph salesmen, anthropologists and folklorists the world over are doing what they can to salvage the remnants of primitive music' (Garcia 2017: 108). The author (probably Winthrop Sargeant, *Time's* music critic) noted that some of the music from Africa 'shows rhythmic resemblances to jazz' (Garcia 2017: 108–109). The emergence of modern anthropology was closely linked to emerging sound recording technology (Garcia 2017: 94, 101). The connections between the industry ('phonograph salesmen') and scientific projects, between the preservation of 'primitive' music and jazz, are a corollary less often noted. Yet the synergies were prominent from the interwar period onwards. Reviews of Katherine Dunham's stage presentations made the connections between primitive musics and the origins of jazz (Garcia 2017: 109, 111). That is, the 'blackness' of the jazz genesis narrative was confirmed scientifically by ethnographic field recordings.

Recordings also intervened in the social function and artistic status of jazz. Parsonage argues that they gave impetus to the transformation of jazz from a dancing to a listening music (Parsonage 2005: 71). That is, the recording not only provided access to jazz, but helped to tilt it towards the category of 'art music', to be appreciated by close mental contemplation rather than by corporeal response. It was against this tendency that the Australian Graeme Bell band reacted with its 'jazz for dancing' policy with such success in London in 1947 (Johnson 2000: 154–156). Similarly, when fans whose only contact with US jazz musicians had been via sound recordings finally saw them on stage, they often experienced a dissonance. Armstrong's (1932) and Ellington's (1933) London performances disappointed many reviewers for compromising what they had come to admire as 'art', with commercial 'entertainment' values and vaudevillian retentions displayed on stage (Parsonage 2005: 239, 240, 249).

The opportunity to repeatedly play a recording also enabled close study of a music that, in performance, was transitory, and this became a pedagogical tool that also encouraged the participation of amateur musicians who lacked formal training (Parsonage 2005: 74). The recording opened up practitioner opportunities outside a professional elite and therefore outside their implicit as well as explicit regulation of membership of the freemasonry of musician. In conjunction with the record-centric clubs, they also created new performance spaces, a new and self-sufficient musical subculture with its own infrastructures. And, as we shall see below, the distinction between music and recording also affected gender politics.

Nation

In recognising the essential role played by modern media and its power relations in the dissemination of jazz, we should already be hearing an alarm bell about the value of geographical borders as discriminators in the formation of jazz. It was, precisely, radio's violation of national borders that required totalitarian regimes to devise strategies through which to address the threat represented by jazz, ranging from proscriptions relating to wireless reception, to attempts to create jazz forms that could be accommodated ideologically. One point to emerge from our overview of jazz under the totalitarian regimes of the Stalinist USSR and the German Third Reich was that there was a discrepancy between policy and practice (see further relevant essays in Johnson 2017C). Proscriptions in the 1930s from Moscow 'barely reached the Azerbaijani capital', Baku, where a distinctive jazz scene was sustained (Naroditskaya 2016: 103). The role and status of jazz in Vichy France was far more complex than the reductive myths about 'resistance' (Fry 2016: 184, 193). Putatively monolithic political formations are an inadequate guide to the local jazz culture.

The most ubiquitous formation deployed in diasporic jazz studies has been that of 'nation', which continues to affect the way jazz musicians are perceived and valued (Picaud 2016: 128). In engaging with diasporic jazz, the idea of nation presents itself as the most obvious structuring principle, but as we have seen, while this is a logical place to begin, it is best seen as a point of departure rather than a stable framework (see further Weisenthaunet 2007; Whyton 2012; Jankowsky 2016). Peter Soleimanipour, leader of the post-1994 revolution Iranian jazz group Atin explicitly sought to disassociate the band from the idea of nation (Nooshin 2016: 133), exemplifying a broader movement towards musical articulations of the tension between nation and culture, as explored in detail in the case of Serbia by Gligorijević (2019).

As discussed above, for example the case of 'Australian' jazz, to essentialise a national jazz culture is to essentialise national identity, eliding important sub- or intra-national heterogeneities. Particularly in the early period, a jazz culture was more often a metropolitan than a national phenomenon, as in the case of Hungary, Portugal, Brazil, Finland, New Zealand (Havas 2018: 6; Cravinho 2016: 83; Fléchet 2016:18; Johnson Forthcoming B; Bourke 2010: 42). Even within individual urban centres there were heterogeneities no less significant than in, say New York, and the 'Uptown/Downtown' distinction in New Orleans. In a city as small as Hobart in Tasmania, reed player Tom Pickering recalled a 'definite schism between established professionals and the Young Turks', the latter being the largely amateur jazz enthusiasts who differentiated themselves from the more traditional dance band musicians (Boden 2016: 118). Picaud has documented the way venues in Paris may be 'distributed in different locations, according to the type of jazz they play and the different music experiences they offer' (Picaud 2016: 129).

The example of Spain as set out by Martínez and Fouce discloses the limits of 'nation' as a conceptual umbrella for the study of music. 'Spain' designates a nation, but one that is riven into various sub-communities distinguished by language, culture and music. There is great heterogeneity encompassed within the physical and conceptual borders of Spain, both diachronically (even the Franco regime evolved) and synchronically, from place to place. This heterogeneity reflects not only the longstanding existence of internally differentiated indigenous communities like Catalan and Basque, but also the imported multiculturalism of increasing migration (Martínez and Fouce 2013B). Perchard argues that jazz in France during the 1970s was 'part of a much broader renewal of interest and faith in the country's provincial cultures' (Perchard 2015: 203). That is, the centrifugal movement of jazz was not just to diasporic metropolitan national centres, but more micro-localised than terms like France or Paris can disclose. Such studies underline the importance of highly localised communities in sharpening the blunt instrument of 'nation' as a discriminator. Ruth Finnegan's benchmark study of music in one city, Milton Keynes in the UK (Finnegan 2007), provides a model that has been replicated in jazz studies by, among others, Helen Southall. Her examination of the musician Will Field and the small, obscure, local jazz/dance band in which he worked in Chester, from the 1930s–1980s, draws on the work of Howard Becker, seeking 'an explanation for the long-term local success of Field and others like him' (Southall 2013: 51). Even more tightly focused is

David Horn's detailed analysis of one recording session, and the paths taken to it by each of the musicians (Horn 2013).

Moving from the micro- to the macro-, the national model tends to obscure one of the distinctive features of the 'jazz journey', that is, the transnational linkages it has established and through which it has been formed (see for example Nicholson 2014: 119–136). The dominant model framing diasporic jazz is that of nation, but that occludes internal heterogeneities relating to such factors as locality, class, and cultural identity, that often reach out beyond nation. These factors suggest different ways of mapping the diaspora, one example of which is provided by John Whiteoak's idea of an antipodean 'Tasman world' (Whiteoak 2009). He notes the extent to which Australia and New Zealand have shared colonial and musical histories, and how the commonalties in this 'intercolonial entity' provide ways of mapping their jazz histories, disclosing both similarities and differences in ways that would not be so evident when they are isolated within 'nation' bounded cells. This approach is richly suggestive of further variations, for example, recognising that the diaspora might be better understood through pathways that cross national boundaries. Thus, for example, there is likely to be more to be learned by a study of port cities in different countries than by the simple nation-based model. A comparative study of the interwar jazz scenes in, say, Stockholm, Liverpool and Shanghai, might well tell us more about the migration of jazz than an attempt to link each of those with rural inland jazz activity in each of those countries, under the umbrella of nation.

The most authoritative modelling for the transnational diaspora of black culture is that articulated by Paul Gilroy who 'shows how different nationalist paradigms for thinking about cultural history fail when confronted by the intercultural and transnational formation I call the black Atlantic' (Gilroy 1999: ix). The question of blackness is touched on elsewhere, but the point argued here is that jazz is an example of a global cultural form that cannot be contained by the simple idea of nation, as conceived geographically. One of the most detailed analyses of the 'Black Atlantic' in relation to jazz is Feld's exemplary study where he invokes the term 'jazz cosmopolitanism' to articulate the complex international networks that shape and are shaped by jazz in Ghana, through stories that are musical equivalents of 'political projects of creating global networks outside of the stranglehold of nation states', representing what he calls 'multilocal belonging' (Feld 2012: 48). Feld illustrates the point by tracing the complicated genealogy of the song 'All for you Louis' that greeted Armstrong on his 1956 visit to Ghana (Feld 2012: 218–219). He concludes that

> To understand Accra's jazz cosmopolitanism then returns us again and again to the acoustic motions of the Black Atlantic sound, to sonic shimmerings, the audible diasporic intimacy of place as washings in and out of race, and to the rich archive of transactional historical synthesis we have in these sound recordings charting hybrid modernities African, Caribbean, European, and American' (Feld 2012: 219).

Nation is a place to begin the study of the globalisation of jazz, but it takes us just so far, and one way out of the cul-de-sac lies in local studies that range from regional to micro-communities, as well as transnational perspectives. It is also productive to imagine alternative groupings, based for example on shipping routes, linguistic affinities, religious and political traditions that override geographical boundaries. Some sense of these possibilities is provided in the 2016 literary history of Europe edited by David Wallace, organised not according to national boundaries, but by various transnational routes. As Mischa van Kan argues throughout his study of the reception of Swedish jazz in the US, it is a dubious essentialism to reduce a jazz culture to the bland homogeneity implied by nation (van Kan 2017).

Genesis Myth: Geographical

The limitations of 'nation' in providing anything but the most provisional map of diasporic jazz, points to a more general difficulty with the application of geo-political formations in tracing the music's history, including its origins. The study of the international diaspora also turns attention back to the case of the US itself. New Orleans remains identified as the single point of origin, from which all flowed. Apart from the explicit narratives, the lace-ironwork imagery of Bourbon Street remains the international metonym for a jazz festival (see for example Eales 2013: 13). But a closer exploration of the intra-US diaspora presents nuanced alternatives, with music that we can identify as proto-jazz forms as pre-dating the 'first' jazz recordings in 1917, distributed widely in regions absent from the traditional jazz geography (Gushee 1994). While a great many of the earliest jazz musicians came from New Orleans, a great many did not, and their diverse origins, geographically and musically, are worth closer study. While accepting that the pri-macy of New Orleans in the origins of the music is 'irrefutable' Jeff Taylor, argues that a wide variety of 'syncopated styles' were evolving during the earliest years of the music, including New York, Chicago, the Southwest and the West Coast. 'The result was the bewildering variety of styles and ensembles heard on recordings of the 1920s, many of which have long been accepted as part of the jazz "canon"' (Taylor 2000: 41–42). Alyn Shipton provides provocative glimpses of various music-making practices which we associate with the birth of jazz, but scattered across the country, and from which jazz musicians would emerge, including black marching bands in Salisbury North Carolina, black church music in St Louis, and funerals in various centres. 'Many of the elements of jazz – rhythmic syn-copation, swing, melodic improvisation – were present in these bands' (Shipton 2001: 66–67).

This is sustained by the testimony of veteran jazz performers such as Joe Darensbourg, born 1906, who recalled that black string bands in his home town of Baton Rouge, 'are your first jazz bands', and George Morrison also remembered playing in a string band in 1915 in Boulder Colorado, a reper-toire that included 'Darktown Strutters' Ball': 'We played that as a jazz number'

(Shipton 2001: 30). Conversely New Orleans native Barney Bigard declared that during that the 1910s the local bands mostly had a violinist as a leader, and 'didn't sound anything like the jazz bands that you hear today' (Shipton 2001: 32). Once we loosen our grip on the New Orleans genesis myth, we begin to hear a much more dispersed account of early jazz activity: as for example Missouri-born Wilbur Sweatman's 'Jass Band' recording in 1917 (Shipton 2001: 38), and James P. Johnson and Lucky Roberts recalled as seminal pianists on the New York scene by Ethel Waters from the teens of the century (Waters n.d.: 105). Well-informed observer Leonard Feather declared it his 'firm belief that though New Orleans was a very important center, there were other cities where jazz was developing at the same time' (Shaw 1977: 278–279). One of the seminal jazz 'nurseries' was the Jenkins Orphanage Band in Charleston, South Carolina, the subject of an illuminating 1980 monograph by John Chilton. The list of alumni includes musicians who would go on to be major figures in the jazz world from the 1920s and on. Joe Helbock, who founded 52nd Street's Onyx Club, recalled hearing the Jenkins Orphanage Band at the Harlem YMCA at the age of 14 (ca. 1908), also 'jazz bands at Barron Wilkins' on Seventh Avenue and 134th (Shaw 1977: 54). Following his tour with Mamie Smith in 1921, Garvin Bushell joined the 'sensational' band at Leroy's at 135th and 5th in New York. It included many musicians who had come through the Jenkins Orphanage Band, 'and they could *play*' (Bushell 1988: 28; his italics).

During his extensive touring career from the early 1920s, Bushell recalled jazz bands active in Baltimore, where the musicians 'had more technique than the New York players … very fly, creative musicians. They also had the best banjo players in the world' (1988: 34), and he would later go on to join the band of Baltimore banjo player Elmer Snowden. In St. Louis he heard Charlie Creath, whom he called 'the greatest blues player of his time' (1988: 34), with better range than most New Orleans trumpeters; in general, 'the bands just out of New Orleans seemed more limited' (1988: 35). Bushell regarded Eddie Heywood's father in Atlanta as the 'top pianist of that day in the south' and playing in a 'modern' style (1988: 36). He also reviews an extensive pool of Harlem jazz pianists already active by the early 1920s, most now overlooked, including Alberta Simmons, 'one of the first pianists I heard that played a style that sounded a little different … fewer notes … more expressive … more drive. She played a swinging bass line – tenths seemed the dominant pattern; it wasn't a walking bass line' (1988: 20). Bushell himself came from Springfield in Ohio, a state that, in the context of the New Orleans profile, produced pioneer jazz musicians in surprising numbers, including Don Frye, Cecil and Lloyd Scott, Luther Wilson, Dave Wilborn, Quentin 'Butter' Jackson, Claude Jones, Earle Warren, Vic Dickenson and McKinney's Cotton Pickers came out of Springfield Ohio (1988: 9, 10). Likewise the now disdained Ted Lewis, whom Bushell recalled as his first major influence, was from Circleville Ohio (1988: xi, 1, 10, 18). The case of Lewis reminds us that, dismaying as it might now be to purists, the distinction between jazz and vaudeville style novelty was not a strong one. James Reese Europe's initial understanding of jazz was as the black theatre music in Washington (Bohlman 2016: 177).

Accounts such as Bushell's remind us that 'jazz' is a coverall term, but that there are actually many instruments used to play jazz, and each of those can have its own genealogy and local style, as in 'Texas tenor', 'Harlem stride piano', and Bushell several times refers to the distinctive quality of Ohio banjo players. He speaks of Harlem in the early 1920s as being a 'melting pot' in which various regional styles for different instruments were brought together:

> many styles from different parts of the country were introduced by musicians who came to live there. Johnny Dunn brought his style from Memphis. The clarinet style I played was something I just concocted there in New York. Dope Andrews was also a New Yorker. ... He hadn't heard Jonas Walker yet, or Honore Dutrey in Chicago. He was more or less the New York trombone style – also similar to what they played in the circus bands'
>
> *Bushell 1988: 23*

Bushell's early peripatetic career discloses a national sweep and exposure to regional styles that present a picture much more nuanced than jazz flowing out of New Orleans to the rest of the country. There was already an understanding and performance of jazz throughout the US, as disclosed in the glossary of musicians with whom Bushell worked (1988: 179–187). The New Orleans approaches were regionally distinctive and deeply impressed Northerners. But the evidence is that it wasn't a new music genre, rather, a new jazz style. 'Once in the world, jazz shows affinities and differences that question a place-based authenticity of jazz' (Higgins 2016: 359).

Genesis Myth: Cultural

As these examples suggest, the 'origin myth' as a cultural, as well as a geographical, construct is also far more complex than black essentialism and African retentions can disclose. The prominence of 'genesis' mythologies in histories of jazz deflects attention from the fact that the music is itself not simply the originary fountainhead of a diaspora, but a stage in a larger tangle of migrations, as diversely fed as the stream it feeds. New Orleans itself is a moment in a continuing diaspora, and jazz emerges from a far more heterogeneous weave of cultural threads than the black/white tapestry that underpins accounts of its beginnings. The fact that the city largely fades from the narrative after it has given birth to jazz has, as in the case of Africa, the effect of freezing its own cultural dynamism, not only in relation to what has followed, but also in relation to what preceded that moment. To explore the idea of what went before would 'demystify that which historians have rendered neat, tidy, and to some extent miraculous' (Pellegrinelli 2008: 39).

The basic black/white template for the cultural origins of jazz is starkly manifest in the durable formulaic opening evocation (predominantly by white historians, as for example Ramsey and Smith 1939: 7–8) of the music and dance events in New Orleans's conveniently named Congo Square, where we witness 'an actual transfer of totally African ritual to the native soil of the New World' (Gioia 2011: 4). There could be no more unqualified assertion of uncontaminated African retentions at the 'birth' of jazz. As in most if not all such essentialist models in the narrative, however, the proposition invites – and has received – closer inspection (see for example Raeburn 2011, 2012; Garcia 2017).

As Garcia's fine (in both senses) study of the subject has amply documented, while the sound of Africa is unquestionably part of the jazz amalgam, its transmigration is by no means, to use Gioia's notion, uncomplicatedly 'total'. The most frequently posited relationship between African cultures and jazz focuses on the commonalties in rhythmic feel, but when Mary Lou Williams performed with African drummers in Carnegie Hall, she found that they 'couldn't play the rhythm of jazz', and deduced that 'when the Africans were brought here as slaves, they lost the drum thing and developed a different style' (Garcia 2017: 223). A similar disconnection was reported by French ethnographer André Schaeffner who, having declared the African roots of the music in his book *Le Jazz* in 1926, was then 'dismayed' to discover that when he played jazz records to locals during a field trip to Dakar-Djibouti 'that the Africans paid no attention to the music' (Plastino and Bohlman 2016: 26). Franz Kerschbaumer's research led him to the conclusion that the 'melodic-rhythmic swing' drum patterns underpinning jazz since the 1920s 'have their roots in the rhythmic melodies of Northern European folk music', and that discussions 'with scholars of African studies … provided no evidence of any comparable rhythmic phenomena in the music of Africa' (Kerschbaumer 2012: 13).

It is of course recognised that 'black' origins were also mingled with European influences, but the latter have been overwhelmingly subordinated to the African heritage. More recent studies have given more recognition to this stream, particularly its contribution to tonality and repertoire (see for example Youngren 2000; Cherchiari 2012B). French writers since Delaunay have in fact argued for France as the birthplace of the music (as did Sidney Bechet; see Perchard 2015: 44), though often more for political than musicological reasons (Fry 2016). The personal testimony of New Orleans pioneers provides ample confirmation of the importance of European traditions. Opera, for example, was important in the musical upbringing of Louis Armstrong, Sidney Bechet and Jelly Roll Morton (Youngren 2000: 24). Even allowing for some intra-racial snobbery that assigned higher status to Creoles, and Morton's *déclassé* jazz enthusiasm, his account of his musical education assigns far more importance to the Franco/European aspects of his musical identity than to African. He identifies his antecedents as French and Spanish, and proudly declares that he was named after the Spanish king Ferdinand (Lomax 1950: 3–4, 32). His early music exposure was exclusively to 'classical selections' and he was first taught guitar by a 'Spanish gentleman', acquiring a repertoire that was strong on late Victorian parlour songs; his parents tried to steer him towards 'art music' and it was at an operatic recital that he was inspired to take up piano (Lomax 1950: 6, 8). On the basis of both primary and secondary sources, it is reasonable to assert that 'without European musics – and cultures – jazz itself would not exist' (Cherchiari 2012B: 98).

This being so, the arguably disproportionate emphasis on the African elements requires some furtive conceptual contortions in the attempt to locate jazz within the larger framework of 'American' music. The awkwardness is exemplified in the following, by no means infrequent, use of the term 'Americanisation': 'By the time Bolden and Bechet began playing jazz, the Americanisation of African music had already begun, and with it came the Africanisation of American music' (Gioia 2011: 5). This begs a question that takes us to the heart of the diasporic flow. Something is left out in this model: what was 'American' music before, or apart from, its Africanisation? Surely what is left out is the 'Europeanisation' of American music. The implication is that the European strands in American music were so 'natural' that they do not need to be considered as the outcome of the same diasporic process that Africanised the music. This makes no sense, in that it implies that prior to the European influence, there was no 'American' music at all. I take this up further below.

The same aporia is present in: 'The work song, another frequently cited predecessor to jazz, is more purely African in nature – so much so, that some examples recorded in the southern United States earlier this century show almost no European or American influence' (Gioia 2011: 8–9). Given that, by Gioia's own account, the first documented presence of Africans in the 'New World' was in 1619 (Gioia 2011: 7) – one year before the Pilgrim Fathers – what does 'American influence' mean here? It means that 'African-ness' is consigned to alien status in relation to 'American-ness'. Simply in terms of chronology, why might it not make more sense to talk about the priority of African influence, and why might we not think that 'American music' starts out by being 'African', that subsequently receives a European imprint? Was the African component of the populace musically silent until the nineteenth century? Of course not, and one of the first manifestations of African musicality was in fact of the kind that has later been so fetishised as central to jazz: drum rhythms, which were sufficiently pervasive as to have been banned by the eighteenth century – Gioia himself refers to the ban on the use of drums by slaves in South Carolina after the Storno Rebellion of 1739, and in Georgia the banning of drums, 'horns and other loud instruments' (Gioia 2011: 7). The traditional jazz narrative has it that African music became an influence on the 'centre', Euro-American music. Why not, by at least equally convincing cultural-historical logic, that European music became an influence on the 'centre', African-American music? The answer seems to be because of a colonialist model of centre and periphery, of cultural hierarchy, of the politics of 'othering'; *in simple*, of who is writing the story. Africans are an 'other' to the American self – a model of political subordination/domination translated to the cultural sphere. It would be productive to construct a historical narrative in which it was the

Europeans who were the cultural 'other', especially given that in the *mythos* of jazz authenticity, that is precisely where they are often located. That is, while originally the African influence is the American 'other', in the jazz narrative the 'other' became the 'white' culture. It is a question for further enquiry as to where and why this transition occurred.

A further problem with the black/white *schema* that frames the diasporic mix flowing into New Orleans is that blackness was not monolithic, as is widely recognised in the category 'creole', which itself embraced greater heterogeneity than the usual understanding as French, Spanish and African (Raeburn 2011: 413). And even this breakdown is far from adequate to articulate the complex multicultural profile of the city, which varied from precinct to precinct (Raeburn 2011: 399). Italians, and especially Sicilians, flowed into the mix, and within this category there were further cultural distinctions (Raeburn 2011: 414). The cultural melting pot embraced Jewish, Caribbean, Latin, Mexican in various permutations and combinations (Raeburn 2011, 2013; Santoro 2000). 'Blackness' was not just a racial characterisation, but had a cultural and class dimension, and many of these groups 'were identified under segregation as "black" (African Americans and Creoles of color). Within New Orleans's incipient jazz community, Jews and Sicilian Americans especially were ... exposed to African-American vernacular music culture' (Raeburn 2011: 390). In the eyes of 'the white elite, Sicilians were considered to be "non-white," as were Hispanics, Jews, Creoles-of-color, and African Americans' (Raeburn 2011: 403 n. 39). All of these groups brought their own traditions to their contributions to the music of the city as performers and teachers, and across their subcultural boundaries, producing a music distinctive to the city (Raeburn 2011: 392, 417). Thus, for example, Neapolitan song became 'part of the contribution to the making of jazz by Italian Americans' (Plastino 2016: 315; see similarly 313, 332 n. 7). It would be gratuitous to go on repeating here the detailed primary research cited in the foregoing. It makes the point clearly enough that in seeking to understand the diasporic flow out of which jazz in New Orleans emerged, the black (African)/ white (European) model is deeply misleading in what it leaves out, and with pernicious political implications.

I conclude by noting another of the cultural streams almost completely neglected in the standard histories, an omission with even more multi-layered political implications. Earlier I raised the question of what was 'American' music prior to either the African or the European traditions. The answer is so obvious, it is extraordinary how rarely it is brought into the discussion of jazz, all the more so because it is a pervasive presence in the primary sources: that is, the music of Native Americans.

Let us begin with the testimony of Jelly Roll Morton. The fact that his Library of Congress recorded reminiscences with Alan Lomax are coloured by self-aggrandisement is well recognised, but the following details would contribute nothing to that end, and I think may be taken at face value as recollections, especially given other supportive evidence. And Morton's account suggests that Native American culture, which I shall also call Indian, in the manner of my witnesses, was as much of a presence in the consciousness and festivities of New Orleans as was the European tradition. All Morton references are to Lomax 1950. He speaks about the proliferation of clubs and associations in New Orleans (including one called the Iroquois (11)), each with its own band that would publicly parade every Sunday (12), and recalls that one of the most popular clubs was called the Indians, even out-drawing audiences for the Mardi Gras parade. Their 'sign' was the call *Ungai-ah! Ungai-ah!*

> When I was a child, I thought they really was Indians. They wore paint and blankets and, when they danced, one would get in the ring and throw his head back and downward, stooping over and bending his knees, making a rhythm with his heels and singing – *T'ouvais, bas q'ouvais* – and the tribe would answer – *Ou tendais'*. [He provides the words of the song]. 'And then they would stop for a minute, throw back their heads and holler … They would dance and sing and go on just like regular Indians, because they had the idea they wanted to act just like the old Indians in years gone by and so they lived true to the Indian style. They went armed with fictitious spears and tommyhawks and so forth and their main object was to make their enemy bow (14–15).

What Morton's account makes clear is that the indigenous culture and its music were a living presence in the New Orleans community out of which jazz emerged, and, on the evidence of the 2011 television series *Treme* (On the DVD, see 'Special Features'>'The making of Treme'>'Beyond Bourbon Street'>'Iko Iko'), set in the wake of the 2005 Hurricane Katrina, although eclipsed in public perceptions outside New Orleans by the city's jazz branding, it remains so today. Raeburn notes the 'African American and Creole Mardi Gras Indian gangs who used tresillo as the ground rhythm for their chanting when roaming the streets on Mardi Gras and St. Joseph's Day', a rhythm which became a standard feature of 'second line' parades, citing the song 'Tu Way Pocky-Way' in Morton's Library of Congress recordings; the Mardi Gras Indian tradition was also documented by Samuel Charters (see *The Music of New Orleans:* 1958; Raeburn 2012: 24, 41). Morton himself adapted 'an ancient Mardi Gras Number, associated with the Indians and appearing in a strain of Robert Hoffman's "Dixie Queen Rag" of 1906, sometimes called "Tee-nah-nah" or "If You Don't Shake (You Get No Cake)"' (Schafer 2008: 205; the song can be heard at www.youtube.com/watch?v=KFrW2F3IvVo). Louis Armstrong recalled that 'with lighter skin than the average piano players', Morton got work in the District 'because they did not want a Black piano player for the job. He claimed he was from an Indian or Spanish race. No Cullud at all' (Shipton 2001: 92). Whatever the truth of this, clearly the claim of being an Indian jazz pianist was not stretching credibility.

Both groups were of course nationally dispersed, and Garvin Bushell had vivid memories of Indians in his own region: 'They still had Indians near Springfield and down in southern Ohio. I used to hear them sing when we'd go out to have our hogs butchered' (Bushell 1988: 5). It was his opinion that

> the influence of the American Indians on jazz has been underestimated. There were plenty of Indians back of our house in Springfield, and part of my family is Indian. There were Indians throughout the South, Southeast, and Southwest. When the slaves ran away, Indians often took them in because Indians hated the white man too. How do you think there came to be so many Negroes with Indian blood?
>
> *Bushell 1988: 19*

As two profoundly marginalised communities, it is not surprising that African-Americans and Indians would find much common ground. Doc Cheatham recalled that 'back in those far off days there was a lot of hanky-panky going on, between the Indians, the black folks, the white folks'; Cheatham's own paternal grandfather was a 'native North American Indian' (Shipton 2001: 16), and the roll call of black jazz musicians with Indian blood or family connections is as long as any other mixed ancestry category. It includes: Frank Trumbauer and, presumably, a Harlem pianist called Seminole (Gioia 2011: 94), Charlie Parker, Cecil Taylor, Anthony Braxton (Heffley 2005: 232), Lee Wiley, Mary Lou Williams, Oscar Pettiford (Shaw 1977: 258), Mildred Bailey's mother was Indian, and she threatened to sue anyone who anyone who wrote that she was a 'Negro' (Szwed 2015: 118), Garvin Bushell, Dave Wilborn, Harold Gossett, Ray Price, and Bill McKinney (Bushell 1988: 5, 6), and trombonist Claude Jones was 'half Indian, from Oklahoma … he used to whoop and do his Indian dance out in the street' (Bushell 1988: 13). Stiegler provides further lists 2009: iv, 43, 44).

These connections flowed into their music, as in the cases of performers from Morton as noted above, to Anthony Braxton (Heffley 2005: 232). Don Cherry recalled that 'in growing up, my parents have American Indian background, so I've always been listening to different American Indian songs and trying to have that feeling in my whole way of life' (cited Stiegler 2009: 42–43). As these comments suggest, American Indian music is one of the traditions flowing into the jazz stream. Native American music has an ancient heritage, and significantly it shares more with African than with early modern European music. André Coeury and André Schaeffner, writing in *Le Jazz* in the 1920s, recognised a wide range of possible influences on jazz, including 'Native American' (Mawer 2014: 46). Both are improvisatory (Nettl and Russell 1998: 5,6). It is instructive to compare the circle dancing in Congo Square described by B. H. Latrobe in the nineteenth century (Parsonage 2005: 107) with archetypal circular formations in non-Western and pre-modern dances, and most particularly with Native American dance formations. The music of both cultures also gives prominence to percussion, to *objets trouvés* instruments and voice (regarding the African tradition, this is recognised by Gioia 2011: 9–11), Garvin Bushell identifies Indian and Irish influences as of major importance (Bushell 1988: 19, and at www.youtube.com/watch?v=zaUwd_ lTNoA at 1'44" to 1'49", accessed 17 June 2018).

An extended account of these affinities is to be found in Morgen Stiegler's 2009 thesis, including general musical parallels and cross references (1, 5, 6, 9, 19, 22–24, 27, 32), the role of improvisation (27); circular dance (25, 26, 28), and broader cultural connections (2,7, 10 to 18, 20, 34). Apart from this unpublished Master's thesis, and relatively brief essays such as Welburn 2002, there is a sur- prising dearth of studies on the relationship between jazz and American Indian music, in spite of the data reviewed above. In their study of Western music's 'Others', Born and Hesmondhalgh write that 'it is not so much that the question of origins … takes the form of an essentialist ideology of the non-Western musi- cian, but, on the contrary that the myth of obscured or impossible or irrelevant origins is itself highly ideological … it can conceal and naturalise domination, both economic and aesthetic, in the cultural sphere' (Born and Hesmondhalgh 2000A: 30). In a similar vein, Howard Mandel paraphrases Norman C. Weinstein to the effect that the identification of Africa as the source of jazz 'would appear to be ideological wish fulfilment, rather than musicological history' (Mandel 2000: 561). The silence surrounding the synergies between the jazz and the music of Native Americans is emblematic of the politics that distort the entire narrative of the jazz diaspora leading to, as well as from, the music, within New Orleans and the US, and internationally. The story is a political one, about relations of power and ownership.

Gender

The mythology surrounding US jazz and its adaptation to diasporic sites manifests other silences that the canon brings with it, and one of the most striking of these relates to gender. While there are many areas of the history and definition of jazz that continue to be bitterly and loudly contested, there is relatively speaking a dearth of debates over gender. It is not my primary intention here to comment on the significance of gender in the history of jazz in the US, on which there is a growing and deeply researched literature, much of which is reviewed in Tucker 2011/2005, and again more recently in Rustin and Tucker 2008B: 10–19. My interest in the topic is firstly as it relates to sites outside the US. And within that category my main focus will be on the period in which, I argue, the feminisa- tion of the music was at its strongest, the interwar period, and particularly the 1920s. At the same time, however, this is the period in which it has been most overlooked: Ake (2002: 64) declares that 'jazz has remained, *since its earliest days*, an overwhelmingly male domain'; similarly Rustin and Tucker 2008: 16), '*From its birth* … jazz history and criticism has [sic] been couched in the language of nation, race, and masculinity' (all italics mine). Unquestionably jazz is aggressively masculinised, as has been abundantly documented (see, for example, Elworth 1995; Rustin and Tucker 2008: 17–19).

I want to suggest, however, this was not the case in the 1920s, certainly in diasporic spaces. The argument is framed by the role of the 'New Woman' in the understanding of modernity. Few associations were so internationally recognised (and feared) as that between jazz and the modern woman. Black American jazz musicians might be demonised as a threat to received values, but they were, for the most part, somewhere else. Young women, by contrast, were everywhere, and everywhere induced a nervousness among conservatives of both genders. Their new freedom was literalised in images of travel and flight (Melman 1988: 95). As early as 1917/1918 a London poster for the musical show *Going Up* by Otto Harbach and Louis A. Hirsch had presented women piloting an aeroplane into the sky (see Figure 5.1).

This foreshadowed the phenomenon of the jazz flapper as portrayed in the 1920s Australian sheet music for 'Flappers in the Sky', which spoke of how the young modern woman soared aloft leaving 'man, mere man' in her wake. The sense of emancipative transgression was graphically proclaimed on its cover, depicting an aircraft called Sky Pirate full of young women smoking, drinking and engaging in homo-erotic conduct (see Figure 5.2).

Even Al Capone, during his 1929–1930 prison term for possession of firearms, lamented the contemporary decline in values, complaining that the 'trouble with women today is their excitement over too many things outside the home.

FIGURE 5.1 Poster for the musical *Going Up*

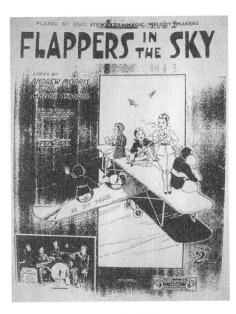

FIGURE 5.2 Sheet music for 'Flappers in the Sky'

A woman's home and her children are her real happiness. If she would stay there, the world would have less to worry about the modern woman' (Allsop 1961: 406).

In Portugal, writer António Ferro, associated modern lifestyles with women and their emancipation (Roxo and Castelo-Branco 2016: 204), an association also suggested in the English song 'That Ragtime Suffragette' (Parsonage 2005: 22). In her study of the flapper in the UK, Billie Melman cites primary sources that located the essence of modernity in young women (Melman 1988: 24), summarised in the image of the flapper, described in *Punch* as the emblem of women's literal enfranchisement, 'the catchword for an adult woman aged twenty one to thirty, when it is a question of giving her the vote under the same qualification as men of the same age' (Melman 1988: 29). For the conservative English press, the flapper represented all that was wrong with modern society, from the threat to patriarchy to international socialism (Melman 1988: 15–37). Unsurprisingly, one of the main points of focus of this gendered moral panic was sexuality. The 1920s saw an efflor-escence of novels and films presenting a sexual imaginary for young women that would have scandalised their Victorian and Edwardian mothers. Melman devotes a full chapter (1988: 89–104) to the mythologisation of the Rudolph Valentino 'lust in the dust' 1921 movie, *The Sheik*, based on the 1919 novel by E. M. Hull (Edith Maude Winstanley), which was so familiar that shot 14 of the shooting script for the 1926 film *Greenhide* (see further below) specifies that this is the book being read by its 'New Woman' heroine Margery. Popular music of the 1920s abounded with narratives about the liberated young woman, 'Wild Wild Women', as the title of the 1919 instrumental Murray Pilcer recording put it (Parsonage 2005: 123). In other songs she could enjoy her 'Breakaway' ('It's got the snappiest syncopation'), and amorous initiatives ('I've gotta have some loving … I'm burning up for kisses') (Johnson 2000: 119).

In an England in which the male population was reduced and maimed by war and traumatised by modern military technology, young women were inclined to take greater sexual initiative and engage with modern recreational technology with enthusiasm. The flourishing early silent film industry in Australian abounded in films about the new lifestyle and moral choices available to women, who also made up the bulk of cinema attendees (see further Johnson 2000: 69). In the 5 February 1920 issue of Harmsworth's *Daily Mail*, in an article called 'A Million Women Too Many', the overabundance of unmarried women is blamed for the decline of the family, and warned of the threat to morality of the 'modern independent girl' pursuing pleasure for pleasure's sake, and imaging this threat as 'the frivolous, scantily clad "jazzing flapper", irresponsible and undisciplined' (Melman 1988: 18, 19). The flapper is an ambiguous image in significant ways, simultaneously sexually predatory, yet also androgynous, marking a deep dislocation of the position of women, a heightened awareness of sexual and erotic possibilities, and the consequent sense of modernity's destabilisation of Anglo-European patriarchy.

Within this dynamic, it is unsurprising that young women felt a particular affinity with the most pervasive music of defiant modernity, jazz. The flapper's aggressive invasion of male spaces and androgynous appearance were deeply embedded in the idea of 'The Jazz Age', from images in lifestyle magazines to the jazzing Japanese 'moga' or modern girl (Atkins 2001, 102). In Finland, she gave her name to The Flappers Dance Band (all male). In Australia, she appeared in the silent film *Should a Girl Propose?* (1926), advertisements for which declared 'The modern Girl jazzes, smokes, and indulges in athletes [sic], enters law and politics, and, in short, does most things a man does, and in most things, does better. WHY SHOULD SHE NOT PROPOSE?', and her modern lifestyle accessories included the 'jazz corset' (See Haavisto 1996: 14; Johnson 1987: 6, 7, 8; Johnson 2000: 4; see Figure 5.3).

It was the modern woman who was most susceptibly attuned to the new music. In the advertisement for the film *Does the Jazz Lead to Destruction?*, shown at the Jazz Week in Sydney's Globe Theatre in 1919, it was Mr McWowse's responsibility to protect Mrs McWowse from the perils of jazz (though by the end of the week he too had succumbed; see Figure 5.4).

In John Bulloch Souter's notorious, and only briefly exhibited, 1926 painting 'The Breakdown', referred to above, a dinner suited black saxophonist is playing to a white woman who has removed her clothing and engaging in a trance-like dance (see Figure 5.5).

The foregoing is a very selective sample of the evidence. In terms of gender politics, women were the main conduit through which jazz entered the diasporic cultural consciousness, especially when the music was regarded as an imported challenge to embedded moral and socio-political traditions, a sonic impostume

FIGURE 5.3 Poster for the film *Should a Girl Propose?*

(see further: UK, Parsonage 2005: 21; Spain, Martínez and Fouce 2013A: 3; Portugal, Cravinho 2016: 97, South Africa, Ballantine 2011: 495; Ballantine 1993, 46–50; Australia, Johnson 2000: 59–76; New Zealand, Bourke 2010: 20). The Swedish song 'In Spare Moments' ('På lediga stunder') from 1929 lamented the modern woman's neglect of house-keeping and child-rearing in favour of dancing to jazz (Fornäs 2003: 218–9). Australian writer Dulcie Deamer reported that when women '*do* jazz', it was a form of 'mild … sex adventure' (Johnson 2000: 66).

Apart from the politics of the New Woman, there were a number of ways in which this gendering was consolidated. One was by virtue of the fact that during the interwar years women were a relatively frequent presence in jazz bands as instrumentalists. One of the 'Flappers in the Sky' referred to above is playing what appears to be a banjo or guitar, or, like Margery in *Greenhide*, a ukulele, all associated with what was understood as modern popular music, in particular, jazz. It was common to see women performing in the early diasporic jazz bands. Cravinho mentions the importance of imported orchestras in Portugal in fostering interest in modern dance styles, including all-women aggregations (Cravinho 2016: 90 n. 53, 92 n. 60). In South Africa black women were involved in early jazz groups,

FIGURE 5.4 Poster for Sydney Jazz Week

thus finding a public space through which they became models of female independence, as in the case of Johanna Phahlane, 'the versatile and brilliant founder
of the (all female) Merry-Makers of Bloemfontein' in the 1930s (Ballantine
2011: 495: Ballantine 1993: 46–50; a strong sense of the contrast post-World War
Two can be gained from Muller and Benjamin, 2011). In New Zealand in the
1930s there were many women in urban dance bands; Bourke lists Elsie Nixon's
Gala Girls Dance Band (Auckland), Wellington's McLoughlin's Ladies Band, and
Pemble's Popular Players led by Thelma Pemble and Wanganui's Tempo Teasers.
Pianist/singer Vora Kissin, secretary of the Newly formed Auckland Rhythm Club

FIGURE 5.5 John Souter's 'The Breakdown'

in 1937 at the age of 22, gave lectures on her musical experience in Sydney and on marijuana and its impact on the US scene; she also organised jam sessions (Bourke 2010: 60).

One of the reasons for the presence of women was that they more frequently received piano lessons as part of their preparation to become domestic acoustic adornments, and thus provided a pre-existing musical labour pool to meet demands related to new technologies. In New Zealand Women musicians, generally pianists, 'were often the backbone of silent film pit orchestras' (Bourke 2010: 60). Whiteoak has documented the same situation in Australia, noting that it was women who were most prominent in these early public improvisational practices (Whiteoak 1999: 14, 66. For further discussion of women in Australian dance/jazz bands, see Dreyfus 1999). It was not only as public performers, but in ancillary roles that women in Australia made a significant contribution to interwar jazz, as for example in the cutting of ragtime and jazz player-piano rolls (Whiteoak 1999: 148–149), radio MDs and studio accompaniment, as in the case of Beryl Newell (Johnson 2000: 119), and as teachers. Beryl Hayward (b. Beryl Williams?) wrote a memoir called *Jazz Pianist of the Twenties*. It is undated, but she appears to have begun her 'jazz career' in 1919 (Hayward n.d.: 13), even though she was probably pre-teen at that time. For some period between about 1922 and 1928 (in her teens), she played every night for dancing, including novelty numbers and 'In a Persian Market' 'to Jazz time' (Hayward n.d.: 18). Of dances at the Palais Royal and the Bondi Casino, she recalled that 'The Charleston, a hectic dance, became the rage but I preferred the English Charleston which was a kind of hopping and stepping dance to the tune of "Valencia" which I played often on the piano because of its popularity' (Hayward n.d.: 25). This memoir provides a rare if not unique account of how a young woman of the 1920s understood, and taught herself jazz, and as such is worth quoting at some length:

I had devised my own method of playing the piano, realising when one is the only person supplying the music there has to be more volume than music as it is written, so I played everything in octaves. A friend of mine, who is also a Jazz Pianist calls them chords. I fill in the other notes with my middle fingers. When playing for any entertainment it is also necessary to play from memory (or playing by ear as some people call it). It is not possible to play for a dance having to read music and turn pages over. I rarely play music as it is written. I improvise most of the time, except for a few tunes, and transpose in order to find a suitable key for people to sing to. I find the keys of F and C the most popular and to me they are the easiest to play. My mother was really fantastic. She preferred to play the black keys! However, I play "Moonlight and Roses" in 4 flats and "Oklahoma" is written in 5 flats which seems unnecessary so I transpose it into C and no one is any the wiser. I can memorise well over 200 old songs and some not so old, but I've never bothered with the latest 'hits' as I find them to be boringly repetitious and untuneful.

Hayward n.d.: 38

As contemporary band photographs disclose, Beryl Hayward was just one performer in a cohort of women who were significant if not essential in antipodean jazz from its beginnings. Australia's first jazz band billed as such was nominally led by an ex-London 'lady baritone' Belle Sylvia, shortly replaced by Australian Maybelle Morgan, who had worked in both the US and in the UK (Whiteoak 1999: 170). That this provoked no surprise suggests that, while the music was from the outset racialised by reputation, it was not yet gendered, nor was its primarily vaudeville setting conspicuously masculinised.

If this gendering seems surprising, it is perhaps because we forget just how deeply implicated the word jazz was with dance, that dancing was a means of creating jazz. In his study of the performers and entrepreneurs who provided entertainment in the Hongkew district of Shanghai in the 1930s, Atkins invokes the very useful model of a 'frontier' as a discriminator. And he identifies this frontier as 'hypermasculinised'. But not taken into account in this assessment is the fact that by the end of the decade there were between 2,500 and 5,000 women taxi dancers working in the precinct, a figure literally relegated to a footnote (Atkins 2011: 469 n. 22). It seems to me that declaring this a hypermasculinised frontier depends very much on how we understand 'performers' or 'actants'. And in the 1920s, dancing flappers were inextricably linked to the idea of jazz. In 1929 Konrad Haemmerling, writing in German under the name Curt Moreck, ruefully catalogued contemporary 'indulgences', in his book *Das Genuss Leben des modernen Menschen*, and included among them an illustration of 'Moderne Jugend (Charletonstunde)', showing a young woman in bobbed hair, tuxedo top and short dress, dancing the Charleston to a record player, while a young man and a grandmotherly figure look on in disdainful disapproval (Moreck 1929, 411, similarly

405). In a room decked with static images of an aristocratic past (ancestral portraits, coat of arms), this dancing 'New Women' is the centre of energy (see Figure 5.6).

The construction of phrases such as 'The modern Girl jazzes', or women 'do jazz', which now seems odd, only makes sense if, as we have seen, we understand that in the earliest stages, 'The Jazz is a dance'. And the dancing flapper is central to the image of jazz in the 1920s. A poem by C. L. Graves 'in the style of Swinburne' ca. 1926 includes the lines:

> And agile maidens, dainty and dapper,
> Sleeker of head than the orb of the plum,
> Each with her chosen whipper-snapper,
> Forth to the Foxtrot nightly come;
> And above the chatter of midnight meals
> The cornet bleats and the saxo squeals
> And the sandalled hoofs of the fearless flapper
> Follow the beat of the furious drum
>
> cited in *Johnson 2000: 59*

In the 1926 Australian film *Greenhide*, there is a jazz sequence extended well beyond plot requirements in which the heroine Margery establishes her independent New Woman status through an improvised unaccompanied dance in front of the band, her 'jazz solo' (See further Johnson 2000: 69–76). Such jazzing was the site at which young women publicly advertised their modernity and emancipation (in

FIGURE 5.6 'Moderne Jugend'

England, Parsonage 2005: 41; Lawson-Peebles 2013: 27; in Spain, Alonso 2013: 78, 80, 81, 82, 87). A woman journalist in New Zealand wrote in 1928 that 'We learn new steps with new, fascinating names, and we have forgotten the old dances and all the pomp and the ceremony that attended them. Today girls do whatever they like in the ballroom. Emancipated from chaperones and gloves and long skirts, they dart, unescorted, across the floor' (Cited Bourke 2010: 42).

I mentioned above that cinema attendance was one sign of the readiness of young women to engage with new recreational technologies in the 1920s. By the early 1930s, jazz was providing another, the use of the microphone in perform-ance. The following is based on arguments set out at length in Johnson 2000: 81–135), and which it would be gratuitous to repeat in detail here, so I confine myself to summary. With the increase in the size and noise levels of metropolitan ballrooms, it became necessary to increase the volume of the orchestras, leading to the formation of the 'Big Band'. In these aggregations, certain low volume 'voices' found themselves at a disadvantage, and from the early 1930s, were switching from various megaphone-based devices to experiments with electrical amplification, in particular, the bass, the guitar and the vocalist (see above). In the US the most prominent microphone crooners were men like Rudy Vallee (who took credit for introducing the vocalist's microphone), Bing Crosby and Frank Sinatra. In Germany women were virtually absent as jazz vocalists (Kater 1992: 69). With the Third Reich's sophisticated understanding of the propaganda potential of the technology, the public amplified voice was politicised and authorised through the male voice. Yet in Australia, the pattern is reversed. There are few surviving recordings of women singers in jazz contexts from the early 1920s, but from the introduction of the microphone in the early 1930s, women come to dominate as jazz/Swing vocal innovators.

To set out the full range of reasons for this would involve a separate mono-graph on Australian cultural history, which in the first instance reminds us that the jazz diaspora cannot be understood without reference to the specificity of its ports of call. In the case of Australia, the reasons are very much related to the balance of valorisations in such binaries as modernity/tradition, and urban/rural. In the earliest stages of white convict settler society, the physical survival of the community depended on the manly virtues that could 'tame' the land, hard and honest labour, the rural values of what in Australia is called 'the Bush'. A major reason is the conspicuous outdoors masculinism of Australian colonial history, when men had heavily outnumbered women (see for example Blainey 2003: 336; Macintyre 2004: 30, 71). The gender demographic, the reliance on primary industry and frontier expansion, underpinned nineteenth-century values and myths. To an unusual extent, the physical survival of this settler society was dependent on male strength and comradeship, and national character was defined through rural narratives associated with outdoor labour through which a man realised his spirit and resourcefulness and validated the work ethic. The city, on the other hand, softened and feminised, and exposed one to trivial diversions or at worst the depraved imported contamination of 'jazz parties'.

In this dynamic, modern urban lifestyles were emasculating and enervating. The main musical accompaniment to depraved modern lifestyles, jazz was decadent, transgressive, and its association with immodest modern dance and its most notorious exponent the young female flapper, carried the suggestion of degraded effeminisation. It is a narrative endlessly repeated in public discourses, especially in early Australian film (see for example the analyses in Johnson 2000: 69–76). In the patriarchal conservatism of Australian public life, the alliance between women and jazz was a powerful marker of cultural change (Whiteoak 1999: 66; Johnson 2000: 59–77).

All this provides a context for the Australian reception of microphone singing from the early 1930s. As mentioned earlier, the original function of the microphone in live performance was to make singers and softer instruments competitive with rising volume. But in a social context such as I have just crudely sketched, using a microphone was a sign of weakness, of lack of vocal strength. The 'crooning' enabled by the use of the microphone was widely regarded as degradingly effeminate. Al Jolson disdained it, and in general singers who had won their professional spurs by long and hard 'Bel Canto' vocal disciplines regarded the microphone as an insult to their masculinity, a 'demonstration of vocal infirmity, inadequacy or impotence' (Pleasants 1974: 39; see further Johnson 2000: 94–98). In wartime 1942 the BBC banned male crooners in order to increase the 'virility' of their popular music content (Baade 2008: 93, 104). British crooner Al Bowlly felt compelled to address this charges of effeminacy in a series of articles republished in Australia's leading professional music magazine in 1934, in which he recognised that to become a singer in the modern microphone manner is to risk the charge of doing 'something shameful and unmanly' (Johnson 2000: 96; see similarly McMullen 2008: 132). Put simply: for a male singer trained in the pre-microphone era, there was strong pressure against the use of the microphone, and especially in a society that accorded special value to traditional manly virtues of strength and self-sufficiency.

But it was no shame for a woman to be called 'effeminate', quite the contrary. Although there were male 'microphone singers' in Australia in the 1930s, it was largely a female domain. In turn, this meant that women were more active in experimentation with its possibilities in the field. Barbara James was probably the most famous big band and jazz vocalist in Australia in the 1930s. She had begun as a child playing both saxophone and xylophone under the mentorship of her father Will James who had led one of Sydney's earliest jazz bands. Possessed of a fine voice, she largely abandoned the instruments in favour of her more portable vocal skills, and made her first recording in 1933 (presciently, it was Noël Coward's 'Twentieth Century Blues'). Close analysis of her recording output from 1931 to the 1950s, together with a series of interviews I conducted with her, led to a number of conclusions that bear on the gendering of the development of jazz singing in Australia.

As the house vocalist with Frank Coughlan's orchestra in the country's newest metropolitan dance palais the Sydney Trocadero, which opened in 1936, she performed nightly, using a microphone to bring her volume up to the band level without shredding her voice. But she discovered that by deploying a 'microphone technique' as she called it, she could also develop different approaches to vocalising, one employing a guttural, closed throat 'dirty' style (as on her version of 'It Don't Mean a Thing' from 1937), and on the other hand, a more natural, almost conversational manner that eschewed the tendency to shrill high register projection of her first recording. Both of these pointed towards the development of popular music vocalising away from the declamatory projection of pre-microphone theatre, towards a 'black' ecstatic style and the understated intimacy of what was then called 'crooning' and which is sustained today in the work of such singers as Nora Jones. Had James been a male singer, it is highly unlikely that the imperatives of masculinity would have enabled this, as tends to be confirmed by the increase in the number of female crooners in Australia throughout the 1930s.

But there was a further outcome of this research which pertains to gender politics in a more unexpected, and perhaps more far-reaching way. The use of the microphone enabled a woman to project without artificially raising her pitch. From the time she began performing live with a microphone, Barbara James's register as disclosed on recordings extended downwards. The microphone enabled women be 'female' without deploying a shrill register. This represents a major change from the traditional connection between feminine sexuality and vocal register. In opera, contralto and low female registers generally signified undesirable women: older, villainous, witches. The desirable heroine was a soprano. The microphone, used in popular music, enabled them to project themselves as women in a more natural manner, rather like being able to dispense with tight dresses and stiletto heels. And finally, and even more important, as Margaret Thatcher recognised, there is a well-established connection between the projection of power and vocal register (Karpf, 2006: 226–229). The emergence of the microphone in (Australian) jazz vocal performance, and its associated gender politics, put women at the forefront of new vocal styles as well as enabling them to deploy a register that was both more natural and associated with a perception of increased authority.

The foregoing arguments raise the obvious question of why has the jazz narrative been so intensely masculinised, including in retrospect. The answer seems to be that this masculinisation was imposed during the decade or so following World War Two. Examining the neglect of the prolific career of outstanding black US pianist Hazel Scott in the jazz literature, Kristin McGee identifies the emergence of this now familiar jazz mythology from the late 1930s, that

> attempted to authenticate a romanticized, masculinized, and racialized image of improvised jazz, one that envisioned and even demanded a local

performative instrumentalism dissociated from earlier theatrical and visually mediated forms to assert its value in what was perceived to be a more
authentic, non-commercial realm.

McGee 2016: 421

This model gained increasing momentum in the post-war decade, part of a more
general attempt to push women back into the domestic sphere from which wartime conditions had to a large extent released them. Diasporically, this shift in
the centre of gender gravity in the jazz *mythos* is disclosed in fascinating detail in
Ursel Schlicht's study of Hot Club activities in Germany in the 1950s, focusing
on a debate in the music's leading journal in that country, *Jazz Podium*, founded
in 1952 (Schlicht 2008). In the April issue of 1956, Peter Kunst, director of a
Hot Club, initiated a forum on women and jazz with an article entitled 'Zur
Diskussion gestellt: Die Frau und der Jazz', prompted by his curiosity as to why so
few women seemed interested in his club's activities, and he invited women jazz
fans to join the forum (Schlicht 2008: 299).

Without rehearsing the details of the subsequent debates as presented by
Schlicht, in summary what followed was a disclosure of a shift in the culture
of jazz that was evident in mission statements in other German jazz clubs. To
express it in simple terms, jazz was ceasing to be a site of pleasure and becoming
a site of intellectual labour, partly as a way of distinguishing the music from its
'inauthentic' commercial forms (Schlicht 2008: 296). This micro-study is particularly valuable as a finely detailed manifestation of a process that was occurring
internationally: purging jazz of its associations with 'entertainment' in order to
locate it within a framework of aesthetic gravitas. But in addition, the *Jazz Podium*
disclosed the corollaries of this process in much broader terms: this aestheticisation
also involved the sacralisation of the record collection and its close study, and the
valorisation of the collector as the 'true' jazz fan (301, 302). The women who
participated in the debate argued that this intellectualisation of jazz engagement
represented a gendered distinction between the idea of 'joy and fulfilment', as
opposed to hard work in the engagement with jazz, but also insisting that the
former was a different but no less significant form of fandom (Schlicht 2008: 313).
One correspondent, Rosemarie Weibe, characterised the culture of collecting,
filing data, compiling dates, personnel, becoming an 'expert', as 'masculine', but
bereft of 'the spontaneity, vibrancy, and emotional liveliness of the music itself'
(Schlicht's paraphrase: 315). At bottom, the terms of the debate very much evoked
the woman=nature, man=culture stereotype. I am certainly not defending that
stereotype, but, rather, drawing attention to the fact that the changing status of jazz
from entertainment/pleasure to art/discipline from the late 1930s, from engaging
with the music through people (corporeal interactions like dance), to objects (analysis of recordings), was also felt to be a shift in its gender politics.

It is demonstrably not the case that jazz as it was understood during the 1920s
(certainly in its diasporic locations where it was so often seen as a threat to local

traditions) can be simplistically characterised as a site of masculinity, quite the contrary. The debates in *Jazz Podium* suggest that the gendering of, for example corporeal excess, pleasure, emotion, abandonment, all as opposed to serious intellectual labour, remained intact. In this connection a study of evolving performance deportment, gesture and costume is instructive (see further below). But these aspects of jazz were being increasingly banished from the 'authentic' jazz experience in the process of aestheticisation and intellectualisation. They went underground, disdained along with 'foot-tapping', dancing, and ecstatic abandonment. And as that happened, the 1920s complicity of women in jazz vanished under the new weave.

PART 4
Last Eight

Counternarratives and Further Directions

6

ALTERNATIVE METHODOLOGIES

Introduction

The foregoing study makes several arguments abundantly clear. One is that if we are to engage with jazz as the global phenomenon for which it demands attention, then its diasporic manifestations are essential to the story, for a range of reasons that include the simple quantitative fact of the extent of its international presence. But in addition, the discourses and infrastructures that have sustained it are themselves in many cases creations of the diasporic process and can only be understood as such. It is, furthermore, in the course of that process that the music has continued to develop new musical formations and practices as part of larger musical and cultural migrations that characterise the modernity of which jazz is held to be the musical exemplar.

This section introduces some of the larger implications of these extrapolations that constitute the remainder of this study. They involve revisions of jazz history and historiography, but also of the dynamics of the socio-political structures within which the music has lodged. Thus, for example, studies of jazz in authoritarian regimes have begun to reconfigure our understanding of totalitarianism. The standard canonical model shaping the story of jazz is simply inadequate to provide such insights. Apart from paying scant attention to jazz outside the US, its determination to characterise the history of jazz as an irresistible teleological ascent to an increasingly pure and distinctive art form, what Gioia, writing of the Armstrong/Hines 'Weather Bird', describes as 'jazz, pure and simple, freed from both the shadow of ragtime and the dictates of dance music' (Gioia 2011: 63), leaves out so much of what happened in the US itself. One result is the imposition of 'a kind of deadening uniformity of cultural meaning on the music' (DeVeaux 1998: 505). The canon has borrowed from Western art discourse a model of autonomous music which, dubious enough in the Euro-centric tradition, is clearly inappropriate to the conditions within which jazz flourished, writing out of the narrative anything that disrupts that tidy ascent to perfection of form (see further Walser 1995: 105, 171, 184). In the words of David Ake, 'jazz does not simply entail a smoothly evolving series of musical styles but rather an array of individuals and communities engaging with diverse, often-times conflicting, actions, ideals, and attitudes' (Ake 2002: 5).

This is emphatically *not* to argue for the abolition of a canon. In any history of cultural production, a canon is an essential reference point against which to construct a repertoire of alternative discourses that might reflect more effectively the specificity of the practice (Gabbard 1995: 6). The problem with the established narrative is not that it is US-canon centred, but that it continues to present itself as the only narrative, *The History of Jazz* (Gioia 2011). What is needed are supplementary parallel and counter-narratives. One such, for example, is testimony-based. Gioia goes on to assert that for Jelly Roll Morton, the dividing line between jazz and ragtime was 'elusive', leading to categorisations that 'few jazz historians would agree with' (Gioia 2011: 20). This foregrounds a number of issues relating to jazz historiography in general and the importance of the diaspora in particular. First, it is as clear a confirmation that one could wish for that the 'meaning' of jazz is itself a diasporic creation, for it says in effect that the community from which jazz emerged did not understand the term as it has later been articulated internationally. But at the same time, it is a solipsism that underlines a retrospective cultural colonialism pervading jazz historiography: the early New Orleans musical community did not subscribe to *our* understanding of the genre jazz, and so were clearly, at best, incapable of making the necessary 'subtle delineations', and at worst simply confused.

Personal Testimony

Rather than condescendingly declare that Morton and his contemporaries didn't know what they were talking about, an instructive alternative path here would be to ask why they articulated these positions. In fact, Morton never said he didn't have a clear understanding of the distinction between jazz and ragtime; quite the contrary, he articulated it with considered and pedantic precision (see for example Lomax 1950: 61–62). The problem is that it is not the understanding that was later sanctioned, based on subsequent diasporic developments that inform our 'hindsight'. *Why* were terms like 'jazz' and 'blues' applied to musics that, much later, we do not categorise in this way? That enquiry will take us much further into the cultural history of the music than a musicologically based *ex post facto* ruling that they should not have been. The two accounts *taken together*, are richly instructive regarding the history of the music and its discourses, and the diasporic process which is central to the dynamics of modern culture.

It might be argued that such testimonies are merely anecdotal and unscholarly, but if we trace most jazz primary sources back to their origins, they are generally anecdotal, ephemeral, or based on sound recordings, with their own problems addressed elsewhere. As a general principle of research, especially in the context of the New Cultural History (to which the New Jazz Studies can be regarded as cognate), it is important to 'let the subject speak', and thus distribute the evidentiary burden more evenly, supplementing rather than displacing other primary sources. Discussing Louis Armstrong's professed admiration for the music of Guy Lombardo, which has dismayed so many purists, Elijah Wald observes: 'we cannot understand an artist like Louis Armstrong without making an effort to explore the breadth of his taste and education, nor do we do either ourselves or his memory any favors if we dismiss his opinions as ridiculous' (Wald 2007: 144). In a sardonic aside invoking André Hodeir's 1956 study, saxophonist Bruce Turner commented that the 'autobiographies by Billy Holiday and Bechet came closer to explaining jazz than all the clinical arguments about evolution and essence' (Turner 1984: 138).

The reference to Bechet's autobiography, however, should remind us that such testimony is itself not necessarily reliable. Burton Peretti (1995: 118) analyses the problems presented by the evidence of oral histories: the subject's veracity, the biases and background knowledge of the interviewee, the cultural, personal and historical positions of both. As Ake points out, Sidney Bechet's memoir *Treat it Gentle* was actually transcribed by Desmond Flower, John Ciardi and Joan Williams, and archived correspondence from Flower and Ciardi suggests that Williams 'interjected a great deal of rather florid prose between Bechet's commentary' (Ake 2002: 182). In many cases, for example that of Morton, we must accept that some self-aggrandisement might be at work, as Gioia recognises (2011: 36). And even the most dispassionately personal account is still drawn largely from memory, a process that is constructed out of a complex weave of that makes it a useful subject for analysis in itself, as in Michael May's account of the veteran Russian jazz musician Oleg Lundstrem. Lundstrem became interested in jazz in 1932 and worked through the worst period of Stalinism, yet insists that for him, 'oppression did not exist' (May 2000: 185). May's juxtapositioning of various historical accounts with these recollections exemplifies the value of drawing together disparate sources including personal testimony.

Jazz-Specific Methodologies

Framed by the appropriate checks, the particular case of testimony also points towards research models which are specific to jazz as a cultural practice. A music which not only has its own distinctive forms and performance protocols, but which has always been in conditions of such vigorous flux, is not going to be tractable to an aesthetic of fixity inherited from art music (see DeVeaux 1998: 505; Johnson 2011; Johnson 2002B: 102–107). One of the remarkable ironies of jazz scholarship is that at the same time as it glories in the exceptionalism of jazz *vis-à-vis* the Western art music tradition, it seeks to enclose, understand and validate it within an aesthetic paradigm derived from precisely that tradition. The limitation of the canon-based model is that in significant respects it elides the specificity of jazz as a practice. That specificity may be articulated under two headings. The first is the sonic modality of jazz – a distinctive phenomenological, cognitive and affective foundation. Hearing is not simply another way of channelling information that is also received visually, but an 'acoustemology' that sets up its own distinctive relationships with the particular cultural and historical moment (see for example Sterne 2003: 90–93; on the term 'acoustemology', see Feld 1994). These relationships produce various protocols for listening, 'listening dispositions', which have particular force in a music so dependent on the ear as jazz (Garcia 2017: 80).

This takes us to a second aspect of 'jazz-specificity'; that is, the distinctiveness of jazz from other sonic expressive forms. In the formation of the jazz *mythos*, those forms have most often been in relation to 'classical' music. The latter's narrative is also canon-based, with its point of reference the scored opus, which is inadequate as a way of engaging with jazz. The relationship between a jazz musician and a recording is so different from the relationship between an art music composer and a score, that linking them as 'texts' is deeply misleading. As suggested above, while there is some warrant for basing the idea of an *oeuvre* on scored music as the basis for defining and assessing the 'work' of a composer, that warrant disappears in the case of a jazz musician – apart from the obvious inappropriateness of the idea of a scored opus to improvisational jazz practice, even the recorded output represents the barest minimum of her/his 'work'. 'Work' means something different: even for the most prolifically recorded jazz musician, the sum of those recordings represents not only the merest fraction of her/his 'work' (see further Rasula 1995), but the ways in which musicians address a formal recording date is generally very different from the way they address the conditions of the weekly or nightly gig, where the music is shaped by an array of subjective, distracted memories coloured by conditions that are not musical or 'artistic' in the usual sense. A recording session could either be regarded as a trivial diversion from gig activity (see Condon's account of sessions with Fats Waller, Condon 1948: 158–162), or, especially in more recent years, as an occasion of high seriousness.

Even within a jazz musician's recorded *oeuvre*, the idea of the 'masterpiece' that becomes his contribution to the canon (again, the gendering is pointed – how many female instrumentalists are represented in the canon of jazz masterpieces?), represents an infinitesimal fraction of a body of recordings that is itself but an infinitesimal fraction of his 'work'. There is some logic in this process for a Eurocentric art music canon, based as it is on a body of scores that represent the sum of compositional output. But for the particular nature of jazz and the conditions which have nurtured it, these models have very little explanatory value. There is a significant tension between the 'great man/work' approach to jazz history, and the idea of 'representativeness'. As for all jazz performers, one recording of 'Ko-Ko' constitutes the merest fraction of a musician's performance output – and in a primarily oral form like jazz, performance is central. Parker himself said that his break on 'Night in Tunisia' (released as 'The Famous Alto Break') was a once-in-a-lifetime achievement: 'I'll never make that break again' (Russell 1972: 212). Furthermore, a focus on these rare 'masterpiece' moments by defin-ition does not give us the kind of representative sample of a musician's output that enables us to locate him in a working tradition. The fact is that

> the vast majority of jazz musicians do not perform in regally appointed con-cert halls or in hip downtown New York performance spaces. Rather, most gigs occur in all many of small-scale restaurants and bars. ... on any given night one can find in every city a group competently going about the jazz business of swinging, improvising, and creating a pleasant mood for dining, romancing, and dancing.
>
> *Ake 2002: 60*

The work of Charlie Parker, simply by virtue of its rare excellence (as we judge it), can give only the slightest glimpse of the day-to-day contours of the enfolding musical landscape. In principle, it cannot be a representative sample of what went on nightly in Mintons, in New York, in the USA or in the global context on which the claim of jazz's significance as a modern music is based. Parker had off-nights, on which he would have fallen back on the formulae which do in fact constitute the basic templates we are trying to discover as historians.

The great majority of musicians sustaining the music as hard-working jour-neymen would also provide a more reliable picture of what was actually going on, as well as being aspired to, than a single recording sanctified as a masterpiece. We know, for example, that Louis Armstrong's 'West End Blues' was not an effusion of spontaneous brilliance, but the outcome of a lengthy period of often more or less repetitive workshopping in performance (Harker 2011: 50). Gioia wants to judge ragtime by its 'finer moments' (2011: 20), and certainly there is a place for this kind of canonical identification of great works. But they are peaks that tell us little about the plains on which most jazz activity was conducted and through which the music – including the 'masterpieces' – was formed. This is all the more so in the case of assessments based on the analysis of solos not only deracinated from the other musicians against which they are constructed, but also from the larger soundscape with which the performance is negotiating. To gain access to some of what would be regarded as 'inferior moments', of ordinary, night-after-dull-night of the kind of performance from which the flesh of 'genius' has been stripped, is to hear the bare bones that define the basic structure of the music-in-practice. This will disclose a 'history' no less illuminating than those canonical works defined by how exceptional they are. It is instructive to hear diasporic bands before they have reached the stage of being indistinguishable from recorded source material which is itself not necessarily representative of the general standard of performance.

It is necessary to develop alternative narratives and methodologies, to continue to shift emphasis from the 'text' to the larger historical and cultural contexts, but also to think in terms of different kinds of discourse. These alternative 'off-centre' perspectives will also sustain a healthy scepticism about the criteria of evaluation that are deployed in jazz historiography, including the dubious instrument of 'authenticity' and its associated aesthetics. These include importations from 'art music' such as the autonomy of the text that transcends place and time, and the teleological model of a continuous process of refinement towards some Platonic perfection. It is notable that these models are rarely if ever applied to, for example, tribal musics that are situated as the static and irredeemably 'other'. This teleology is a privilege reserved for Western and Westernised musics.

The persistence of the centre (US)/margins (elsewhere) model is pernicious; even when the attention of canon-based writers goes beyond the borders of the US, the terms of evaluation remain US-centric, as in Mike Zwerin's assessment that Paris became 'the jazz capital of Europe', based on the number of expatriate US musicians who lived there (Zwerin 2000: 545). Increasingly, however, the hier-archical binary 'US/elsewhere' is being demolished, as for example in the writing of, among many others, E. Taylor Atkins (2001, 2003) and Stuart Nicholson (2005, 2014), and in Heffley's argument that the European free jazz movement marked the displacement of the US as 'centre' (2005: 91–95). Once the 'centre' is displaced, we are able to find interest and value in any performance as an engage-ment with place and history. This includes music played in the US itself. Sudhalter and Shipton are two of a substantial cohort of scholars who have observed a complex chain of touring 'territory' itineraries that nurtured as well as dispersed jazz well beyond the 'up the river from New Orleans to Chicago' mythology (Sudhalter 2000: 156; Shipton 2001: 51).

But the displacement of that centre/margins model, by which the jazz story is dominated and shaped by the US-based canon, invites us to think not just of new narratives, but of new narratologies and methodologies. As Scott DeVeaux argued, new supplementary narratives need to be created 'for an approach that is less invested in the ideology of jazz as aesthetic object and more responsive to issues of historical particularity. Only in this way can the study of jazz break free from its self-imposed isolation' (DeVeaux 1998: 505). If we can escape the canonical paradigm, which is tailored to a cultural tradition against which jazz is defined by its otherness, we are more likely to learn something by allowing the music to disclose its own theoretical and discursive frameworks. Indeed the idea that a single master narrative will accom-modate jazz is at odds with the diversity of forms and contexts that characterise the music, a point taken by Ake in his 2002 study: 'no single methodology dominates this book. Instead, my goal is to shape the analytical tools to the subject at hand' (2002: 4).

Narratologies

Apart from growing numbers of contextual studies exploring, for example, medi-ation and mediatisation, and, as in this case, the global diaspora, jazz scholars are investigating different approaches to the way in which the narrative can be structured apart from through the model of a canon punctuated by masters and masterpieces. These include the idea of jazz as a process, which 'tends to valorize change, risk, surprise, and the development or discovery of fresh varieties of expression and beauty' (Harris 2003: 120), and jazz not as a monolithic totality but as a set of textual and contextual threads each with own history, such as instrumentation, formal parameters, practices (improvisation, orchestration), gender, ethnicity, politics (Cugny 2012). Ake suggests a closer study of the music that moves away from the point of view of the composer/performer to the listener/consumer (Ake 2002: 290). Of course, whichever model one adopts is going to be porous: jazz audiences are not passive consumers, but 'produce' the music through forms of feedback in the moment, and performers must also be 'consumers', or there would be no co-ordinated collectivity. In the course of a carefully articulated argument about the limitations of sound recordings as jazz 'texts', Jed Rasula notes that a synchronic rather than a diachronic study offers its own distinctive insights into the music (Rasula 1995: 140).

Rasula also enlarges the horizon further by suggesting that 'history might already be inscribed in some medium other than writing, that truth might be conveyed by "word of mouth" or even the more fleeting record of rhythmic signatures in music and dance' (Rasula 1995: 137). This takes us beyond the question of what aspect of the music we study, to the alternatives to a linear, schematic cause-and-effect teleology which is inscribed in 'texts'. The established jazz narrative is colonised by textuality, by models of narrative orderliness, linearity, teleology, by figure/ground, centre/margins, like a well-composed story or painting. One effect of shifting attention away from that master narrative (black/male/US centric) to its 'off-centre' forms, its diaspora, is to destabilise all those models.

In seeking to articulate a system of explanations for the complex field of African retentions in various musics including jazz, Garcia resurrects the 1987 model of the rhizome as proposed by Deleuze and Guattari, which establishes 'connections between semiotic chains, organisations of power, and circumstances relative to the arts, sciences, and social struggles' (Garcia 2017: 19). We are moving here towards a challenge to the traditional idea of narrative itself, departing from the coherence of a classical scientific historiographical discourse. One portal to that other space is Henry Louis Gates's concept of 'signifying', paraphrased by Richard Middleton as a 'continual reworking of a "changing same" – as the master-trope of black cultural practice' (Middleton 2000: 73). Gary Tomlinson cites Gates's identification of signifying's use of repetition and revision as 'fundamental to black artistic forms', but also his recognition that this 'theory of criticism' is not exclusively black, and that perhaps 'critics of other literatures will find this theory useful as they attempt to account for the configurations of texts in other traditions' (Tomlinson 2011/1991: 33).

This is worth some consideration especially because, although originating as a mode of literary criticism, 'signifying' has become such a frequent model in jazz discourse. Although Gates recognises that it is not exclusively a 'black' model, he accords it Ur-status. But this rather reverses matters historically and hierarchically, and it is instructive to consider why that reversal has occurred. I suggest that 'signifying' is just one example of a rhetoric that is, in the larger historical context not the exception but the norm, and as such reflects an underlying non- and pre-scientific epistemology that is articulated in all expressive forms, from the graphic (painting) to the verbal (poetry), in medieval illuminated manuscript, and in music, from Hebridean hymn-singing to other ritual song. It is a way of conceiving the relationship between language and the world that lies outside the scientific model as articulated in the work of Francis Bacon and later institutionalised by the Royal Society. These in effect laid down the scientific principles of English prose, by which any function other than lexicographic denotation was anathematised as releasing ambiguities which would unpredictably enlarge rather than circumscribe meanings. What is most interesting about 'signifying' is not what it is, but why it has become so pervasive *in a race-based form*.

I suggest that the answer to this might well be the same as the answer to the question as to why jazz itself, a rich hybrid, has for so many people been reduced to a race-based music. Like 'signifying', the formal characteristics of jazz are not unique, but can be found not just in other black-based musical forms (gospel, blues), but in other musics that lie outside the Western art music tradition. As I suggest elsewhere in this study, it is not so much jazz that is 'exceptionalist'; the 'exceptionalist' music is Western art music. Signifying is one form of the vast 'Other' to the scientific discursive paradigm; jazz is one form of the vast 'Other' to Western art music. The question is: why identify that Other as 'black' when there are so many other 'Others' that are not? And my hypothesis is that this is underpinned by the very specific racial politics that framed the music's arrival when and where it did. It is, in short, a complex tapestry of racism in itself, woven out of the late enlightenment and colonialism, with all their own aporias and contradictions. I suggest further that, given the global dispersal and dominance of jazz in the twentieth century, it might well be the most instructive possible musical vehicle for the analysis of one of the dominant modernities that formed largely under the influence of white US, for whom the most immediately present, visible and troubling other was black.

The appearance of jazz in the US provided white society with a musical 'Other' that was simultaneously alien yet categorisable as such. It was intelligibly a cultural form, available to be bounded and described as radically Other in musical, aesthetic and moral terms, and could plausibly be attributed to the troubling racial Other – black Americans. As something recognisable as a form of social practice it could be accommodated within a cultural scheme, and as such could be controlled discursively, and in time also commercially. It seems to me to be no coincidence that over the same period that jazz as a set of musical practices became standardised and institutionalised, its historical narrative was also being tidied up.

As jazz internationalised it was generally accepted to be a music having roots in primitive blackness, but nowhere did that have the same intense meaning, the same ambiguous sensitivity, as in the US, nowhere else did blackness have exactly the same political resonance, nowhere else was it so important, and in so many ways, to articulate that connection, because by articulating it, by manufacturing the discourse, all that it represented could be then controlled. The jazz narrative is thus, in the truest sense, a myth, a collection of stories that 'made sense' of something that could not otherwise be explained, that situated the 'heart of (American) darkness' within a largely 'sense-making' scheme. That narrative cannot be translated wholesale into other cultures, simply because the specific configuration of US race politics does not exist in other cultures. Different 'Others' are needed to establish the resonance – Jews, for example, had to be recruited more prominently into the version fostered by the Third Reich. In the USSR, when jazz was 'Othered' negatively, it was as music of the capitalist US, and in fact one of its positive valorisations was based on the idea that it was the music of blacks, though it was the political subordination that this led to that became the centre of gravity. One avenue for understanding the dynamics of the global diasporas then is not just to think about how jazz was accepted and assimilated, but to pay more attention to how and why it was not, in what terms was it 'Othered'.

In this endeavour, it is useful to relocate jazz outside the domain of aesthetics. This is not to deny that it is music, but that the attempt to draw it into the dominant models of music aesthetics can only obscure its character. The creative dynamics of non-musical improvisation for example are likely to be more illuminating than those framing non-improvisational music, as in improvisational group theatre sports and other unscripted ('unscored') team activities. That shift may be understood as going beyond musicological-based methods of analysis to embrace a broader range of disciplines such as the 'new anthropology' anticipated by ethnographer Katherine Dunham from the 1930s and 1940s (Garcia 2017: 61). She also foreshadowed the possibilities of more radical alternative research modes when, as a dancer she evolved a terpsichorean 'discourse', or ethnochoreology, that also challenged prevailing scientific discourses in their attempts to engage with Caribbean music and jazz (Garcia 2017: 180–184). Her dance/music presentation *Heatwave*, premiered in 1943, incorporated a satire on 'anthropology's and jazz criticism's obsessions with the scientific pursuit of musical origins and its authentic iterations' (Garcia 2017: 181). It is thus a notable early refusal of the mediating analytic prose of scientific debate, in favour of the corporeal immediacy of dance and music themselves. Gilroy urges that in attempting to engage with 'black cultural forms', one has to recognise the 'specific dynamics of performance' (Gilroy 1999: 75). In light of my discussion above, however, I would locate such forms not for their black 'exceptionalism', but as high profile exemplifications of a more general category of non-textual or otherwise unauthorised forms of 'knowledge production' that have a particular predominance in groups subordinated and marginalised by such factors as gender, class, generation, place, race and ethnicity.

Epistemologies

That is, at the centre of what appear to be issues of 'ontology' – of what jazz is – there is a prior question of epistemology – how do we know and represent what jazz is? This is not just a question about documentary sources and evidence for 'what happened', records, documents, testimonies; it is more fundamentally: how do we *know*? By what means do we know? Do we know, for example by reading 'texts'? One of the reasons these questions can be asked of improvised music in general is because of its plasticity, and its open significations, as compared with what could be called visual texts: wherever it goes, even though of course its meaning changes, a novel, a printed poem retains its form; likewise a painting framed on canvas, a sculpture. So, too, music that is decisively scored. This does not apply to jazz in performance, which therefore invites us to think more carefully about historiographical method than we might do in relation to fixed and permanent documents (including sound recordings). In the words of Rasula:

> Having learned from the music how to hear the world differently ... few have been aroused to a corresponding revision of their writing practice, and those purporting to write "history" have never paused to examine the terminological and conceptual presupposition involved.
>
> *Rasula 1995: 153*

Discussing a famous recorded Miles Davis solo, 'My Funny Valentine' from 1964, on which there are notorious fluffed notes, Robert Walser argued that to understand Davis's success 'may require rethinking some of our assumptions about what and how music means' (Walser 1995: 167).

To a significant degree, then, as one of the escape trajectories from the gravitational pull of a canon-centric model of cultural history with its attendant fetishes of 'universality' and 'autonomy', this project is about historical method and even more fundamentally, epistemology. When we draw jazz into the paradigms of Western art music, its aesthetics, its teleologies, its sacralisation of the score, its regimentations and criteria of mastery, it is already understood that this is to enclose it within an alien template, a Procrustean bed which it will not fit without serious deformations. That deformation goes deeper than the aesthetic, to the question of epistemology, a way of knowing. It demands alternative and complementary ways of knowing culture and history, that recognise the place- and time-specificity of all cultural practices and productions, humanising them, embedding them in the realities of their circumstances.

7

CONCLUSIONS AND FUTURE DIRECTIONS

Introduction

This study has been an attempt to provide some answers to the question, 'What might we learn about jazz by escaping the gravitational pull of the US-centric canonical model which quarantines the music from broader fields of enquiry? Of the many escape trajectories, I have concentrated on the diaspora, which, especially in the early period, presents us with musics that are often regarded as unworthy of serious attention, raising the question of how we engage with music that, by all the analytical tools deployed by music scholars, is 'bad'. The paradox is taken up from various perspectives in, among others, Björnberg and Stockfelt 1996; Johnson 1994:40–41; Washburne and Derno 2004. How do we write about the 'mediocre' and formulaic jazz – and music in general of less than 'masterpiece' status - that serves the vast majority of musical appetites across the globe, even at high profile professional events, as in Goddard's account of a Nice Jazz Festival (Goddard 227–234)?

To turn our attention to jazz that lies outside the canon centred on musical masterworks offers the chance to locate it within a larger field of musical practices with which it has affinities. It is a manoeuvre that can expand the horizons of jazz studies beyond the field of music, however. Collective improvisation is, after all, the condition of everyday urban modernity, and the interactive dynamics in jazz practices have lessons for the conduct of civil society (Johnson 2000: 182). While music is capable of carrying, and even generating, serious social tensions (Johnson and Cloonan 2008), its therapeutic potential is a matter of common knowledge. And there are attributes of the jazz experience which can be deployed to that end with particular effectiveness. Both Ballantine and Feld have pointed beyond musical practice to larger issues relating to the welfare of the public sphere (Ballantine 2019; Feld 2012: 126).

The following discussion embraces what I believe are the most far-reaching arguments in this study. Its direction can be signposted by noting that the paradigm framing the canonical model and all its corollaries is based on an aesthetics that is fundamentally visual (see further Johnson 2013: 103–104). Its 'texts' are sound recordings, but the scholarly analysis of those recordings relies on converting sonic messages into written transcriptions, and this has become more so as the music has been increasingly conceived as moving away from the dance towards a more cerebral order. For this reason, the increasing 'material turn' in jazz studies is one of the promising signs for future development (Schuiling 2019), and a corollary to that trajectory is the growth of detailed micro-studies that have been referred to and exemplified in the foregoing discussions (see further Whyton 2019).

Micro-Case Study

I conclude this study by drawing together two dimensions of enquiry which converge on one aspect of jazz practice: corporeality and, more particularly, dancing. As we have seen, the two were virtually equated in the interwar period, and the severing of that equation is one of the most potentially instructive directions for further enquiry. This is partly because it is a site at which two apparently distant approaches to further research converge: cognitive theory and micro-case studies. As far as I am aware, dancing, in its broadest sense of expressing the self corporeally, is universal, transcultural. Yet the idea of a 'dance' as a formal social practice, is so culturally bound that simply deploying the term in that sense elides an enormous range of socially sanctioned practices. I begin with a 'micro' study in survey that, on the face of it, is situated at the other end of the spectrum from the broader horizons of cognitive theory to which I turn below. But for all the apparent distance separating them, each richly informs the other, macro theory in micro practice. And I shall stay with the connection between jazz and the body, in particular, dance.

Perhaps the most useful lesson to be drawn throughout the foregoing study is of the radical inadequacies of taxonomies that underpin the US-centred canonical jazz narrative, as frameworks for understanding jazz in its quintessential role as the archetypal music of twentieth-century modernity. The term 'jazz' itself, now understood as a practice conducted by musicians before an audience, elides what was central to the meaning of the word for the first half century of its history: a modern dance and a music for modern dancing. It still remains largely so behind that mythical space called 'the cutting edge'. If the current 'state of the art' means literally its current manifestations, then the state of the art is still quantitatively anchored in the mainstream spectrum, and in jazz venues around the world, it is still a music that is corporeally engaging, danced to, a 'foot-tapping' music.

But even to try to imagine ourselves in the great era of the connection between jazz and dance is to conjure an image of a dedicated site of leisure like a nightclub filled with couples enjoying a relaxing evening of re-creation through recreation, dining, drinking, courting, or a venue dedicated specifically to dance: a ballroom, a palais de danse. There is an orchestra of professional musicians with a command of up-to-the-minute developments in modern dance including US jazz and Swing influenced music. It is an image largely perpetuated in US-based cinematic narratives. 'The jazz is a dance', from Charleston to jitterbug, in which the dancers are lithe, hip youngsters fully competent in the latest jive moves, or formally dressed urban sophisticates in a nightclub or restaurant.

Let us consider, however, a brief case study that exemplifies the inadequacies of that imaginary in the diasporic realm, what is left out by that simple idea of 'going to a dance'. I shall take the example of a typical public dance event in Finland in the interwar period, because I happen to know this area well enough to be able to describe it with informed confidence. This account is condensed from Johnson Forthcoming B, but also supplemented by crucial local primary sources, retrieved and translated by historian of Finnish popular music and film, Anu Juva, to whom I owe a great debt of thanks for discussions enlarging my understanding of the field.

The venue for a demographically 'typical' dance at that time would be a rural village. If it is high summer, it is likely to be held on a wooden dance floor by a lake, or even at a crossroads. If indoors, as it would be for much of the year, it would be in the local community hall. Unless it was an exceptional occasion when, say a professional Helsinki dance orchestra like Dallapé was touring the countryside, the band would most likely be amateur musicians servicing villagers in the local area. Remote from the sophistication of a metropolis like Helsinki or Turku, at its most ambitious the instrumentation would probably be based on salon orchestras or the traditional Finnish brass septet the torviseitsikko, but with the addition of a drummer and with the violinist doubling on a saxophone if the band were intent on giving the younger couples the sense of jazz up-to-dateness. Even so, the repertoire would be highly traditional. (An invaluable archive from the Helsinki City Museum that includes photographs of dance and jazz bands from the period is online at www.helsinkikuvia.fi/search/ and search (in Finnish, 'haku') 'jazz', accessed 1 February 2019.)

What a public dance involved in that time and place bore almost no resemblance to its equivalent in the major metropolitan palais de danse produced by the inter-national craze for public dancing from the early twentieth century. The halls in which dances were held were usually owned or managed by local associations – sporting, agricultural, co-ops, local amenities groups. They generally manifested political orientations, Red or White depending on location. In the 1920s such associations would hold lotteries to raise money for local amenities, including schools, libraries or fire brigades. Pubs, one of the main public leisure sites in other Western countries, are notably absent from the list of leisure venues, because from 1919 prohibition was in force in Finland, and even after it was lifted in 1932, the sale of alcohol has remained tightly controlled by the government. Conducted in these club halls, the phrase 'community dance' should not conjure up an image based on more familiar Anglo-US models. In some parts of rural Finland, popular secular entertainment was regarded with some suspicion, associated with a Lutheran work ethic, and so opportunities for many forms of popular recreation were limited. These halls were venues for various community amenities and events including study circles (in the case of the Reds, these would especially promulgate the principles of socialism), workers' libraries, plays, choirs, poetry readings, and educational courses.

In such venues, public dancing events were part of a larger programme that incorporated various 'self-improvement' activities, at the end of which a dance might be held. 'Self improvement' apart, the programmes were a means of avoiding a tax imposed on dances, dating from 1914, originally fixed at around 10%, but raised as high as 50% during World War One. The rate was generally lower for dances sponsored by associations, and the tax was not finally lifted until 1989. The tax could also be avoided by selling the same tickets more than once (which presumably reduced the apparent number of people attending according to the numbers of the tickets remaining unsold). Depending on date and place, a dance was tax-free if it lasted no longer than one hour and was part of a larger programme of other events, such as poetry readings, plays, study groups. This impacted on the profile of dance musicians, since a mixed event meant that musicians who could also participate in other kinds of programme were in high demand. When dancing became prohibited, initially as inappropriate to the solemnity of wartime (beginning 7 December 1939 and continuing erratically until 9 September 1948), secret 'corner dances' would be held, either indoors or outdoors, sometimes subjected to strict police enforcement, as we have seen above. One way of circumventing the bans was to offer dance classes involving less than half an hour a day, or through private house parties, though these were considered public events if attended by too many people. And even at weddings, the married couple were permitted one waltz, with the guests allowed only to watch. The ban could also be circumvented by having another event – a play reading, a poetry recital for example – ready at a moment's notice from the lookout of a police raid.

As the reference to regional heterogeneities above sought to foreshadow, we cannot characterise these dancing venues monolithically in terms of demography, class or politics, all of which in one way or another intersect with the fostering of jazz, which increasingly spread into rural centres throughout the 1920s. Jazz was for dancing, but dancing and its venues were implicated in complex and heterogeneous contemporary dynamics. What this example of diasporic jazz and dance confirms is the importance of engaging with local practices and cultures if we want to build a working model of the full history of jazz as the template for modern music and its international migrations and coming-into-being. This was a dance in Finland in the first half of the twentieth century, a site of recreation, often courtship and memory creation. But notwithstanding the shared categorisation, the US-centred canonical model of jazz will tell us nothing about the distinctiveness of this diasporic jazz/dance event.

From Methodologies to Epistemologies

Given the ubiquity and durability of the jazz/dance connection, a case such as this is a reminder of how dangerous it is to generalise from essentialised categories. But if we drill down far enough, what is at issue here is not just methodological, but epistemological. Pondering the great appeal of jazz for South Africans in the mid-twentieth century, Carol Ann Muller suggests that an answer like 'cultural imperialism' is inadequate and we might well move to an answer 'that examines the nature of listening to music specifically' (Muller 2016: 294). I emphasise the word 'listening' here, rather than 'music', because I wish to draw attention to the fact that hearing is not simply a supplement to seeing, but as we have noted, a different kind of knowing, an 'acoustemology'. The way we deploy that form of knowledge can cast new light not just on jazz itself, but on the dynamics of glocalisation. There is a well-developed literature addressing different dimensions of these questions, with a valuable overview of various theorisations of music and its role in identity formation, its diffusion, and its cultural politics in Born and Hesmondhalgh (2000B). Since the late twentieth century these arguments have increasingly turned to the role of corporeality in music cognition and affect (see for examples Walser 1991, 1995; Leppert 1993; Sloboda and Juslin 2001). Because of the significant role played in jazz performance by memory and corporeality, it is also a promising platform for the further study of the perception and organisation of time (Doffman 2019). Discussions of kinaesthetics in the creation of music point us towards the role, nature and function of cognition in the music experience, and in particular in the case of collective improvisation and the concept of 'flow' (on kinaesthetics and jazz practice, see for example Pressing 1987, Johnson 2000 177–179, and on flow, Hytönen-Ng 2013).

Sonic Cognition and Jazz Studies

I wish to extrapolate from such studies towards relatively recent theories of cognition, articulated under such labels as extended mind theory (Menary 2010; Clarke 2011), embodied cognition (Weiss and Haber 1999; Chemero 2011), cognitive ecology (Tribble and Keene 2011), vibrant matter (Bennett 2010), kinaesthetic empathy (Reynolds and Reason 2012). While each of these has its own distinctive inflections and emphases, they are broadly united in questioning the sharp distinctions we make between cognitive and non-cognitive entities, thus problematising the mind/body split that has traversed studies of cognition, as articulated most famously in Descartes 'I think, therefore I am'; that is, the essence of the self lies in a separate cognitive centre.

   The following arguments have been set out in various publications (for sources on acoustic ecology, see Johnson 2017A, and relating to live music, Johnson 2017B), but as far as I am aware they have not been developed at any length in relation to jazz. I therefore briefly rehearse them here. The binary in which the mind is privileged over the body in our conception of human value, has under-pinned a neglect of the physical in the study of culture. This is reflected in the centralising of the mediating effects of culture and ideology in our interpretation of social practices, including music. Relatively rarely, however, is the question asked in music studies how our knowledge of these practices gets into the interpreting mind, that is, through a more enfolding mediation we call the body. And that mediation is itself no more 'transparent' than the ideologies it admits. How does the sensorium itself filter our interpretation of what is 'out there'? In the case of music, the primary sense is hearing, and it is useful to think of music first just as sound rather than as culture. This turns our attention to the mechanics of sound and the physiology of hearing, and how these 'mediate'.

The space in which we hear sound already begins to lay down the foundations of interpretation: the potential of reverberation, for example, to predispose the listener to a state of awe or fear has been recognised since antiquity. Like rever-beration, noise whose source we cannot easily locate, such as sound coming from above or apparently all around us, or low frequency sounds, will also set up unbalanced power relations that produce emotions ranging from irritation to awe to terror. The CRESSON sound research centre in France calls this the 'Ubiquity Effect' (see Augoyard and Torgue 2006: 130–139), and it has been understood and deployed especially by architects and dramatists from antiquity and down to film music composers and sound engineers. The reasons that we cannot locate these sources and the anxieties they therefore cause, are panhistorical, transcultural, and trans-special. This is because they are to do with the general physics of sounding and the physiology of hearing, the mediating body. Put simply the Ubiquity Effect is a function of where our ears are and how we locate sound sources.

The next stage in the journey of the sound to the interpreting consciousness is from the ear to the brain. But here again, physiology has priority over culture in the process of interpretation. Our first responses to external stimuli are emotional and are generated in the amygdala. The musical signal arrives at the amygdala via two paths, one of which travels through the auditory cortex, which can identify the precise nature of the stimulus by sorting through our memory, identifying a particular song we have already heard, for example. But the other path is direct from the ear to the amygdala, and is called a quick and dirty path. Quick, because that signal arrives first; dirty, because it has a lower level of discrimination, but is a primary survival mechanism, preparing us for fight-or-flight: I am not sure what I am hearing, but it is threatening. This response is involuntary, inescapable and almost irrevocable. This signal establishes a constraint on what culturally based interpretations we may then bring to a sound – it is normally impossible, for example, to interpret someone yelling in your ear as an expression of tenderness (see further Johnson 2008A).

Since what we think of as the body therefore plays a primary role in the for-mation of music affect, these processes raise the question of where the 'body' stops and the interpreting 'mind' begins, echoing a perennial debate over the tensions between sensuous and rational responses to music. And that question in turn destabilises the conceptual models that have sustained cultural theory, such as the binaries 'subjective/objective', 'culture/nature' and 'mind/body' (see further Johnson 2017A: 17–18). I want to emphasise the source of these perturbations. Although we conventionally think of ourselves as connected with the world through five senses, in our public transactions, most of these – touch, taste, smell – are regarded as either deficient in the articulation of complex exchanges, or simply inappropriate as public mediations, leaving sight and hearing as the main channels. Sight enables and reinforces the binaries I mentioned; hearing challenges them. Hearing is not simply a supplement to seeing, it is a portal to a different order of knowledge, with its own distinctive materiality.

I want to follow a line of thought implicit here, by means of acoustemology, to link a music like jazz (that is, collective, improvised, aurally processed rather than notated for the eye) to the possibility of breaking down the binaries rooted in the scientific revolution and Enlightenment reason on which a politics of separation is based. Jazz as sonicity (as opposed to score-based music) has particular aptness because, in addition to the importance of live performance, its global dispersal was so closely associated with twentieth-century sound technologies. In contemplating the African diaspora through music, Garcia recognises the importance of 'the materiality of sound' in relation to the rapid developments in sonic technologies over the 1930s and 1940s, and discusses the relationship between sound, space and affect (Garcia 2017: 75–76). Such reflections, along with Feld's work among the Kaluli community in Papua New Guinea (for example Feld 1994), open the door into an enormous space for a radical exploration of the relationship between Euro- and non-Euro-centric cultures of listening. We are accustomed to the fact that, in John Berger's words, there are 'ways of seeing' (Berger 1972); there are also 'ways of listening'. It is not simply that audition is generically different from vision neuro-physiologically, but that there are many species of audition differentiated culturally, what Garcia refers to in relation to hearing 'blackness' as 'listening dispositions' (Garcia 2017: 80).

Let us develop these observations in conjunction with the cognitive theories alluded to above, to make the point that there is a close affinity between audition and theories that question the division between mind and body. Cognition has been conventionally understood as a function of the mind. This has not always been so – 'to learn by heart' is a residue of a pre-Enlightenment assumption that the heart was an organ of cognition. But since Descartes, it is generally taken for granted that we receive information via the body, process it in the brain, and then represent the outcomes of that processing through bodily gestures, words and the manipulation of objects (like a pen, brush, keyboard). The array of approaches mentioned above, such as extended mind theory, question these assumptions, arguing that cognition is a larger complex feedback ecology involving 'mind', 'body' and their interaction with the external world – such as, in the present study, a musical instrument and an (active) audience: 'It is a thesis that takes the bodily manipulation of external vehicles as constitutive of cognitive processes' (Menary 2010: 21). Distributing cognitive processes beyond the brainpan clearly has radical implications regarding the status of the body. Our gestures and the material accessories they engage with are not 'mere' representations of ideas fully thought out in the mind. Gesture *is* cognition (see for example Goldin-Meadow, 2003: 242–244; McNeill 2005: 147–148, 195–206). In the model I am summarising, these physical 'gestures' are not just outward manifestations of thinking, *they are thinking*. Prevent them, and 'thinking' cannot take place. In the case of Barbara James's vocal experiments discussed above, we have outcomes that could not have eventuated without mutually reinforcing collaboration between her 'mind', the microphone, and her manual manipulation of the technology, an exemplary model of an extended cognitive system.

One benefit of theories of extended mind or embodied cognition is thus to give stronger recognition to what the church once called 'adiaphora' – social practices which seem to be a representation of inner belief, ritual gestures that are regarded as less important than internalised doctrinal positions. The rich potential of deploying adiaphora in our understanding of the relationship between music, gesture and belief systems is strikingly illustrated in Tribble and Keene's study of the essential role of the act of metrical psalm singing in the formation, not just the representation, of belief in the English reformed church in Renaissance England (Tribble and Keene 2011: 89–106). Similarly, in his study of Byzantine devotional singing, Tore Lind explores the relationship between sounding, ecclesiastical architecture and identity and belief systems: 'Right singing creates the correct unity of *doxa* (belief) and *praxis* (practice) that is the conservative essence of Orthodox Christianity' (Lind 2012: 160). The monastic chants are not simply the performance of religiosity: 'the musical activity is a means of creating and embodying a strong sense of group mentality and identity' (Lind 2012: 48). Proscribe the gesture and you extinguish the 'thinking'; those who sought to extirpate various devotional rituals, and those who died for them, all too well understood their essential role in shaping belief. Likewise in other secular 'adiaphoric' practices including handbooks of appropriate posture and mien for learning, reading and performing music. Ake (2002: 105) cites C. P. E. Bach's eighteenth century guide to performance practice, 'that a musician's facial expressions and bodily gestures are oftentimes – and should be – conscious choices, inseparable from "the music"'. These kinds of practices are usually regarded as being merely supplementary to the main business of composition and public performance. A 'cognitive ecology' approach gives us a far richer understanding of how essential these behaviours and their contexts are to the formation and maintenance of knowledge and belief systems. While the model might seem startling, it articulates what has long been implicit in a number of fields of enquiry, from field theory to gestalt therapy (see further for example Johnson 2017B: 22 and Garcia 2017: 74–75). Indeed, it is a disconcerting reminder of the power of deeply entrenched academic theory, to realise that the proposition that gesture is cognition is entirely consistent with common sense and common practice. Think of the person who is counting on her fingers, who moves his lips as he reads, a vote teller who points to those with their hand raised.

And, I now add, the complicity of mind and body in musically based improvisation. Drummer Cuba Austin recalled a recording session in 1928 with McKinney's Cotton Pickers, at which the sound of the musicians tapping their feet while playing was muffled, by removing their shoes and putting their feet on pillows, but which kept sliding away. The worst foot-tapping offender was reed player Prince Robinson, so Don Redman decided to lash his ankles and knees together. It worked until Robinson started his solo. He began to bob up and down 'with his feet tied together, and finally gave up in the middle of it – looked up at Don and said, "Aw, Don, I can't play tied up like this."' (Shapiro and Hentoff 1955: 191). The play of the body is most evident when performance is not regimented by a score (nor audience behaviour by the conventions of an art music concert), but in what has been called 'real-time composition'. This in fact is a way of understanding the role of kinaesthetics in instrumental improvisation. There are times when the mind, as a problem-solving engine of artistic design, simply drops out of gear, and lets the fingers do the thinking. Music improvisations are not shaped just by the creative mind, but by *bodily* memory and habit. That is what those hours of practice are for. Embodied cognition has been described as an extension of the 'bodily' or 'corporeal' turn in cultural studies (see further Sheets-Johnstone 2009). I now want to bring into convergence the foregoing discussions of theories of extended mind and sonic affect, to argue that jazz was the first globally influential music from the early twentieth century in which this 'bodily turn' and the idea of 'extended mind' were most clearly manifest. It is noteworthy that in one of the very few references to non-visual examples in arguments for extended mind theory, Clark refers in passing to jazz improvisation (Clark 2011: 24).

He also refers to dance. As we have seen, it appears that amidst all the heterogeneous understandings of 'jazz' in its earliest diasporic forms, it was universally associated with modern dance, and indeed often identified as such – 'the jazz', as in 'the tango', 'the foxtrot'. As such it signified a changing attitude to the mind/body relationship, with the corporeal being accorded more freedom. This was true for both the dancers themselves and for the performers (if that distinction can be made). I want to revisit the fact that most diasporic destinations received written reports of jazz performance well before recordings. In the case of Australia, these reports tell us at least as much about extravagant stage deportment as about the sound of the music. The following reviews all refer to performances in 1918 (all cited Johnson 1987: 4); the first was cited earlier in another connection.

> the 'Jass' band consists of a pianist who can jump up and down, or slide from one side to the other while he is playing, a 'Saxie' player who can stand on his ear, a drummer whose right hand never knows what his left hand is

doing, a banjo (ka) plunker, an Eb clarinet player, or a fiddler who can dance the bearcat.

Each instrumentalist is not only a skilled performer, but also something of a dancer and a humorist.

The act used to conclude with 'Oh! You Drummer', a rag in which the band apparently went mad, playing with heads, arms, and bodies swaying to the music. The drummer concluded by throwing all his instruments up into the air. The pianist stood on his chair playing the frenzied melody, while the trombone and saxophone players fell over totally exhausted, gasping for breath.

The pattern is further documented by John Whiteoak who also cites reviews that noted a connection between these physically rhythmic movements and dance, it 'helps the dancers to keep in time' (Whiteoak 1999: 177). This corporeal connection is also adverted to by drummer Jo Jones talking about rhythm: 'when an artist is performing on an instrument he breathes in his normal fashion, and he has a listening audience that breathes along with him', and if the artist is 'breathing improperly, it's like the audience is left with a little case of indigestion' (Shapiro and Hentoff 1992: 408). This throws attention forward to the role of 'mimetic participation' in theories of extended cognitive systems. Arne Cox discusses the role of mimetic participation in music experience: 'part of how we understand music involves imagining making the heard sounds for ourselves, and this imagined participation involves covertly and overtly imitating the sounds heard and imitating the physical actions that produce these sounds' (Cox 2006: 46).

Whiteoak also notes that this corporeal extravagance was a frequent feature of 'imitation African-American performance practice', including 1910s ragtime performers' (Whiteoak 1999: 177). The reference to African-American practice is a reminder of the general alignment of white (European) with rationality and restraint, and black (African-American) with abandoned physicality. This *schema* has of course been a perennial model in jazz historiography, as for example in the way Bill Evans has been represented (Ake 2002:99). This 'intellectualisation' is in vivid contrast with the earliest profiles of jazz activity. Whether as a flamboyant dance like the Charleston or as a band performance, jazz was perceived and performed as a music of corporeal excess, and all the more so in its diasporic sites. Photographs of the earliest Australian jazz bands prior to the arrival of the first US groups emphasise the kind of physical zaniness referred to in press reviews – standing at odd angles on the piano and drum stools, almost recumbent on the stage (see for example Will James's Jazz Band, Johnson 1987: 66). Likewise early cinematic footage indicates that in the absence of sound, a band proclaimed its jazz credentials by clowning and extravagant prancing about, as for example in the film *Greenhide* from 1926, in which improvised physical abandonment is equally displayed in the woman's solo dance that accompanies the band (discussed above).

Such images raise several lines of enquiry. Why, for example, did these 'cornball' performance representations tail off into the 1930s, giving way ultimately to the physically constrained demeanour of jazz groups from the 1950s, as exemplified by the MJQ. The usual suggestions relate to the increasing intellectualisation of jazz, but it appears there is also a parallel in material culture: the coming of sound film. In what is regarded as Australia's first sound film *Showgirl's Luck* (1931) a film about making a sound film, the band footage shows the same clownish animation as in the silent *Greenhide*. By the time of *The Squatter's Daughter* (1933) there is an important shift in the cognitive ecology of jazz: the acting conventions of the sound movie were more established, and sound film has made jazz gestures redundant: the jazz-inflected dance band manifests dinner-suited dignified composure. And as an umbrella over these suggestions, I think there is an argument to be developed that these patterns are most apparent in diasporic jazz. As a parallel, it is notable that comparisons with images of jazz events closer to 'home' (whether 'home' is New Orleans as compared with elsewhere in the US, or the US as compared with the rest of the world), suggest that the physical grotesqueries became more exaggerated with diasporic distance (for 'at home' examples, see the early sections of Keepnews and Grauer Jr. 1968). This invites further enquiry as to why there might be a connection between extravagance of gesture and diaspora, the importance of 'thinking' jazz corporeally.

The spontaneous corporeal flamboyance evident in early jazz performance and dance signalled new attitudes to the body. In his 'A idade do jazz-band' (The Age of the Jazz Band), first published in Brazil in 1922, Portuguese modernist António Ferro connected improvisation, spontaneity and the accelerated pace of life with jazz and modern dance, all proclaiming 'new perceptions of civilisation and the adoption of new guises, conceptual attitudes and relations with the body' (Cravinho 2016: 88). As we have seen, it was these 'relations with the body' that have underpinned some of the most strident objections to modern dance and jazz since the 1920s. A press report from 19 May 1921 lamented that a meeting of London dance teachers had decided that the 'shymmy' [sic] could be regarded as socially acceptable: 'Before Europe understood itself to have an obligation to educate the inferior races: now it copies them. Is this the end of the prestige?' Similarly in 1923 we find objections to 'savage dancings … real rhythmic epilepsy', 'a great musical chorographic [sic] drunkenness', linked with 'black Africa' (Cravinho 2016: 85). The nervousness about the corporeal dimensions of jazz was also evident later among jazz spokesmen themselves, dismissive of 'foot-tapping' music in their flight to the aesthetic high ground on which the canonical narrative was erected (see further Johnson 2002B). While Dave Brubeck lamented the intellectualisation of jazz that spurned dance (Shapiro and Hentoff 1992: 393, 409), Stan Kenton's high art aspirations for the music summarised the prevailing view among the 'progressives': 'The modernists deserve the credit for proving that jazz doesn't have to be danced to. As a matter of fact, I don't think that jazz was meant to continue as dance music' (Shapiro and Hentoff 1992: 387–388).

Vernacular dance does not carry the same cultural capital as instrumental skill. Dancing appears to be abandoned corporeality, instrumental performance is disciplined and more cerebral. In addition, dance is also more feminised – as noted in the earlier discussion of gender, the stereotypical image of the irresponsible 'jazz age' is the dancing flapper.

I want to suggest that it is the repudiation of the corporeal which stands in the way of jazz's potential as a platform for the further exploration of various forms of embodied cognition. Initially I also found the focus on performance deportment as opposed to sound in early reviews disappointing, but that was because I thought of these antics as incidental to the understanding of the music (except in foregrounding the sometimes-overlooked continuities between jazz and vaudeville). Studies of gesture suggest however that these stage antics are not merely incidental. A more far-reaching implication of these 'secular adiophora' is that if we want to engage with the jazz diaspora it is useful to think of gestural repertoire as actually integral to jazz consciousness of the time, rather than merely mannered attempts to represent the music – a forerunner of the performer and audience demeanour of rock and later 'headbanging' music. As such, it seems more than possible that part of the evolution of the actual sound of jazz (and other musics), is directly related to the evolution of its gestural vocabulary, including that of the 'audience'. Hence, the importance of close micro-studies of local sites of jazz experience that take into account the corporeal dimensions of those experiences in relation to the socio-cultural dynamics which frame them.

In the present context, the point is that, although anathematised for their physicality, in these forms of social conduct, it is difficult – I would say impossible - to disentangle the cognitive from the corporeal. In music performance, and especially in its least mediated forms like singing and dancing, where does the 'cognitive' end and the 'corporeal' begin? I repeat an earlier comment: the dancer is the dance. It is difficult to recapture now the conceptualisation, especially in its earliest diasporic forms, that 'The Jazz' was as much a dance as a musical genre. If a couple does the tango, do we say they are providing what is merely a representation of 'tango thinking', or would it be more accurate to say that they are 'thinking through tango'? It is part of jazz orthodoxy that at some point in its ascent to high art status the music was severed from dance and became a 'listening' music. That point is most often identified as the arrival of 'undanceable' bop. But, as an aside, in spite of the ubiquitous identification of early jazz with dancing, it had already been in some instances a 'listening' music. Examples include the Ylä-Opris Restaurant in Helsinki which presented high profile jazz but with a strict no-dancing policy (Haavisto 1996: 13), London jam sessions in the 1930s as recalled by Frank Coughlan, above, and in New Zealand from the late 1930s through the 1940s (Ward 2017: 174). Conversely, bop was evidently regarded as danceable: apart from the recorded virtuoso bop tap-dancer Baby Lawrence, Mary Lou Williams remembered seeing 'the Savoy Ballroom kids fit dances to this kind of music' (Shapiro and Hentoff: 1992: 351). Even some forms of 'free jazz', are 'much more body-related than is generally assumed' (Jost 2012: 282). Amiri Baraka noted that contrary to widespread belief, people danced to bop, and fans (as well as musicians including Dizzy Gillespie) moved between Birdland and The Palladium ('The Temple of Mambo) where they could enjoy the dance contests accompanied by the Afro-Cubans (Santoro 2000: 527). In general, jazz writing has neglected this aspect of the music, as Catherine Tackley has noted: 'the development of jazz criticism and scholarship has been intimately linked with the evolution of listening over dancing ... as the primary mode of reception' (Tackley 2013: 193).

These aporias aside, in its century-old history, in spite of a putative shift to a 'listening' music, jazz has remained a highly corporeal experience. As noted above, when the Graeme Bell band in England opened the Leicester Square Jazz Club in February 1948, in re-affirming the connection with dance they vastly increased the youthful following for the music (see further Bell 1988: 105–109; Johnson 2000: 153–157). English saxophonist Bruce Turner's account of his conversion to jazz is a familiar story. A friend played him a recording of Ellington's 'Hot and Bothered'.

> It made my feet tap, and I felt as if I wanted to shout for joy. I'd never felt that way about a piece of music. I believe I even crouched forward a little, head bowed in an attitude of respectful attention.
>
> *Turner 1984: 25*

The deep complicity between corporeal and mental responses had been imaginatively exploited by Hugues Panassié in his presentations on jazz. He sought to persuade those who attended his record sessions to experience jazz 'somatically rather than intellectually' (Perchard 2015: 30) and deployed elaborate gestural theatre which he invited his audience to mimic (Perchard 2015: 30–31). The discourse is littered with similar examples (see for example Benedikt 2006: 1′001′02′ to 1′01′22; Perchard 2015: 26) but the implications have scarcely been extrapolated. They run parallel with studies of 'flow' (see Hytönen-Ng 2013), and point towards developments in cognitive research involving mirror neurons, gestural cognition and extended mind theory.

The 'bodily turn' has begun to infiltrate jazz study, though generally *en passant*. Referring to the 'process model of musical identity', and citing Paul Gilroy's arguments about the connectedness of black identity formation and 'bodily significations', Born and Hesmondhalgh (2000B: 55) speak of the importance of gesture in identity formation. Bohlman and Plastino recognise that the jazz 'scene is not just an abstract space; rather, it assumes its identity through the physical places of jazz, around and on the *body*. The bodily presence of jazz is crucial to its most intimate attributes for the individual' (Bohlman and Plastino 2016A: 5). The argument is taken up by Claire Levy in her discussion of Bulgarian musician Milcho Leviev, in the Bohlman and Plastino collection, arguing for a 'natural interaction between musical and cultural, social, and psychological energies.

In other words, representations of the body, psychologically grounded forms of desire, and sociomusical action are in constant contact' (Levy 2016: 86).

Ake has pointed to some of the potential lines of enquiry into 'the way that musicians' bodily gestures reinforce certain possible meanings for their audiences while delimiting contrasting interpretations' (Ake 2002: 83), by reference to Bill Evans and Keith Jarrett, and the 'pivotal role that the body … plays for both of these musicians in communicating' (Ake 2002: 84). He cites Orrin Keepnews's liner notes to the 1961 Bill Evans Trio album *Sunday at the Village Vanguard*, which include the comment

> I find myself so absorbed that consciousness of my body disappears and I become as one large ear, equipped only with a psyche. I am not aware of the act of listening. I am suffused by the music and become one with the music.
>
> *Ake 2002: 90*

This kind of statement is not uncommon among rhapsodic responses to music, and we are inclined to interpret them as transcendence of the body, the body 'disappearing', leaving only the higher mind, as Keepnews himself implies, only a psyche. But in the context of the present discussion it is instructive to consider that it is 'consciousness' that disappears, the faculty separate from the body, or even that it is the *separation* that disappears, obliterated by the ear, by the phenomenology of listening; that is, to explicitly recognise the potential explanatory power of theories of extended cognitive systems. These approaches are re-establishing the linkages between thought, the body and the material world that had been severed by Cartesian dualism.

Nowhere is this more fully evident than in what has historically and culturally been the most widespread form of music making: collective improvisation. If we are looking for an extended cognitive system to study, we could not do better than to start with collective musical improvisation. If we retrieve the corporeality of jazz experience, not only do we re-establish a connection with what has been historically one of its more ubiquitous features – the dance – it enables us to situate the study of jazz centrally in the articulation of the emerging developments in cognitive theory. The diasporas were not incidental footnotes to the story of jazz, as implied in canonical narratives. They are essential to the importance of the music and to its narrative. If jazz had never left New Orleans it would have remained just another of the multitude of local folk forms that emerged out of America's hybrid formation. If jazz had not left the US, it could not have become the master template for the modern processes of musical globalisation on which its importance is based. Nor could its horizons have been so broadened as a potential site of radical innovation in such fields as cultural analysis and cognitive theory.

BIBLIOGRAPHY

In the course of this study, particularly in Chapter 2, I have made passing reference, often at second-hand, to a number of early jazz publications, but have not included all of them in this bibliography

NOTE: A number of the publications listed below were republished in various collections or editions. I provide details for both the original and the reprint in this bibliography, but my in-text referencing gives the date of the reprint, which is generally now more accessible.

Ake, D., 2002. *Jazz Cultures*. Berkeley, Los Angeles and London: University of California Press.

Allsop, K., 1961. *The Bootleggers: The Story of Chicago's Prohibition Era*. London: True Crime Library.

Alonso, C., 2013. Aphrodite's Necklace Was Not Only a Joke: Jazz. Parody and Feminism in Spanish Musical Theatre (1900–1939). *In:* Martínez and Fouce, 78–89

Altman, R., 2004. *Silent Film Sound*. New York: Columbia University Press.

Anagnostou, P., 2016. Towards a History of Jazz in Greece in the Interwar Era. *Jazz Research Journal*, 10 (1–2), May/November, 54–74.

Appel, A. Jr., 2002. *Jazz Modernism: From Ellington and Armstrong to Matisse and Joyce*. New Haven: Yale University Press.

Arndt, J., 2012. European Jazz Developments in Cross-Cultural Dialogue with the United States and their Relationship to the Counterculture of the 1960s. *In:* Cerchiari, Cugny and Kerschbaumer, 342–365.

Atkins, E. T., 2001. *Blue Nippon: Authenticating Jazz in Japan*. Durham and London: Duke University Press.

Atkins, E. T. (ed.), 2003. *Jazz Planet: Transnational Studies of the "Sound of Surprise"*. Jackson: University Press of Mississippi.

Atkins, E. T., 2011. Jammin' on the Jazz Frontier: The Japanese Community in Interwar Shanghai. *In:* Whyton, 463–474. First pub., *Japanese Studies*, 1999, 19, 5–16.

Augoyard, J.-F and H. Torgue, eds, 2006. *Sonic Experience: A Guide to Everyday Sounds*. Trans. Andra McCartney and David Paquette. Montreal: McGill-Queen's University Press. Originally published in French, 1995.

Baade, C., 2008. "The Battle of the Saxes": Gender, Dance Bands, and British Nationalism in the Second World War. *In*: Rustin and Tucker, 90–128

Bailey, D., 1992. *Improvisation: Its Nature and Practice in Music*. London: The British Library National Sound Archive.

Bakriges, C. G., 2003. Musical Transculturation: From African American Avant-Garde Jazz to European Creative Improvisation, 1962–1981. *In*: Atkins, 99–114.

Ballantine, C., 1993. *Marabi Nights: Early South African Jazz and Vaudeville*. Johannesburg: Ravan Press.

Ballantine, C., 2003. Music and Emancipation: The Social Role of Black Jazz and Vaudeville in South Africa Between the 1920s and the Early 1940s. *In*: Atkins, 169–189.

Ballantine, C., 2011. Concert and Dance: The Foundations of Black Jazz in South Africa Between the Twenties and the Early Forties. *In*: Whyton, 475–500. First pub. 1991 *Popular Music*, 10 (2), 121–45.

Ballantine, C., 2019. Jazzing for a Better Future: South Africa and Beyond. *In*: Gebhardt, Rustin-Paschal and Whyton, 327–338.

Barber, C., 2013. Recorded interview, Edinburgh, 26 July. Unpublished. My thanks to interviewer Martin Cloonan for a transcript.

Beale, C., 2000. Jazz Education. *In*: Kirchner, 756–765.

Bell, G., 1988. *Graeme Bell, Australian Jazzman: His Autobiography*. Frenchs Forest NSW: Child and Associates.

Bendrups, D. and R. G. H. Burns, 2011. Subject2Change: Musical Reassemblage in the Jazz Diaspora. *In*: D. Bendrups and G. Downes, eds, *Dunedin Soundings: Place and Performance*. Dunedin NZ: Otago University Press, 67–79.

Bennett, J., 2010. *Vibrant Matter: a Political Ecology of Things*. Durham NC and London: Duke University Press.

Berger, J., 1972. *Ways of Seeing*. London: Penguin

Bergh, J., 1991. Booklet accompanying the CD *Sigaret Stomp: Jazz in Norway 1940–1950*. Unpaginated. See Discography below.

Bergmeier, H. J. B. and R. E. Lotz., 1997. *Hitler's Airwaves: The Inside Story of Nazi Radio Broadcasting and Propaganda Swing*. New Haven & London: Yale University Press.

Berliner, P. F., 1994. *Thinking in Jazz: The Infinite Art of Improvisation*. Chicago and London: University of Chicago Press.

Bierman, B., 2019. Jazz and the Recording Process. *In*: Rustin-Paschal, Gebhardt and Whyton, 209–220.

Birdsall, C., 2012. *Nazi Soundscapes: Sound, Technology and Urban Space in Germany, 1933–1945*. Amsterdam: Amsterdam University Press

Bisset, A., 1987 *Black Roots White Flowers: a History of Jazz in Australia*. Sydney: ABC Enterprises (Updated from the original 1979 edition).

Björnberg, A. and O. Stockfelt, 1996. *Kristen Klatvask fra Vejle*: Danish Pub Music, Mythscapes and 'Local Camp'. *Popular Music*, 15 (2), 131–147.

Blainey, G., 1966. *The Tyranny of Distance: How Distance Shaped Australia's History*. Melbourne: Sun Books.

Blainey, G., 2003. *Black Kettle and Full Moon: Daily Life in a Vanished Australia*. Camberwell Victoria: Viking/Penguin.

Boden, M. J., 2016. Tom Pickering: Jazz on the Periphery of the Periphery. *Jazz Research Journal*, 10 (1–2) May/November, 109–125.

Bohlman, P. V., 2016. Jazz at the Edge of Empire. *In:* Bohlman and Plastino, 153–180.

Bohlman, P. V. and G. Plastino, 2016A. Introduction. *In:* Bohlman and Plastino, 1–48.

Bohlman, P. V. and G. Plastino, 2016B. *Jazz Worlds/World Jazz.* Chicago: University of Chicago Press.

Born, G. and D. Hesmondhalgh, 2000A. Introduction: On Difference, Representation, and Appropriation in Music. *In:* Born and Hesmondhalgh, 1–58.

Born, G. and D. Hesmondhalgh, eds, 2000B. *Western Music and its Others: Difference, Representation and Appropriation in Music.* Berkeley, Los Angeles, London: University of California Press.

Boulton, D., 1959. *Jazz in Britain.* London: The Jazz Book Club.

Bourke, C., 2010. *Blue Smoke: The Lost Dawn of New Zealand Popular Music 1918–1964.* Auckland: Auckland University Press.

Braggs, R. K., 2016. *Jazz Diasporas: Race, Music and Migration in Post-World War II Paris.* Berkeley: University of California Press.

Breen, M., 1997. Popular Music. *In:* S. Cunningham and G. Turner, eds, *The Media in Australia: Industries, Texts, Audiences,* 2nd ed. St Leonards NSW: Allen & Unwin, 143–162.

Brennan, M., 2017. *When Genres Collide: Down Beat, Rolling Stone, and the Struggle between Jazz and Rock.* New York and London: Bloomsbury.

Breyley, G.J., 2017. From the 'Sultan' to the Persian Side: Jazz in Iran and Iranian Jazz since the 1920s. *In:* Johnson 2017C, 297–324.

Brown, M., 2008. Let's All Sing! – The Community Singing Movement in New Zealand and its Publications. *Crescendo,* 79, 13–17.

Brown, M., 2011. Locating the Vernacular in the Māori Guitar Strumming Style. *In:* W. Pond and P. Wolffram, eds, *World Music is Where We Found It—Essays by and for Allan Thomas.* Wellington: Victoria University Press, 116–130.

Brown, M., 2012. *Making Our Own—Two Ethnographic Case Studies of the Vernacular in New Zealand Music: Tramping Club Singsongs and the Māori Guitar Strumming Style.* Unpub. Doctoral dissertation, Victoria University of Wellington/Massey University, New Zealand School of Music.

Brown, M., 2013. Off the Beaten Track: The Vernacular and the Mainstream in New Zealand Tramping Club Singsongs. *In:* A. Bennett, J. Taylor and S. Baker, eds, *Redefining mainstream popular music.* New York: Routledge, 177–189.

Brown, M., 2017, 'A Piano in Every Other House'? The Piano in New Zealand Trade Statistics 1877–1931. *New Zealand Journal of History,* 51 (2), 26–53.

Brusila, J., 2003. *Local Music, Not from Here: The Discourse of World Music Examined Through Three Zimbabwean Case Studies: The Bhundu Boys, Virginia Mukwesha and Sunduza.* Helsinki: Finnish Society for Ethnomusicology Publications.

Büchmann-Møller, F. and H. Welsgaards-Iversen, 2008. *Montmartre Jazzhuset 1 St. Regnegade 19, Kbhvn K, 1959–1976.* Odense: Jazzsign & Syddansk Universitets.

Burke, P., 2019. Race in the New Jazz Studies. *In:* Gebhardt, Rustin-Paschal and Whyton, 185–196.

Bushell, G., as told to Mark Tucker, 1988. *Jazz from the Beginning.* Wheatley Oxford: Bayou Press.

Cappelletti, A., 2012. Across Europe: Improvisation as a Real and Metaphorical Journey. *In:* Cerchiari, Cugny and Kerschbaumer, 123–140.

Carey, J., 1992. *The Intellectuals and the Masses: Pride and Prejudice among the Literary Intelligentsia 1880–1939.* London and Boston: Faber and Faber.

Carr, I., D. Fairweather and B. Priestley, 1987. *Jazz: The Essential Companion.* London: Grafton Books.

Cashman, S. D., 1989, *America in the Twenties and Thirties: The Olympian Age of Franklin Delano Roosevelt*. New York and London: New York University Press.

Celenza, A.H., 2019. The Birth of Jazz Diplomacy: American Jazz in Italy, 1945–1963. *In*: Rustin, Gebhardt and Whyton, 315–326.Cerchiari, L., 2012A. Introduction. *In*: Cerchiari, Cugny and Kerschbaumer, vii–xviii.

Cherchiari, L., 2012B. Sacred, Country, Urban Tunes: The European Songbook; "Greensleeves" to "Les Feuilles Mortes" ["Autumn Leaves"], "Gigolo" to "O Sole Mio". *In*: Cerchiari, Cugny and Kerschbaumer, 98–122.

Cerchiari, L., L. Cugny, F. Kerschbaumer, eds, 2012. *Eurojazzland: Jazz and European Sources, Dynamics, and Contexts*. Boston: Northeastern University Press.

Chemero, A., 2011. *Radical Embodied Cognitive Science*. Cambridge Mass and London: The MIT Press.

Chilton, J., 1980. *A Jazz Nursery: The Story of the Jenkins' Orphanage Bands*. London: Bloomsbury Book Shop.

Clark, A., 2011. *Supersizing the Mind: Embodiment, Action, and Cognitive Extension*. Oxford: Oxford University Press.

Clarke, J., 1994. *All on One Good Dancing Leg*. Sydney: Hale & Iremonger.

Clunies-Ross, B., 1979. An Australian Sound: Jazz in Melbourne and Adelaide 1941–51. *In*: G. Spearritt and D. Walker, eds, *Australian Popular Culture*. North Sydney: George Allen & Unwin: North Sydney, 62–80.

Collier, J. L., 1981. *The Making of Jazz: A Comprehensive History*. London: Macmillan (first pub. Granada, 1978).

Condon, E., 'Narration by Thomas Sugrue', 1948. *We Called it Music: A Generation of Jazz*. London: Peter Davies.

Cooke, M., 2008. *A History of Film Music*. Cambridge: Cambridge University Press.

Cooke, M. and D. Horn, eds, 2002. *The Cambridge Companion to Jazz*. Cambridge: Cambridge University Press.

Coplan, D., 1985. *In Township Tonight: South Africa's Black City Music and Theatre*. Johannesburg: Ravan Press. Note that an updated edition was published in 2007 as *In Township Tonight! Three Centuries of South African Black City Music and Theatre*. Auckland Park: Jacana. I am indebted to Jonathan Eato for this information, but have not been able to access a copy at the time of writing.

Corbett, J., 1995. Ephemera Underscored: Writing Around Free Improvisation. *In*: Gabbard, 217–240.

Cox, A., 2006. Hearing, Feeling, Grasping Gestures. *In*: A. Gritten and E. Kinf, eds, *Music and Gesture*. Aldershot: Ashgate, 45–60.

Cravinho, P., 2016. Historical Overview of the Development of Jazz in Portugal, in the First Half of the Twentieth Century. *Jazz Research Journal*, 10 (1–2), May/November, 75–108.

Cravhino, P., 2017. A Kind of 'In-Between': Jazz and Politics in Portugal (1958–1974). *In*: Johnson 2017C: 218–238.

Crease, R. P., 2002. Jazz and Dance. *In*: M. Cooke and D. Horn, 69–80.

Crowdy, D. and M. Goddard, 1999. The Pedagogy, Culture and Appropriation of Jazz in Papua New Guinea. *Perfect Beat: The Pacific Journal of Research into Contemporary Music and Popular Culture*, 4 (3) July, 48–65.

Cugny, L., 2012. Did Europe "Discover" Jazz? *In*: Cerchiari, Cugny and Kerschbaumer, 301–341.

Davidson, J., 1983. *A Showman's Story: The Memoirs of Jim Davidson*. Adelaide: Rigby.

DeVeaux, S., 1998. Constructing the Jazz Tradition: Jazz Historiography. *In*: R. G. O'Meally, ed., *The Jazz Cadence of American Culture*. New York: Columbia University Press, 483–512. First published in *Black American Literature Forum*, 25 (3), 1991, 525–560.

DeVeaux, S., 2000. (first pub 1997) *The Birth of Bebop: A Social and Musical History*. London: Picador.

DeVeaux, S. and G. Giddins, 2009. *Jazz*. New York and London: W.W. Norton and Company.

Dimbleby, J., 2016 (1st edn. Viking 2015). *The Battle of the Atlantic: How the Allies Won the War*. UK: Penguin, Random House.

Doffman, M., 2019. Time in Jazz. *In*: Rustin, Gebhardt and Whyton, 163–172.

Dorin, S., 2016. Editorial: The Global Circulations of Jazz. *Jazz Research Journal*, 10 (1–2), May/November, 5–12.

Dreyfus, K., 1999. *Sweethearts of Rhythm: the Story of Australia's All-Girls Bands and Orchestras to the End of the Second World War*. Sydney: Currency Press.

Duby, M., 2017. "Fanfare for the Warriors": Jazz, Education, and State Control in 1980s South Africa and After. *In*: Johnson 2017C, 268–293.

Eales, A. C., 2013. 'They've Really Gone to Town with all that Bunting': the influence and (In)visibility of Glasgow's Jazz Festival. *Journal of Jazz Research*, 7 (1), 9–21.

Eato, J., 2017. A Climbing Vine through Concrete: Jazz in 1960s Apartheid South Africa. *In*: Johnson 2017C, 241–267.

Elsdon, P., 2019. Figuring Improvisation. *In*: Rustin, Gebhardt and Whyton, 221–230.

Elworth, S. B., 1995. Jazz in Crisis, 1948–1958: Ideology and Representation. *In* Gabbard, 57–75.

Evans, S., 2016. Expressive Identity in the Voices of Three Australian Saxophonists: McGann, Sanders and Gorman. *In*: Johnson 2016, 248–266.

Feld, S., 1994. From Ethnomusicology to Echo-Muse-Ecology: Reading R. Murray Schafer in the Papua New Guinea Rainforest. *In Soundscapes Writings from the Acoustic Ecology Institute*. Online at www.acousticecology.org/writings/echomuseecology.html, accessed 15 September 2018.

Feld, S., 2000. The Poetics and Politics of Pygmy Pop. *In*: Born and Hesmondhalgh, 254–279.

Feld, S., 2012. *Jazz Cosmopolitanism in Accra: Five Musical Years in Ghana*. Durham NC and London: Duke University Press.

Fernández. R. A., 2003. 'So No Tiene Swing No Vaya' A La Rumba': Cuban Musicians and Jazz. *In*: Atkins, 3–18.

Finnegan, R., 2007. *The Hidden Musicians: Music-Making in an English Town*. Middletown: Wesleyan University Press. First published 1989, Cambridge University Press.

Fléchet, A., 2016. Jazz in Brazil: An Early History (1920s–1950s). *Jazz Research Journal*, 10 (1–2), May/November, 13–34.

Ford, J., 1995. *Meet Me At The Trocadero*. Cowra NSW: Joan Ford.

Fornäs, J., 2003. Swinging Differences: Reconstructed Identities in the Early Swedish Jazz Age. *In*: Atkins, 207–224.

Fry, A., 2016. That Gypsy in France: Django Reinhardt's Occupation Blouze. *In*: Bohlman and Plastino, 181–199.

Gabbard, K., 1995A. Introduction: The Canon and Its Consequences. *In*: Gabbard, 1–28.

Gabbard, K., ed., 1995B. *Jazz Among the Discourses*. Durham NC and London: Duke University Press.

Gabbard, K., 2002. The Word Jazz. *In*: Cooke and Horn, 1–6.

Galbraith, J., 2016. Sex and the Sonic Smorgasborg: The Necks – Extending The 'Jazz' Piano Trio Format. *In*: Johnson, 2016: 267–284.

Garcia, D. E., 2017. *Listening for Africa: Freedom, Modernity, and the Logic of Black Music's African Origins*. Durham and London: Duke University Press.

Gebhardt, N., N. Rustin-Paschal, and T. Whyton, eds, 2019. *Routledge Companion to Jazz Studies*. New York: Routledge.

Gelatt, R., 1976. *The Fabulous Phonograph: 1877–1977*. New York and London: Collier. Second Revised Edition. First published, 1954. Note, the Author's 'Foreword' identifies this as the Third Edition.

Gelly, D., 2014. *An Unholy Row: Jazz in Britain and its Audience, 1945–1960*. Sheffield and Bristol: Equinox.

Gendron, B., 1995. "Moldy Figs" and Modernists: Jazz at War (1942–1946). *In*: Gabbard, 31–56.

Gennari, J. 2006. *Blowin' Hot and Cool: Jazz and its Critics*. Chicago and London: University of Chicago Press.

Gilroy, P., 1999. (first published 1993). *The Black Atlantic: Modernity and Double Consciousness*. London, New York: Verso.

Gioia, T., 1988. *The Imperfect Art: Reflection on jazz and modern culture*. New York and Oxford: Oxford University Press.

Gioia, T., 2011. *The History of Jazz*, 2nd ed. New York and Oxford: Oxford University Press.

Giuffre, L., 2016. The Lost History of Jazz on Early Australian Popular Music Television. *In*: Johnson, 2016: 117–134.

Givan, B., 2003. Django Reinhardt's Left Hand. *In*: Atkins, 19–39.

Godbolt, J., 1984. *A History of Jazz in Britain 1919–1950*. London, Melbourne and New York: Quartet Books.

Goddard, C., 1979. *Jazz Away from Home*. New York and London: Paddington Press.

Goffin, R., 1945. *Jazz: From the Congo to the Metropolitan*. Trans. Walter Schaap and Leonard Feather. New York: Doubleday, Dorin & Co.

Goldin-Meadow, S., 2003. *Hearing Gesture: How Our Hands Help Us Think*. Cambridge Mass and London: The Belknap Press of Harvard University Press.

Gould, T., 2018 *Masters, Mongrels and Madness: Recollections and Observations on Art Music in Australia*. Tony Gould.

Gligorijević, J., 2019. *Contemporary Music Festivals as Micronational Spaces: Articulations of National Identity in Serbia's Exit and Guča Trumpet Festivals in the Post-Milošević Era*. Unpub. Doctoral Dissertation, Faculty of Humanities, School of History, Culture and Arts Studies University of Turku Finland. My thanks to Gligorijević for making available a pre-submission copy.

Gronow, P., 1996. *The Recording Industry: an Ethnomusicological Approach*. Tampere: University of Tampere.

Guerpin, M., 2012. Why Did Art Music Composers Pay Attention to "Jazz"? The Impact of "Jazz' on the French Musical Field, 1908–1924. *In*: Cerchiari, Cugny and Kerschbaumer, 47–80.

Gushee, L., 1994. The Nineteenth-Century Origins of Jazz. *Black Music Research Journal*, 14 (1), 1–24.

Haavisto, J., 1996. *Seven Decades of Finnish Jazz: Jazz in Finland 1919–1969*. Trans. Roger Freundlich. Helsinki: Finnish Music Information, Helsinki.

Hardie, R. and A. Thomas, eds, 2009. *Jazz Aotearoa: Notes Towards a New Zealand History*. Wellington: Steele Roberts.

Harker, B., 2011. *Louis Armstrong's Hot Five and Hot Seven Recordings*. Oxford: Oxford University Press.

Harris, J., 2003. Jazz on the Global Stage. *In*: Monson, 103–134.

Hart, P., 2005. *Bloody April: Slaughter in the Skies over Arras, 1917*. London: Cassell.

Hasse, J. E., 2012. "A New Reason for Living": Duke Ellington in France. *In*: Cerchiari, Cugny and Kerschbaumer, 189–213.

Hastings, M., 2004. *Armageddon: The Battle for Germany 1944–45*. London: Pan/Macmillan.

Havas, Á., 2018. *Simultaneous Aesthetic Hierarchies: The Mainstream/Free Jazz Distinction* (unpub. manuscript, unpaginated). This is a modified a version of Ádám Havas, 2017. A szabadság dogmatizmusa és a dogmatizmus szabadsága: különbségtételek rendszere a mainstream-free jazz dichotómiában. ('The Dogmatism of Freedom and the Freedom of Dogmatism: The Logic of Distinctions in the Mainstream/Free Jazz Dichotomy') published in the Hungarian journal *Replika* No. 101–102, 169–196.

Hayward, B. [ca. 1981] *Jazz Pianist of the Twenties* [no publication details].

Heffley, M., 2005. *Northern Sun, Southern Moon: Europe's Reinvention of Jazz*. New Haven and London: Yale University Press.

Heffley, M., 2012. Revisioning History Lived: Four European Expats, Three Men and One Woman, Who Shaped One American Life in Two American Cultures. *In*: Cerchiari, Cugny and Kerschbaumer, 381–406.

Heining, D., 2012. *Trad Jazz, Dirty Boppers and Free Fusioneers: British Jazz, 1960–75*. Sheffield and Bristol: Equinox.

Helasvuo, V., 1987. The 1920s: Fresh Breezes from Europe. Trans. William Moore. *Finnish Music Quarterly*, 3–4 (87), 2–10.

Hellhund, H., 2012. Roots and Collage: Contemporary European Jazz in Postmodern Times. *In*: Cerchiari, Cugny and Kerschbaumer, 431–446.

Herbert H., 2012. Contemporary European Jazz in Postmodern Times. *In*: Cerchiari, Cugny and Kerschbaumer, 431–446.

Hersch, C., 2008. Reconstructing the Jazz Tradition. *Jazz Research Journal*, 2 (1), 7–28.

Higgins, N., 2016. In Search of Compatible Virtuosities: Floating Point and Fusion in India. *In*: Bohlman and Plastino, 338–363.

Hobsbawm, E. J. (writing as Francis Newton). 1989. *The Jazz Scene*. London: Weidenfield and Nicolson. First published London: MacGibbon and Kee, 1959.

Holbrook, D., 1974. Our Word JAZZ. *Storyville*, December 1973–January 1974, 46–58.

Horn, D., 2002. The Identity of Jazz. *In*: Cooke and Horn, 9–32.

Horn, D., 2013. *An Exercise in Stop-Time: The Complexity of a Musical Moment*. www.scribd.com/document/188192972/Exercise-in-Stop-Time-The-Complexity-of-a-Musical-Moment, accessed 20 December 2018.

Hurley, A. W., 2006. *Summertime* in Indonesia? *Perfect Beat: The Pacific Journal of Research into Contemporary Music and Popular Culture*, 8 (1) July, 3–21.

Hurley, A. W., 2008. Beyond the *Sakura Waltz*: Reflections on the Encounter Between German and Japanese Jazz, 1962–1985. *Perfect Beat: The Pacific Journal of Research into Contemporary Music and Popular Culture* , 8 (4) January, 25–43.

Hurley, A. W., 2009. *The Return of Jazz: Joachim-Ernst Berendt and West German Cultural Change*. New York and Oxford: Berghahn Books.

Hytönen-Ng, E., 2013. *Experiencing 'Flow' in Jazz Performance*. Farnham: Ashgate.

Ielmini, D., 2012. Orchestral Thoughts: Jazz Composition in Europe and America: An Interview with Composer-Director Giorgio Gaslini. *In*: Cerchiari, Cugny and Kerschbaumer, 235–252.

Iglesias, I., 2013. Swinging Modernity: Jazz and Politics in Franco's Spain (1939–1968). *In*: Martínez and Fouce, 101–111.

Iglesias, I., 2017. Performing the 'Anti-Spanish' Body: Jazz and Biopolitics in the Early Franco Regime (1939–1957). *In*: Johnson 2017C.

Jackson, J. H., 2011. Making Jazz French: The Reception of Jazz Music in Paris, 1927–1934. *In*: Whyton, 463–474. First published, *French Historical Studies*, 2002, 25, 149–170.

Jalkanen, P., 1989. Alaska, *Bombay Ja Billy Boy: Jazzkulttuurin murros Helsingissä 1920-luvulla*. Helsinki: University of Helsinki.

Jalkanen, P., 1996. Popular Music. *In*: K. Aho, P. Jalkanen, E. Salmenhaara, K. Virtamo, eds, *Finnish Music*. Trans. T. Binham and P. Binham. Keuruu Finland: Otava 1996, 206–238.

Jankowsky, R. C., 2016. The Medium Is the Message? Jazz Diplomacy and the Democratic Imagination. *In*: Bohlman and Plastino, 258–288.

Johnson, B., 1982. Is There an Australian Jazz?, *Jazz: The Australian Contemporary Music Magazine*, February, 20–23.

Johnson, B., 1987. *The Oxford Companion to Australian Jazz*. Melbourne: Oxford University Press.

Johnson, B., 1994. Klactovesedstene: Music, Soundscape and Me. *In* H. Järviluoma, ed., *Soundscapes: Essays on Vroom and Moo*. Finland: Department of Folk Tradition/Institute of Rhythm Music, 39–47.

Johnson, B., 1998. Doctored Jazz: Early Australian Jazz Journals. *Perfect Beat: The Pacific Journal of Research into Contemporary Music and Popular Culture*, 3 (4), January, 26–37.

Johnson, B., 2000 *The Inaudible Music: Jazz, Gender and Australian Modernity*. Sydney: Currency Press.

Johnson, B., 2002A. The Jazz Diaspora. *In*: Cooke and Horn, 33–54.

Johnson, B., 2002B. Jazz as Cultural Practice. *In*: Cooke and Horn, 96–113.

Johnson, B., 2003. Naturalizing the Exotic: The Australian Jazz Convention. *In*: Atkins, 151–168.

Johnson, B., 2004. Tools Not of Our Making: Shaping Australian Jazz History. *In*: P. Hayward and G. Hodges, eds, *The History and Future of Jazz in the Asia-Pacific Region: refereed Proceedings of the inaugural Asia-Pacific Jazz Conference (September 12th–14th 2003)*. Queensland: Central Queensland University Publishing Unit, 6–17.

Johnson, B., 2008A. "Quick and Dirty": Sonic Mediations and Affect. *In*: C. Birdsall and A. Enns, eds, *Sonic Mediations: Body, Sound, Technology*. Newcastle-upon-Tyne: Cambridge Scholars Publishing, 43–60.

Johnson, B., 2008B. Australian Jazz. *In*: S. Homan and T. Mitchell, eds, *Sounds of Then, Sounds of Now: Popular Music in Australia*. Hobart: ACYS Publishing: 113–130.

Johnson, B., 2010. Deportation Blues: Black Jazz and White Australia in the 1920s. *IASPM Journal: Journal of the International Association for the Study of Popular Music*, 1 (1). Online at www.iaspmjournal.net/index.php/IASPM_Journal/article/view/297/546 Accessed 25 September 2018.

Johnson, B., 2011. Hear Me Talkin' To Ya: Problems of Jazz Discourse. *In*: Whyton, 21–32. Originally published 1993. *Popular Music*, 12 (1), January, 1–12.

Johnson, B., 2013. I Hear Music: Popular Music and its Mediations. *IASPM@Journal: Journal of the International Association for the Study of Popular Music*, 3 (2), 96–110; online at www.iaspmjournal.net/index.php/IASPM_Journal/article/view/606/pdf_1 Accessed 11 September 2018.

Johnson, B., 2015. We Can't Sleep in the Movies any More. *Screen Sound Journal*, 5, (appearing in 2015), 5–18; at www.screensoundjournal.org/issues/n5/05.%20SSJ%20 n5%20Johnson.pdf Accessed 13 October 2018.

Johnson, B., ed. 2016 *Antipodean Riffs: Essays on Australasian Jazz*. Sheffield and Bristol: Equinox.

Johnson, B., 2017A. Sound Studies Today: Where are We Going? *In:* J. Damousi and P. Hamilton, eds, *A Cultural History of Sound, Memory and the Senses.* New York and London: Routledge, 7–22.

Johnson, B., 2017B. In the Body of the Audience. *In:* J. Tsioulakis and E. Hytönen-Ng, eds, *Musicians and Their Audiences: Performance, Speech and Mediation.* New York and London: Routledge, 15–33.

Johnson, B., ed., 2017C. *Jazz and Totalitarianism.* New York and London: Routledge.

Johnson, B., 2019. The Jazz Diaspora. *In:* Rustin, Gebhardt and Whyton, 17–26.

Johnson, B., Forthcoming A (scheduled 2020). Jazz Outside the US. *In:* D. Horn and J. Shepherd, eds, *Bloomsbury Encyclopedia of Popular Music of the World.* Vol. XIII. *Genres: International.* New York & London: Bloomsbury Academic.

Johnson, B., Forthcoming B. Jazz in Finland, 1918 to 1940. *In:* W. van der Leur, ed., *The Oxford History of Jazz in Europe.* Oxford University Press.

Johnson, B., Forthcoming C. John Grant Sangster. *In: The Australian Dictionary of Biography.* Melbourne: Melbourne University Publishing.

Johnson, B. and M. Cloonan, 2008. *Dark Side of the Tune: Popular Music and Violence.* Aldershot: Ashgate.

Jones, A. F., 2003. Black Internationale: Notes on the Chinese Jazz Age. *In:* Atkins, 225–243.

Jost, E., 2012. The European Jazz Avant-Garde of the Late 1960s and Early 1970s: Where did Emancipation Lead? *In:* Cerchiari, Cugny and Kerschbaumer, 275–297.

Kajanová, Y., G. Pickan, R. Ritter, eds, 2016. *Jazz from Socialist Realism to Postmodernism (Jazz under State Socialism).* Frankfurt am Main: Peter Lang.

Karpf, A., 2006. *The Human Voice.* New York: Bloomsbury.

Kater, M. H., 1992. *Different Drummers: Jazz in the culture of Nazi Germany.* New York and Oxford: Oxford University Press.

Keepnews, O. and B. Grauer, Jr., 1968 (rev. ed., first pub. 1955). *A Pictorial History of Jazz: People and Places from New Orleans to Modern Jazz.* Middlesex: Hamlyn/Spring Books.

Kennaway, J., 2012. *Bad Vibrations: The History of the Idea of Music as a Cause of Disease.* Farnham: Ashgate.

Kerschbaumer, F., 2012. The Influence of Celtic Music of the Evolution of Jazz. *In:* Cerchiari, Cugny and Kerschbaumer, 3–20.

Kernfeld, B., ed., 1988. *The New Grove Dictionary of Jazz,* Two Volumes. London: Macmillan.

Kirchner, B., ed., 2000. *The Oxford Companion to Jazz.* Oxford: Oxford University Press.

Konttinen, M., 1987. The Jazz Invasion. Trans. Susan Sinisalo. *Finnish Music Quarterly,* 3–4 (87), 20–5.

Korman, C. H., 2016. Paulo Moura's Hepteto and Quarteto: 'Sambajazz' as Brazilogical Popular Instrumental Improvised Music. *Jazz Research Journal,* 10 (1–2) May/November, 153–187.

Koyama, K., 2000. Jazz in Japan. *In:* Kirchner, 566–574.

Kuplis, J. 2015. *Ian Pearce, Pianoman: An account of the life and times of Tasmania's gentleman of jazz.* Sandy Bay Tasmania: Jan Kuplis.

Kuplis, J. and T. Pickering, 2012. *Tom Pickering: Jazzmaker.* Sandy Bay Tasmania: Jan Kuplis.

Laird, R., 1999. *Sound Beginnings: The Early Record Industry in Australia.* Sydney: Currency Press.

Lawson-Peebles, R., 2013. The 'Grave Disease': Interwar British Writers Look at Ragtime and Jazz. *Journal of Jazz Research,* 7 (1), 23–48.

Leppert, R., 1993. *The Sight of Sound: Music, Representation, and the History of the Body,* Berkeley: University of California Press.

Levy, C., 2016. Swinging in Balkan Mode: On the Innovative Approach of Milcho Leviev. *In*: Bohlman and Plastino, 79–97.

Lewis, G. Foreword: Who is Jazz?. *In*: Bohlman and Plastino, ix–xxiv.

Lewis, L., 1996. *Arthur and the Nights at the Turntable: The Life and Times of a Jazz Broadcaster.* Wingen NSW: K'Vrie Press (first published 1996, London: Excalibur Press).

Lind, T. T., 2012. *The Past Is Always Present: The Revival of the Byzantine Musical Tradition at Mount Athos.* Lanham, MD: The Scarecrow Press.

Linehan, N., 1983. Dave Dallwitz: The Creation of a Myth'. *Jazz, The Australasian Contemporary Music Magazine,* January/February, 20–21.

Lomax, A., 1950. *Mister Jelly Roll: The Fortunes of Jelly Roll Morton, New Orleans Creole and "Inventor of Jazz".* New York: Duell, Sloan and Pearce.

Lotz, R. E., 2012. Cross-Cultural Links: Black Minstrels, Cakewalks, and Ragtime. *In*: Cerchiari, Cugny and Kerschbaumer, 143–166.

Lücke, M., 2010. The Postwar Campaign against Jazz in the USSR. *In*: Pickan and Ritter, 83–98.

Macdonald, L., 1993. *They Called it Passchendaele: The Story of the Third Battle of Ypres and of the Men Who Fought in It.* London: Penguin (First published 1978).

Macintyre, S., ed., 2004. *A Concise History of Australia,* 2nd ed. Cambridge: Cambridge University Press .

Mandel, H., 2000. Jazz in Africa: The Ins and Outs. *In*: Kirchner, 559–565.

Martin, T., 2000. Jazz in Canada and Australia. *In*: Kirchner, 575–582.

Martinelli, F., ed., 2018. *The History of European Jazz.* Sheffield: Equinox.

Martínez, S. and H. Fouce, 2013A. Introduction: Avoiding Stereotypes: A Critical Map of Popular Music in Spain. *In*: Martínez and Fouce, 1–13.

Martínez, S. and H. Fouce, eds, 2013B. *Made in Spain: Studies in Popular Music.* New York and London: Routledge.

Mawer, D., 2014. *French Music and Jazz in Conversation: From Debussy to Brubeck.* Cambridge: Cambridge University Press.

May, M., 2000. Swingin' under Stalin: Russian Jazz during the Cold War and Beyond. *In*: R. Wagnleitner and E. May, eds, *"Here, There and "Everywhere": The Foreign Politics of American Popular Culture.* Hanover and London: University Press of New England, 178–191.

McGee, K., 2016. A World(ly) Jazz Autonomy: Hazel Scott and Hollywood's Racial-Musical Matrix. *In*: Bohlman and Plastino, 402–428.

McKay, G., 2005. *Circular Breathing: The Cultural Politics of Jazz in Britain.* Durham and London: Duke University Press.

McKay, G., 2018. Festivals. *In*: Martinelli, 707–718.

McMullen, T., 2008. Identity for Sale: Glenn Miller, Wynton Marsalis, and Cultural Replay in Music. *In*: Rustin and Tucker, 129–154.

McNeill, D., 2005. *Gesture and Thought.* Chicago and London: University of Chicago Press.

Meehan, N., 2016. *New Zealand Jazz Life.* Wellington: Victoria University Press.

Meehan, N., 2017. The New Zealand Jazz Tradition: Something Borrowed, Something Blue. *In*: Michael Brown and Samantha Owens, eds, *Searches for Tradition: Essays on New Zealand Music, Past and Present.* Wellington: Victoria University Press, 161–173.

Melman, B., 1988 *Women and the Popular Imagination in the Twenties: Flappers and Nymphs.* New York: St Martin's Press.

Menary, R., ed., 2010. *The Extended Mind.* Cambridge Mass and London: The MIT Press.

Merriam, A. P. and F. H. Garner, 1998 (originally published 1960). Jazz – The Word. *In*: R. G. O'Meally, ed., *The Jazz Cadence of American Culture.* New York: Columbia University Press, 7–31.

Middleton, R., 2000. Musical Belongings: Western Music and its Low-Other. *In*: Born and Hesmondhalgh, 59–85.

Mitchell, Jack. 1988. *Australian Jazz on Record 1925–80*. Canberra: Australian Government Publishing Service.

Monson, I., ed., 2003. *The African Diaspora: A Musical Perspective*. New York, London: Routledge.

Moody, B., 1993. *Jazz Exiles: American Musicians Abroad*. Reno: University of Nevada Press.

Moore, A., 2002. Authenticity as Authentication. *Popular Music*, 21 (2), May, 209–223.

Moore, H., 2007. *Inside British Jazz*. Aldershot: Ashgate.

Moore, J. B., 1998. Studying Jazz in Postwar Japan: Where to Begin? *Japanese Studies*, 1, 18 (3), 265–280.

Moreck, C., 1929. *Kultur und Sittengeschichte der neuesten Zeit: da Genussleben des modernen Menschen*. Dresden: Paul Aretz.

Morgan, P., 2003. *Fascism in Europe, 1919–1945*. London: Routledge.

Morgenstern, D., 2000. Recorded Jazz. *In*: Kirchner, 766–787.

Mulders, F., n.d. *Speaking Frankly: A Lifetime of Reminiscing by Frank Mulders*. Unpublished memoir. This was completed late in his life, which covered the period 14 July 1925 to his death in Adelaide, South Australia, 25 February 2011. In the final section he indicates that this was completed early 2011.

Muller, C. A., 2016. Musical Echoes: Diasporic Listening and the Creation of a World of South African Jazz. *In*: Bohlman and Plastino, 289–306.

Muller, C. A. and S. B. Benjamin, 2011. *Musical Echoes: South African Women Thinking in Jazz*. Durham NC and London: Duke University Press.

Naroditskaya, I., 2016. Azerbaijani *Mugham* Jazz. *In*: Bohlman and Plastino, 98–124.

Nettelbeck, C., 2004. *Dancing with De Beauvoir: Jazz and the French*. Melbourne: Melbourne University Press.

Nettl, B., with M. Russell. eds, 1998. *In the Course of Performance: Studies in the World of Musical Improvisation*. Chicago and London: Chicago University Press.

Neuenfeldt, K., 2016. "I Wouldn't Change Skins with Anybody": Dulcie Pitt/Georgia, a Pioneering Indigenous Australian Jazz, Blues and Community Singer. *In*: Johnson 2016, 192–211.

Nicholson, S., 2005. *Is Jazz Dead? (Or Has It Moved to a New Address)*. New York and London: Routledge.

Nicholson, S., 2014. *Jazz and Culture in a Global Age*. Lebanon: Northeastern University Press.

Nooshin, L., 2016. Jazz and its Social Meanings in Iran: From Cultural Colonialism to the Universal. *In*: Bohlman and Plastino, 125–149.

Oivi, M., H. Salmi and B. Johnson, Forthcoming. *Yves Montand, Cultural Diplomacy, and the USSR*. Basingstoke: Palgrave Macmillan.

Panassié, H., 1944. *The Real Jazz*. Trans. Anne Sorelle Williams. New York: Smith & Durrell, Inc.

Parsonage, C. (now Tackley), 2005. The Evolution of Jazz in Britain, 1880–1935. Aldershot: Ashgate.

Parsonage, C. (now Tackley) 2012. Benny Carter in Britain, 1936–1937. *In*: Cerchiari, Cugny and Kerschbaumer, 167–188.

Pedro, J., 2017. 'The Purest Essence of Jazz': The Appropriation of Blues in Spain during Franco's Dictatorship. *In*: Johnson 2017C, 174–189.

Pellegrinelli, L., 2008. Separated at 'Birth': Singing and the History of Jazz. *In*: Rustin and Tucker, 31–47.

Perchard, T., 2015. *After Django: Making Jazz in Postwar France*. Ann Arbor: University of Michigan Press.

Peretti, B. W., 1995. Oral Histories of Jazz Musicians: The NEA Transcripts as Texts in Context. *In*: Gabbard, 117–133.

Pfleiderer, M., K. Frieler, J. Abeßer, W-G. Zaddach and B. Burkhart, eds., 2017. *Inside the Jazzomat: New Perspectives for Jazz Research*. Mainz: Schott Music.

Picaud, M., 2016. 'We Try to Have The Best': How Nationality, Race and Gender Structure Artists' Circulations in the Paris Jazz Scene. *Jazz Research Journal*, 10 (1–2) May/November, 126–152.

Pickhan, G. and R. Ritter, eds, 2010. *Jazz Behind the Iron Curtain*. Frankfurt am Main: Peter Lang.

Piedade, A. T. de C., 2003. Brazilian Jazz and Friction of Musicalities. *In*: Atkins, 41–58.

Pietraszewski, I., 2014. *Jazz in Poland: Improvised Freedom*. Trans. Lucyna Stetkiewicz. Frankfurt am Main: Peter Lang.

Pinckney, W. R. Jr., 2003. Jazz in India: Perspectives on Historical Development and Musical Acculturation. *In*: Atkins, 59–79.

Plastino, G., 2016. Jazz Napoletano: A Passion for Improvisation. *In*: Bohlman and Plastino, 309–337.

Pleasants, H., 1974. *The Great American Popular Singers*. New York: Simon & Schuster.

Portugali, A., 2017. On the Marginality of Contemporary Jazz in China: The Case of Beijing. In Johnson 2017C, 325–243.

Potts, D. and A., 1985. *Yanks Downunder 1941–1945: The American Impact on Australia*. Melbourne: Oxford University Press.

Pressing, J., 1987. The Micro- and Macrostructural Design of Improvised Music. *Music Perception*, 5 (2), 132–172.

Pronko. M., 2019. Quiet About It—Jazz in Japan. *In:* Gebhardt, Rustin-Paschal and Whyton, 271–280.

Prouty, K., 2010. Toward Jazz's 'Official' History: The Debates and Discourses of Jazz History Textbooks. *Journal of Music History Pedagogy*, 1(1), 19–43. (online at www.ams-net.org/ojs/index.php/jmhp/article/view/4/26, accessed 27 July 2016). NOTE: my citations from this article are from the online text which is not paginated, and my page numbers are based on those appearing in the scroll column, which begin at 1).

Prouty, K., 2019. Jazz Education: Historical and Critical Perspectives. *In:* Gebhardt, Rustin-Paschal and Whyton, 45–54.

Radano, R. M., 1995. Critical Alchemy: Anthony Braxton and the Imagined Tradition. *In*: Gabbard, 189–216.

Raeburn, B. B., 2011. Stars of David and Sons of Sicily: Constellations Beyond the Canon in Early New Orleans Jazz. *In*: Whyton, 389–418. First published in *Jazz Perspectives*, 2009, 3: 123–152.

Raeburn, B. B., 2012. Beyond the Spanish Tinge: Hispanics and Latinos in Early New Orleans Jazz. *In*: Cerchiari, Cugny and Kerschbaumer, 21–46.

Ramsey Jr., F. and C. E. Smith, 1939. *Jazzmen*. New York: Harcourt, Brace and Company.

Rastrick, Ó., Forthcoming. 'Not Music but Sonic Porn': Negative Reception of Jazz, Identity Politics and Social Reform. *Cultural History: Journal of the International Society for Cultural History*.

Rasula, J., 1995. The Media of Memory: The Seductive Menace of Records in Jazz History. *In*: Gabbard, 134–162.

Rasula, J., 2002. The Jazz Audience. *In*: Cooke and Horn, 55–68.

Reimann, H., 2017. Four Spaces, Four Meanings: Narrating Jazz in Late Stalinist Estonia. *In*: Johnson 2017C, 69–93.

Reimann H., 2019. Conceptualizing Jazz as a Cultural Practice in Soviet Estonia. *In*: Gebhardt, Rustin-Paschal and Whyton, 129–138.

Reynolds, D. and M. Reason, eds, 2012. *Kinesthetic Empathy in Creative and Cultural Practices.* Bristol and Chicago: Intellect.

Ritter, R. 2017. Jazz in Moscow after Stalinism. In Johnson 2017C, 50–66.

Ross, B. C., 2016. The Reception of Jazz in Adelaide and Melbourne and the Creation of an Australian Sound in the Angry Penguins Decade. *In*: Johnson 2016, 84–102.

Ross, L., 2003 *African-American Jazz Musicians in the Diaspora.* Lewiston: The Edwin Mellen Press.

Roxo, P., 2017. Jazz and the Portuguese Dictatorship before and after the Second World War: From Moral Panic to Suspicious Acceptance. *In*: Johnson 2017C.

Roxo, P. and S. El-S. Castelo-Branco, 2016. Jazz, Race, and Politics in Colonial Portugal: Discourses and Representations. *In*: Bohman and Plastino, 200–235.

Russell, Ross. 1972. *Bird Lives!* London: Quartet Books.

Rustin, N.T. and S. Tucker, eds, 2008A. *Big Ears: Listening for Gender in Jazz Studies.* Durham NC and London: Duke University Press.

Rustin, N.T. and S. Tucker, 2008B. Introduction. *In*: Rustin and Tucker, 1–28.

Sangster, J., 1988. *Seeing the Rafters: The Life and Times of an Australian Jazz Musician.* Ringwood Victoria: Penguin.

Santoro, G., 2000. Latin Jazz. *In*: Kirchner, 522–533.

Schafer, W. J., 2008. *The Original Jelly Roll Blues: The Story of Ferdinand Lamothe, A.K.A Jelly Roll Morton The Originator of Jazz, Stomps and Blues.* Fulham London: Flame Tree Publishing.

Schenker, F. J., 2019. Listening for Empire in Jazz Studies. *In*: Gebhardt, Rustin-Paschal and Whyton, 231–238.

Schlicht, U., 2008. "Better a Jazz Album than Lipstick" (Lieber Jazzplatte als Lippenstift): The 1956 Jazz Podium Series Reveals Images of Jazz and Gender in Postwar Germany. *In*: Rustin and Tucker, 291–319.

Schuiling, F., 2019. Jazz and the Material Turn. *In*: Gebhardt, Rustin-Paschal and Whyton, 87–96.

Scott, D. B., 2001. *The Singing Bourgeois: Songs of the Victorian Drawing Room and Parlour,* 2nd ed. Aldershot: Ashgate.

Scott-Maxwell, A., 2016. Early Jazz in Australia as Oriental Exotica. *In*: Johnson 2016, 47–64.

Seguin, P.-E., 2016. Lydia in Oz: The Reception of George Russell in 1960s Australia. *In*: Johnson 2016, 229–247.

Shaw, A., 1977. *52nd Street: The Street of Jazz.* New York: Da Capo.

Shelemay, K. K., 2016. Traveling Music: Mulatu Astatke and the Genesis of Ethiopian Jazz. *In*: Bohlman and Plastino, 239–257.

Shand, J., 2009. *Jazz: The Australian Accent.* Sydney: UNSW Press.

Shapiro, N. and N. Hentoff, 1992 (first pub. 1955). *Hear Me Talkin' To Ya: The Classic Story of Jazz as Told by the Men Who Made it.* London: Souvenir Press.

Sheets-Johnston, M., 2009. *The Corporeal Turn: an Interdisciplinary Reader.* Exeter: Imprint Academic.

Shepherd, J., D. Horn and D. Laing, eds, 2005. *Continuum Encyclopedia of Popular Music of the World,* Volumes III *Caribbean and Latin America;* V, *Asia and Oceania;* VI, *Africa and the Middle East;* VII Europe. London and New York: Continuum.

Shipton, A., 2001. *A New History of Jazz.* London and New York: Continuum.

Shipton, A., 2012. The New Orleans Revival in Britain and France. *In:* Cerchiari, Cugny and Kerschbaumer, 253–274.

Simpson, D., 2007. Hit Me with Your Rhythm Shtick. *The Guardian,* 30 March, online at www.theguardian.com/music/2007/mar/30/popandrock.worldmusic.

Southall, H.V., 2013. Jazz on the Border: Jazz and Dance Bands in Chester and North Wales in the Mid-Twentieth Century. *Journal of Jazz Research,* 7 (1), 49–77.

Skvorecky, J., 1989. *Talkin' Moscow Blues.* London: Faber & Faber.

Sloboda, J. A. and P. N. Juslin, eds, 2001. *Music and Emotion: Theory and Research.* Oxford: Oxford University Press.

Starr, S. F., 1983. *Red and Hot: The Fate of Jazz in the Soviet Union 1917–1980.* New York and Oxford: Oxford University Press.

Stendahl, B., Jazz in Norway 1920–1940, http://jazzbasen.no/jazzhistorie_1920_1940_eng.html, accessed 10 May 2007.

Sterne, J., 2003 *The Audible Past: Cultural Origins of Sound Reproduction.* Durham NC: Duke University Press.

Stevens, D., 2007. *The Life of Freddie Thomas.* Unpub. Memoir.

Stiegler, M., 2009. *The African Experience on American Shores: Influence of Native American Contact on the Development of Jazz.* MA Thesise, Bowling Green State University. Online at https://etd.ohiolink.edu/rws_etd/document/get/bgsu1244856703/inline on 22 March 2018.

Stites, R., 1992. *Russian Popular Culture: Entertainment and Society since 1900.* Cambridge: Cambridge University Press.

Studdert, W., 2013 'We've Got a Gig in Poland': Britain and Jazz in World War II. *Journal of Jazz Research,* 7 (1), 79–111.

Sudhalter, R. M., 1999. *Lost Chords: White Musicians and Their Contribution to Jazz 1915–1945.* Oxford and New York: Oxford University Press.

Sudhalter, R. M., 2000. Hot Music in the 1920s: The 'Jazz Age', Appearances and Realities. *In:* Kirchner, 148–162.

Sutcliffe, M., 1982. The First Americans. *Jazz: The Australian Contemporary Music Magazine,* December, 22–23.

Sutcliffe, M., 1989. Australians Overseas: The Three Australian Boys. *Australian Record and Music Review,* 1, April, 2.

Szwed, J., 2015. *Billie Holliday: The Musician and the Myth.* London: Windmill Books/Penguin/Random House.

Tackley (née Parsonage), C., 2013. Jazz, Dance and Black Music Identities. *In:* S. Dodds and S. Cook, eds, *Bodies of Sound: studies across popular music and dance.* Burlington, VT: Ashgate, 193–207.

Tackley, C. and T. Whyton., 2013. Editorial: Transnational Perspectives on Jazz. *Journal of Jazz Research,* 7 (1), 5–7.

Tagg, P., 2015. 'Backbeats, Bluenotes and Scotch Snaps: music analysis v. standard historical narrative'. NIMiMS (Network for the Inclusion of Music in Music Studies), Symposium in Helsinki, 20 November 2015. Helsinki University, Musicology, Topelia building. Video: Jouni Eerola / JAPA. At www.youtube.com/watch?v=R5CpMSu4soc, accessed 2 January 2019.

Tagg, P. and B. Clarida, 2003. *Ten Little Title Tunes: Towards a Musicology of the Mass Media*. New York and Montreal: The Mass Media Music Scholars' Press.

Taylor, J., 2000. The Early Origins of Jazz. *In*: Kirchner, 39–52.

Thompson, P. A. and R. Macklin, 2000. *The Battle of Brisbane: Australians and the Yanks at War*. Sydney: ABC Books.

Tipping, N., 2016. Cuba Street Parade: Identity, Authenticity and Self-Expression in Contemporary Australasian Jazz Scenes. *In*: Johnson 2016, 103–116.

Tomlinson, G., 2011. Cultural Dialogics and Jazz: A White Historian Signifies. *In*: Whyton, 463–474. Originally published in *Black Music Research Journal*, 1991, No. 11, pp. 229–264.

Toynbee, J., C. Tackley and M. Doffman, eds. 2014 *Black British Jazz: Routes, Ownership and Performance*. Farnham: Ashgate.

Tribble, E. B. and N. Keene, 2011. *Cognitive Ecologies and the History of Remembering: Religion, Education and Memory in Early Modern England*. Basingstoke: Palgrave Macmillan.

Tucker, S., 2011. Deconstructing the Jazz Tradition: The "Subjectless Subject" of New Jazz Studies. *In*: Whyton, 135–150. Revised version from *The Source: Challenging Jazz Criticism*, 2005, 2, 31–46.

Tucker, S., in collaboration with Dorothy Giles, 1948. *Some of These Days: An Autobiography*. London: Hammond and Hammond.

Turner, B., 1984. *Hot Air, Cool Music*. London, Melbourne, New York: Quartet Books.

van der Leur, W., ed., Forthcoming. *The Oxford History of Jazz in Europe*. Oxford University Press.

van Kan, M., 2016. Cooling Down Jazz: Making Authentic Swedish Jazz Possible. *Jazz Research Journal*, 10 (1–2), May/November, 35–53.

van Kan, M., 2017. *Swingin' Swedes: The Transnational Exchange of Swedish Jazz in the US*. Doctoral Dissertation, Department of Cultural Sciences Skrifter från musikvetenskap, Göteborgs universitet nr 104: University of Gothenburg.

von Eschen, P., 2004 *Satchmo Blows up the World: Jazz Ambassadors Play the Cold War*. Cambridge Mass and London: Harvard University Press.

Wald, E., 2007. Louis Armstrong Loves Guy Lombardo: Acknowledging the Smoother Roots of jazz. *Jazz Research Journal*, 1 (1), 129–145.

Wald, E., 2009. *How The Beatles Destroyed Rock'n'Roll: An Alternative History of American Popular Music*. Oxford and New York: Oxford University Press.

Wall, T., 2019. Jazz on Radio. *In*: Gebhardt, Rustin-Paschal and Whyton, 65–73.

Wall, T. and P. Long, Jazz Britannia: Mediating the Story of British Jazz on Television, *In* Whyton 501–526. First published in *Jazz Research Journal* 3 (2009), 145–170.

Wallace, D., ed., 2016. *Europe: A Literary History*, 1138–1418. Oxford, New York: Oxford University Press.

Walser, R., 1991. The Body in Music: Epistemology and Musical Semiotics. *College Music Symposium*, 31, 118–126.

Walser, R., 1993. *Running With the Devil: Power, Gender, and Madness in Heavy Metal Music*. Middleton Ct.: Wesleyan University Press.

Walser, R., 1995. "Out of Notes": Signification. Interpretation, and the Problem of Miles Davis. *In*: Gabbard, 165–188.

Walser, R., 1999. *Keeping Time: Readings in Jazz History*. New York and Oxford: Oxford University Press.

Ward, A., 2015 New Zealand's First Jazz Recording. *Audio Culture*, 25, November, at www.audioculture.co.nz/scenes/new-zealand-s-first-jazz-recording, accessed 25 September 2018.

Ward, A., 2017. Going to Town in the Big Jam: 'Official' Jam Sessions in the 1940s and the Development of the New Zealand Jazz Community'. *In*: M. Brown and S. Owens, eds, *Searches for Tradition: Essays on New Zealand Music, Past and Present*. Wellington: Victoria University Press, 174–188.

Washburne, C. and M. Derno, eds, 2004. *Bad Music: The Music We Love to Hate*. London and New York: Routledge.

Wasserberger, I., A. Matzner and P. Motyčka, eds, 2017. *Jazz in Europe: New Music in the Old Continent*. Oxford: Peter Lang.

Waters, E. n.d., *His Eye is on the Sparrow: An Autobiography by Ethel Waters*. London: W. H. Allen, a Pinnacle Book.

Watson, D. (compiler), 1994. *The Wordsworth Dictionary of Musical Quotations*. Hertfordshire: Wordsworth Editions.

Webb, M., 1997. A Long Way from Tipperary: Performance Culture in Early Colonial Rabaul, New Guinea, and the Genesis of a Melanesian Popular Music Scene. *Perfect Beat: The Pacific Journal of Research into Contemporary Music and Popular Culture*, 3 (2), January, 32–59.

Weisenthaunet, H., 2007. Historiography and Complexities: Why is Music 'National'? *Popular Music History*, 2 (2), 169–199.

Weiss, G. and H. F. Haber, eds, 1999. *Perspectives on Embodiment: The Intersections of Nature and Culture*. London and New York: Routledge.

Welburn, R., 2000. Jazz Criticism. *In* Kirchner, 745–755.

Welburn, R., 2002. A Most Secret Identity: Native American Assimilation and Identity Resistance in African America. *In*: J. F. Brooks, ed., *Confounding the Color Line: Indian-Black Relations in Multidisciplinary Perspective*. Nebraska: University of Nebraska Press.

Whiteoak, J., 1999. *Playing Ad Lib: Improvisatory Music in Australia 1836–1970*. Sydney: Currency Press..

Whiteoak, J., 2004. Our Jazz-Making Tools and How We Chose to Use Them. *In*: P. Hayward and G. Hodges, eds, *The History and Future of Jazz in the Asia-Pacific Region: refereed Proceedings of the inaugural Asia-Pacific Jazz Conference (September 12th–14th 2003)*. Queensland: Central Queensland University Publishing Unit, 18–28.

Whiteoak, J., 2009. Across the Big Pond: Mapping Early 'Jazz' Activity in New Zealand through Australian Jazz Historiography and Sources. *In*: R. Hardie and A. Thomas, eds, *Jazz Aotearoa: Notes Towards a New Zealand History*. Wellington: Steele Roberts, 14–40.

Whiteoak, R., 2016. Examining the Legend and Music of Australian Saxophonist, Frank Smith. *In*: Johnson 2016, 215–228.

Whyton, T. ed., 2011. *Jazz*. Farnham: Ashgate.

Whyton, T., 2012. Europe and the New Jazz Studies. *In*: Cerchiari, Cugny and Kerschbaumer, 366–380.

Whyton, T., 2019. Wilkie's Story: Dominant Histories, Hidden Musicians, and Cosmopolitan Connections in Jazz. *In*: Gebhardt, Rustin-Paschal and Whyton, 3–15.

Williams, J. F., 1995. *The Quarantined Culture: Australian Reactions to Modernism 1913–1939*. Cambridge: Cambridge University Press.

Williams, L. F., 2003. Interpreting the Creative Process of Jazz in Zimbabwe. *In*: Atkins, 81–97.

Williamson, J. and M. Cloonan, 2016. *Players's Work Time: A History of the British Musicians' Union, 1893–2013*. Manchester: Manchester University Press.

Youngren, W. H., 2000. European Roots of Jazz. *In* Kirchner, 17–28.

Zaddach, W.-G. 2017. Jazz in Czechoslovakia during the 1950s and 1960s. In Johnson 2017C, 114–135.

Zenni, S., 2003. Gianluigi Trovesi's Music: An Historical and Geographical Short-Circuit. *In*: Atkins, 115–125.

Zwerin, M., 1985. *La Tristesse de Saint Louis: Jazz Under the Nazis*. New York: Beech Tree Books.

Zwerin, M., 2000. The Real World Music … or the Full Circle. *In*: Kirchner, 534–547.

FILMOGRAPHY AND DISCOGRAPHY

TV/Video/DVD

Altman, Robert and Alan Crosland Jr. (dir.) 1958–1961. *Peter Gunn*. TV series USA.

Attias, Dan (dir.), 2011. *Treme, The Complete First Season*. HBO Y30043. USA. Duration 607 minutes.

Benedikt, Julian (dir.). 2006. *Play Your Own Thing: A story of Jazz in Europe*. DVD, Euroarts, 2055748.

Burns, Ken (dir.), 2001. *Jazz*. USA. Ten episodes, total duration 1140 minutes.

Whitford, Frank. 1994 *Bauhaus: The Face of the Twentieth Century* Video documentary. BBC/RM Arts.

Williams, Joe (narrator), 2009. *Jump for Jazz*, Part 1, at www.youtube.com/watch?v=zaUwd_lTNoA, accessed 17 June 2018).

Discography (Chronological order)

For older titles on now rare labels, I have generally not included discographical detail if they are available on YouTube.

'Dixie Queen Rag', 1906. Robert Hoffman. Also known as 'Tee-nah-nah' or 'If You Don't Shake (You Get No Cake)'. Available at www.youtube.com/watch?v=KFrW2F3IvVo, accessed 28 July 2019.

'Wild Wild Women', 1919. Murray Pilcer Orchestra. England. Available at www.youtube.com/watch?v=htaXekkzsyI, accessed 6 August 2018.

'Milenberg Joys', 1926. Palais Royal Californians. Australia. Available at www.youtube.com/watch?v=JRI7kU5HSgc, accessed 27 August 2018).

'That Certain Party', 1926. Palais Royal Californians. Australia. Columbia 0517, Master No. R-14. Source Mitchell 1988: 159.

'West End Blues', 1928. Louis Armstrong. USA. Available at www.youtube.com/watch?v=W232OsTAMo8, accessed 18 January 2019.

'Asfalttikukka' (Asphalt Flowers), 1929. Suomi Jazz orkesteri (Finnish Jazz Orchestra), Finland. Available at www.youtube.com/watch?v=0LXW__fBVNw, accessed 30/6/2017.

'42nd Street', 1933. Jim Davidson and his New Palais Royal Orchestra. Australia. Available at www.youtube.com/watch?v=1n1y7Uxgjfo, accessed 6 January 2019.

'Twentieth Century Blues', 1933. Barbara James. Australia. Available at www.youtube.com/ watch?v=o1bHcGKqCck, accessed 6 January 2019.

'Broadway Rhythm', 1936. Rytmi Pojat (Rhythm Boys). Finland. Available at www. youtube.com/watch?v=cA2TpAooA7M, accessed 9 January 2019.

'It Don't Mean a Thing if it Ain't Got that Swing', 1937. Barbara James. Australia. Available at www.youtube.com/watch?v=uMt4RAN4RIQ, accessed 6 January 2019.

'Night in Tunisia', 1946. Charlie Parker. USA. Available at www.youtube.com/watch?v=x_ TcSO0pNtw, accessed 12 January 2019.

The Very Best of Jazz – 50 Unforgettable Tracks 2014 CD compilation. Available at www. youtube.com/watch?v=9f6V-QehbU4, accessed 8 July 2018.

Charlie and his Orchestra, 1940–1943. Germany. Their catalogue is listed, the lyrics transcribed and the music is available on the CD that accompanies Bergmeier and Lotz 1997. Separate tracks available on youtube, search Charlie and His Orchestra.

'L'accordeoniste', 1940 [?]. Edith Piaf. France. Available at www.youtube.com/ watch?v=Vhu-0IBZm5s, accessed 2 January 2019).

'Pål sine høner', 1941. Øvind Berghs Bristolorkester. Norway. Reissued on *Sigaret Stomp: Jazz in Norway 1940–1950*. Norsk Jazz Arkiv HJCD 9002. I wish to thank the Norsk Jazz Archiv for generously making available to me its five CD compilation *Jazz in Norway*.

Africa Speaks, America Answers, 1957. Guy Warren. USA. Decca DL 8446. www.youtube. com/watch?v=RmJfp1ypWMg&list=PL5OGPo_qh6oylrXQP2eggdLWg_Mbusn-w, accessed 29 January 2019.

The Music of New Orleans: The Music of the Streets/The Music of Mardi Gras, Vol 1, 1958. Samuel Charteris. USA. Folkways FA2461, 1958. Available at www.youtube.com/ watch?v=9ONdP-0wKBQ&list=PLFN4zAGpIZKdS0yRxQYyWcO57hu3F8Zhe, accessed 29 January 2019

Sunday at the Village Vanguard, 1961. Bill Evans Trio. USA. Riverside RLP-376. Available at www.youtube.com/watch?v=gZ_rZZusz90, accessed 29 January 2019.

'My Funny Valentine', 1964. *Miles Davis in Concert*. USA. Columbia CS 9106. Available at www.youtube.com/watch?v=3hnjrGvXddo, accessed 30 January 2019.

Stratavarious, ca. 1969, released 1972. Ginger Baker. UK. Polydor. Available at www.youtube. com/watch?v=37sDbvQOJ2I, accessed 29 January 2019.

The Smithsonian Collection of Classic Jazz, 1973. Smithsonian Institution, in association Columbia Special Products. Available at www.youtube.com/playlist?list=PLwT2Q5BE TQuQ0elH1U7R3ZpKZF6RTHTdW Accessed 29 January 2019.

The Troc, 1991. Australia. MBS Jazz 8.

FILMS (Chronological order)

Does the Jazz Lead to Destruction? 1919. Dir. Unknown. Australia. Duration not known. Silent.

The Sheik, 1921. Dir. George Melford. USA. 80 minutes.

Should a Girl Propose?, 1926. Dir. P.J. Ramster. Australia. Duration not known. Silent.

Greenhide, 1926. Dir. Charles Chauvel. Australia. Duration not known. Silent.

The rest are sound film.

St Louis Blues, 1929. Dir. Dudley Murphy. USA. 16 minutes.

Epi Shalfoon and his Melody Boys performing 'E Puritai Tama E', 1930. New Zealand. Duration 57 seconds. Available at: www.youtube.com/watch?v=bm-wTQaKNdw, accessed 25 September 2018.

King of Jazz, 1930. Dir. John Murray Anderson. USA. Duration 105 minutes.

Showgirl's Luck, 1931. Dir. Norman Dawn. Australia. Duration 55 minutes.

The Squatter's Daughter, 1933. Dir. Ken G. Hall. Australia. Duration 104 minutes Australia, 90 minutes English release.

Broadway Melody of 1936, 1935. Dir. Roy Del Ruth. USA. Duration 101 minutes.

The Flying Doctor, 1936. Dir. Miles Mander. Australia. Duration 92 minutes Australia, 67 minutes English release.

Sun Valley Serenade, 1941. Dir. H. Bruce Humberstone. 1941. USA. Duration 86 minutes.

Orchestra Wives, 1942. Dir. Archie Mayo. 1942. USA. Duration 98 minutes.

Cabin in the Sky, 1943. Dir. Vincente Minnelli. 1943. USA. Duration 98 minutes.

Young Man with a Horn, 1950. Dir. Michael Curtiz. 1950. USA. Duration 112 minutes.

The Glenn Miller Story, 1953. Dir. Anthony Mann. 1953. USA. Duration 115 minutes.

The Benny Goodman Story, 1955. Dir. Valentine Davies. USA. Duration 116 minutes.

Pete Kelly's Blues, 1955. dir. Jack Webb. 1955. USA. 95 minutes.

Rock Around the Clock, 1956. Dir. Fred F. Sears. Duration 77 minutes.

Blackboard Jungle, 1955. Dir. Richard Brooks. Duration 101 minutes.

A Touch of Evil, 1958. Dir. Orson Welles. USA. Duration 95 minutes.

The Five Pennies, 1959. Dir. Melville Shavelson. USA. Duration 117 minutes.

Anatomy of a Murder, 1959. Dir. Otto Preminger. USA. Duration 160 minutes.

It's Trad Dad, 1962 (In the US released as Ring-a-Ding Rhythm) Dir. Richard Lester. UK. Duration 78 minutes.

The Pink Panther, 1963. Dir. Blake Edwards. USA. Duration 115 minutes.

Sweet and Lowdown, 1999. Dir. Woody Allen. USA. Duration 95 minutes.

La La Land, 2016. Dir. Damien Chazelle. USA. Duration 128 minutes.

The Green Book, 2018. Dir. Peter Farrelly. USA. Duration 130 minutes.

INDEX

Note: Unless it is self-evident from the title, the category of the item is specified, as for example film, book, recording, band etc.